the vine

DUNN

FOREWORD BY
HIS HOLINESS
THE DALAI LAMA

EDITED BY
G. SHERMAN
H. MORRISON

MESSAGES OF
HOPE FROM
AROUND THE WORLD

the vine

This book is a collection of stories of hope from 47 people in 33 countries. It took nearly three years to complete this project. Letters came from heads of state, royals, refugees, pastors, doctors, architects, scientists, and students, with an age range from 10-94 years old. When I started this project, my hope was to inspire positivity in the world during a very dark time.

The pandemic changed many things for us and in my mind. I wanted to stop for a moment to reflect. To me, this book became more than just stories of hope. It became a snapshot of our humanity and collective consciousness. As Dr. Martin Luther King, Jr. perfectly said, "It really boils down to this: that all life is interrelated. We are all caught in an inescapable network of mutuality, tied into a single garment of destiny. Whatever affects one destiny, affects all indirectly."

We can all share our human experience and inspire others through storytelling. As we emerge from the pandemic, I welcome you to write your own story of hope and share it. If this book moves you, we would love to hear from you. We created an Instagram page to share your stories: @thevineofhope

ISBN: 978-1-951503-82-6 (Hardcover)
ISBN: 978-1-951503-83-3 (Paperback)
ISBN: 978-1-951503-84-0 (Ebook)

Published by Tyler Wagner

Authorsunite.com

Jane Goodall photo credit: Stuart Clarke

Contents

Contents

Contents

Foreword
His Holiness the Dalai Lama

Tibet, Buddhist Monk

All living beings want to lead a happy life in peace. We must therefore think seriously about what would make our world a more friendly and harmonious place. We human beings are social animals; we depend on the community in which we live. From the moment we're born, we are dependent on the care and affection of our mother and family to survive.

We all have seeds of compassion and loving-kindness within us. On this basis, if we make the effort, together we can build a happy human community. In my own experience, when we were still in Tibet, we thought of people from the outside world, especially Europeans and others with their big noses, as different from us. But once we became refugees in India, we became aware of the oneness of humanity and recognized how all human beings are basically the same.

Real happiness is not about having money or power, it's about achieving inner peace. If we have peace of mind, we will be happy day and night. Happiness is related to our emotions, and we all have the potential to cultivate positive as well as negative emotions. Positive emotions will lead to our happiness and will contribute to a more joyful and harmonious environment, while negative emotions cause those around us unhappiness, fear, and anxiety, leaving us equally devoid of the peace of mind we seek.

Since real happiness is related to our mind and emotions rather than material prosperity alone, all of us possess the same potential to be happy and joyful. Although the wealthy may have plenty, if they always want more, then they are unlikely to find the peace of mind that comes with contentment. Being contented on a mental level, over and above mere physical satisfaction, is an important source of happiness.

Modern education is oriented towards material goals, which in turn leads to a materialistic way of life. People brought up this way lack the emotional tools necessary to tackle their destructive emotions and, consequently, they have a limited idea of how to deal with many of the problems they face. Just as we bring up children with an appreciation of physical hygiene, we need to introduce them to an equivalent emotional hygiene. This entails teaching them, for example, how the most effective destroyer of peace of mind is anger, but also how it can be countered by developing concern and compassion for others. Ignorance, another factor clouding the mind, can be dispelled by learning. A great Tibetan scholar once remarked that even if you're to die tomorrow, it's still worth learning something new today.

If education systems fostered inner peace, concern for others and the idea of doing no harm, students would learn how to achieve peace of mind. This is what is required if we are to fulfil the goal of a genuinely peaceful world. I've noticed that those who are more compassionate and warm-hearted tend to be more peaceful. If we have peace of mind, even when we receive bad news, we'll be able to deal with it in a calmer way.

To maintain this kind of inner peace, we need to tackle our disturbing emotions. As far as the mind is concerned, like other animals, we have an array of sense consciousnesses. What sets human beings apart is our intelligence, our ability to think while also considering and planning for the future. Happiness and unhappiness belong to the mind, not the senses. Similarly, mental training takes place on the level of the mind. It is therefore important to become more familiar with the mind itself and how it functions.

To analyze the mind, we need to use reason and intelligence. We need to examine our emotions, to ask ourselves whether we're angry with our opponent's mind, his body, or his actions. If we investigate carefully, we will find our opponent is not intrinsically hostile as he appears to be. In fact, nothing exists intrinsically as it appears. Our opponent has not been our enemy from birth, neither has our friend been someone we've been attached to for all that time. Becoming a friend or an adversary is dependent on circumstances. Considering there is a difference between how things appear and how they actually exist is something I find very useful.

I believe that if we use our intelligence, we can overcome many of the problems we face. According to the new conditions in which we find ourselves, we must adapt and discover new solutions. We must be willing to adopt new ways of thinking. With problems like global warming and climate change, the COVID-19 pandemic, or the gap between rich and poor, we must understand how they have come about, and determine how they can be addressed.

We live in an interdependent world. What affects us affects others too. Climate change, for example, has no respect for national boundaries, and because it is such a serious threat, we need to address it with a strong sense of community, recognizing how in being human we are all the same. Differences between us are secondary. We all share this one planet, our only home. Consequently, we must take better care of it. We must cultivate compassion not only for our fellow human beings, but also for the other animals, birds, and insects with whom we share the world. Affection and concern for others are not luxuries, they are necessary for our survival.

In the past, nations were more or less independent of each other. People lived in villages that were relatively self-sufficient. The words *we* and *us* referred to a small circle of people. Today, the reality is different. The fact that global warming affects us all warns us how we must cooperate with each other to survive. The global economy tells us there is little difference between us, whether we come from east or west, north, or south. The idea of limiting our concern to just a small circle of people is out of date.

Clinging to a strong feeling of *us* and *them* creates problems because it divides us and leads to conflict. Since we can't survive alone, we must think of everyone in terms of *us*.

We live in hope—hope that something good will happen. As human beings we must be realistic and use our intelligence to look at things from different angles to see a more complete picture. Our lives revolve around a desire for things to turn out well. To have hope is to be concerned about the future. Although nothing about the future can be guaranteed, it is more constructive to remain hopeful.

At the age of twenty-four I lost my country, but as a refugee living in India, a democratic, pluralistic, multi-religious society, I enjoy freedom of thought and freedom of speech, and I'm able to share my thinking with other people. It turns out that becoming a refugee has also brought me the opportunity to meet people from around the world and gain experience I would otherwise not have had.

The important point here is to try to transform adversity into opportunity. If we are disproportionately focused on ourselves, we may be confronted by something disheartening. Rather than dwelling on that and letting ourselves become discouraged, it's better to transform our despondency into a determination to lead life in a meaningful way. This will have the effect of relaxing the mind, which will enable consideration and compassion for others to arise naturally. When the mind is anxious and restless, we can't use our intelligence clearly. The solution is to work on creating a deeper sense of peace within ourselves.

It is important to focus on bringing compassion into our everyday motivation. This will strengthen our confidence, which in turn will help us deal with the challenges we face. We must adopt a broader approach to how we view others. We need to be motivated by a vivid sense of the oneness of humanity. Wherever I go and whoever I meet I regard as just another human being like me, a brother or sister. There are differences between us—differences of nationality, color, faith, and social status—but to focus only on these, to the exclusion of what we have in common, is to create problems for ourselves.

Imagine you've escaped from some catastrophe and find yourself all alone. If you see someone in the distance coming towards you,

you'll just be glad to meet another human being regardless of their nationality, color, or faith.

I'm sometimes asked if the world is better now than when I was a child. I believe it is. If we look at the European Union, among its members are people of different nationalities, speaking different languages, and enjoying different cultures who, in the past, fought and killed each other. After the second world war, European leaders founded what has become the European Union. I'm a great admirer of the spirit of this organization and its emphasis on the common good. Since peace has prevailed among the EU's members for more than seventy years, I consider this spirit to be a hopeful sign of human maturity.

During the twentieth century war was rife. Too many people thought the use of weapons was a source of power. This outdated way of thinking can be traced back to feudal attitudes. The use of force at a time when democracy encourages us to think in terms of equal rights is completely inappropriate.

One recent positive move is the signing of a pledge by the five recognized nuclear-weapons states affirming how a nuclear war cannot be won and must never be fought. Disputes between countries should be resolved through dialogue in a spirit of accommodation, understanding, and diplomacy. History provides ample evidence of how violence never leads to lasting peace. Indeed, it is essential for the survival of humanity to exert ourselves in making this a century of dialogue.

Today, it's not enough to simply think about or talk about problems such as global warming and the climate crisis or the gap between rich and poor—we need to take action. As I have already mentioned, we have this unique human intelligence. We should use it to solve the challenges we face, and never give up or tell ourselves there is no hope. When we have a positive goal and are motivated to seek the wellbeing of others, no matter how difficult it is to achieve, we must remain steadfast and realistic in our effort.

I take great inspiration from the advice of an eighth-century Indian Buddhist master who recommended that whatever the circumstances, we should try to see things clearly from different angles. Rather than becoming fixated on a problem we encounter, it's better to develop courage that we can achieve positive change and the confidence to bring it about. If, however, the problem cannot be resolved, simply worrying about it won't be of any help.

Regarding the COVID-19 pandemic, I have great admiration and respect for the efforts of all the doctors and nurses and other front-line workers who have been determined to help those suffering in this crisis, despite the personal danger to themselves. They are enthusiastic and full of concern for their patients. I believe their inner strength affords them some protection. It's important they remain brave and self-confident. Similarly, scientists conducting research into vaccines and treatments must retain their resilience as they employ their professional skills for the benefit of others.

As we look ahead, we clearly cannot change the past, but we can still shape the future. If we focus too much on ourselves, then happiness will elude us, whereas concerning ourselves with the wellbeing of others is the gateway to great joy. If we're serious about happiness in the long term, we need to open our hearts and focus on others as well as ourselves.

Introduction
Adria L. Dunn

United States, Writer

Adria is known as a super connector for philanthropy and a bridge for humanitarian causes. Over the years she established a global network that came to fruition during the pandemic, during which she became known as a "mini-UN in her sweatpants."

Adria grew up in Wisconsin and moved to Chicago to study Journalism at Columbia. She started her career as a futures and foreign exchange broker at the Chicago Board of Trade. After a move to Singapore in 2009 she transitioned into private wealth management and joined Coutts & Co.

Moving back to the USA in 2017, Adria worked as a financial advisor for Morgan Stanley in Florida. She has now left the world of banking to focus her attention on being a writer, philanthropist, and family office advisor. Her passions include all things equestrian, good tea, travel, and most important of all, inspiring hope in others.

* * * * *

Dear World,

Thank you for choosing to read this book and learning about the stories of these amazing individuals from around the globe. They have each agreed to share a personal letter with you from their heart.

This book is a microcosm of humanity as we chose writers across many industries such as business, science, philanthropy, the arts, media, sports, religion, education, activism, and government from more than two dozen countries.

How this book was born is itself a story of hope. Each writer was referred to me through a group chat I created on WhatsApp shortly before the pandemic started, hence the title *The Vine*. The group chat idea came to me while sitting one day on my sofa in Miami. I was exhausted after a long week in New York City and for whatever reason I had an impulse to connect all my friends in philanthropy from across the globe on a single chat, kind of like speed dating for philanthropy. My heart was pounding as my fingers started to add names one by one to the chat. I thought to myself, "Am I mad? Will they be furious for not asking their permission?"

Quite the opposite occurred. The group chat was a hit, but just a few weeks later the pandemic emerged, the mood changed, and I essentially decided to become a kind of mini-United Nations (in my sweatpants, no less). I made countless introductions and hosted Zoom calls with world leaders to simply help. These efforts resulted in lives being saved, millions raised for charity, and countless referrals and connections made around the globe.

These connections also resulted in the collection of stories in this book you are holding now. I didn't have this network of world leaders when I started this project, but because of the chat it bloomed into a worldwide network of family offices, government officials, and other various leaders from more than sixty countries who came together daily for good causes on my cell phone. It's bizarre to me, but what I didn't realize at first was how the more I gave, the more it all came back beyond measure. There is some magic in how this story unfolds, so let me tell you my own story of hope and the vine.

Hope has flowed in and out of my life like a river. Sometimes the river runs deep and wide, sometimes it's turbulent, and sometimes it's gentle, but it is always ever-present. Even though I have had great suffering, like so many others, I have always sought out more reasons to be hopeful in my life than not.

Let me share with you my definition of hope. To me, hope is the little voice inside of us saying everything is going to turn out all right. It says everything is working for us and not against us. As we are blinking, breathing, eating, as birds fly in formation, or bees create honeycombs, as the sun rises and sets, every second the world around us moves in order. We have death, but we also have life. When I was born, my mother used to say I would have rainbows over my future. I had small moments of hope in my grades, my first job, laughter with friends, and in the silence of night. There will be special people, places, moments, and successes, along with failures and tragedy, as well as some faith and beauty mixed in. All these things can be road signs to hope. If we listen carefully, if we pay close attention, they are a guiding light, showing us the way.

One cold, random morning at a coffee shop in Oklahoma City, a man named Brad Bandy gave me a message of hope. Brad is a pastor and runs a non-governmental organization (NGO) called The Spero Project. It helps refugees resettle in the region. I had recently moved back to the United States from Malaysia and had started working in finance for a major Wall Street firm. A few months earlier I had been referred to his organization and became a volunteer. We weren't expecting to run into each other that morning, but apparently there was a bigger plan at work. The person Brad was supposed to meet didn't turn up and my own meeting had been canceled, so we decided to sit down and have breakfast together. After some small talk, he told me how the previous day he had a vision about me, and this is what he said:

"Don't waste your life. You have gift, a gift of building bridges of trust that can bear the weight of truth. People's trust is a very sacred thing, be careful how you steward it. It's not about money, it's the doorway because we need it to live, but my real work (on this Earth) is creating trust between human beings, and I will be a safe place for them. Abundance is in who we all know and remember how we treat others is how God treats us. It defines who we really are. How do we treat those who cannot benefit us? Serving others is key as we are often mentored by the least of these, the greatest leaders you have never heard of…"

For whatever reason that day, I knew his words would be important, so I wrote them down as quickly as I could. I kept this little note in my phone and life moved on. I had forgotten about it until I stumbled across it one day in 2020, right in the middle of the pandemic. I realized I was connecting the whole world—governments, family offices, NGOs, scientists, doctors, lawyers, anyone I felt I could help. I had a burning desire in me and I could not just sit still. I had to do something.

Another incident of hope happened a few years before, in 2016. I had traveled all around the world trying to find myself. My business in Asia had just failed and I was not sure where to go next. I was depressed at the time as I had lost everything. I stopped in Paris to visit my friend Theresa. To cheer me up, she took me to the Chapel of Our Lady of the Miraculous Medal where St. Catherine Labouré is buried. She told me it is a special place of miracles and that I should pray.

I sat in a pew for what seemed like a long time, and nothing happened. As I was about to walk out, I heard a whisper and the number 19 popped in my mind, as well as the flower of life. I could not understand if this was something coming from my brain or somewhere else much deeper, but the number and flower were crystal clear. After returning to my hotel, I decided to search the internet for 19 and the flower of life. Sure enough, I discovered there are 19 circles in the flower of life. I did not know this before. In 2017 I decided to name my next company 19&Co. Fast forward a few years later to 2020 when COVID-19 appears, and a friend called to tell me I should probably think about changing the name of my company. Why? She said because it's the virus backwards! I was floored and didn't know if it was a bad omen or what I should do. It was right in front of me the whole time and I didn't see it. My new company was a beverage product, I was pretty sure no one wanted to drink virus water.

I contracted COVID-19 in the first week of October 2020. It was not a fun experience, but after I healed and had antibodies, I traveled to New York City for work. On the airplane I heard a whisper again and it kept saying *hope*. I was nervous to see how the city had changed after so much loss of life. It saddened me. I have always loved NY—the Statue of Liberty, the street vendors, Central Park, the Hudson River, and so much more. All my relatives had passed through Ellis Island and began their American dream there. New York to me has always been a beacon of light for people from all walks of life.

After I landed, I called my client Ivor in South Africa to check in on him. His son was the first case of COVID-19 in his country, and it was a scary experience for them. His son's fever sky-rocketed and Ivor admitted he was worried he would not make it. I asked Ivor what else he was up to, and he told me he was writing a letter to Joe Biden, who was on the cusp of becoming the next president. This piqued my curiosity, and I asked what kind of letter he was writing. He was writing about having completed the first comprehensive African Youth Survey and the great hopes he had for Africa. He wanted the West to pay attention to Africa.

This is when inspiration struck me. I asked him if he would be interested in writing a letter to the world, perhaps to be included in a book. Then I explained how we could invite others from around the globe to also write letters. In fact, my neighbor in Miami is a publisher, and I could call him and ask about such a project. Ivor enthusiastically said he was absolutely on board, and I had my first writer.

My second call was to Tyler Wagner of Authors Unite. He is a good friend I met at an event a few years before and we've kept in touch. I never thought I would be calling him to pitch a book of hope, but when I told him my idea he was inspired and agreed the world needs hope now more than ever.

The arrival of the novel coronavirus global pandemic in 2020 was a pivotal moment in history. Every one of us became united because of a virus that didn't care about status, location, political or religious affiliation, skin color, or gender. It has taught us how we cannot succeed without the cooperation of others, and most importantly how we are all fallible. It's now 2022 and I am finally ready to share this book with you. The past two years have been incredibly challenging for everyone. It has been a time to reflect. As S.A. Sachs once said, "Hope rises like a phoenix from the ashes of shattered dreams."

Since the pandemic began, there have been many moments of hope in my life, but the most powerful one was 19&Co or COVID-19 backwards. I decided once again to search out the meaning of the flower of life and read it with fresh eyes. I realized what St. Catherine Labouré was saying is how we are all built from the same blueprint. The flower of life symbolizes creation in its totality and serves as a constant reminder of hope from a rainbow in the sky to the stars in the heavens.

With Love and Peace,

Adria L. Dunn

India

Chapter 1

Chaitanya Raj Singh Bhati

King of Jaisalmer

Chaitanya Raj Singh Bhati is the 44th Maharawal (King) of the erstwhile Kingdom of Jaisalmer (Jaisalmer State was a Bhati Rajput kingdom in the far-western part of present-day Rajasthan, India, from the mid-twelfth century CE until 1947. The royal dynasty of Jaisalmer claims to be descended from the deified hero Krishna). He is involved in various sustainable development projects, ranging from agriculture, education, heritage conservation and restoration, and water conservation.

He finished his formal education from Sanskriti School, New Delhi, and has been a student of Politics from the School of Oriental and

13

African Studies (SOAS), University of London. His time at SOAS has made him aware of the global challenges humanity faces today, and how young people can shape their own future.

Chaitanya was one of the main stakeholders in setting up the Gyaan center in Jaisalmer, India, which is a girls' school and women's economic center to uplift women and promote skill development. It was featured on the cover of architectural digest India and has won many design awards nationally and globally. He was also involved in promoting and creating awareness about Industrial Hemp as a product from a policy and consumer perspective in India. He is the founder of Polstrat, which provides a political advisory system led by data and technology to make politics accessible, remove barriers, and empower political candidates and parties.

He learnt his values and sustainable nature from his hometown, Jaisalmer. The city located at the heart of the Thar Desert has always been a source of inspiration for him.

* * * * *

It would not be an exaggeration to say I more-or-less stumbled upon the invitation to be a part of this project and share my thoughts on hope. As I scrolled through the list of contributors, I debated at length on how the views of a late twenty-something fellow like me could offer any substance to a collection of thoughts from some exceptionally experienced people who have achieved immense success in their respective fields and have personally impacted the lives of so many others. I even wondered if the invitation was sent to me in error. Finally, however, I mustered the courage to put pen to paper, and as my first-time writer's cold feet slowly thawed, my contribution to this timeless topic emerged.

To my mind, hope or apêksh (in Sanskrit: अपेक्ष) has always been the underlying unconscious platform for humanity, both at an individual level with the idea of the *spiritual self* at the core of every individual and at the collective level that has allowed the human race to reach previously unimaginable new heights. What strikes me about hope is how universal the emotion is, yet how we all find it in different places and ways. For me, I find it in the history of Jaisalmer. An erstwhile Indian princely state, with a rich 867-year history, Jaisalmer and its history have offered inspiration, guidance, and hope to many. Some of the stories of my beautiful hometown continue to

14

deeply impress me as they continue to shine a beacon of hope for me personally as a fundamental factor in my own journey.

Jaisalmer Princely State was a Bhati Rajput kingdom in the far-western part of present-day Rajasthan, India, from the mid-twelfth century CE until 1947. The state of Jaisalmer had its foundations in what remains of the empire ruled by the Bhati dynasty. Early Bhati rulers reigned over a large empire stretching from Ghazni in modern-day Afghanistan to Sialkot, Lahore and Rawalpindi in modern-day Pakistan to Bhatinda and Hanumangarh in modern-day India. Bhati dominions continued to be shifted southward as they ruled Multan, then were finally pushed into Cholistan. Jaisalmer was the new capital founded in 1156 AD by Maharawal Jaisal, and the state took its name from the founder.

Most of the princely states of the Indian subcontinent, of which there are 565 in total, have thrived in this land not by *ruling* but by *serving* their people. Jaisalmer has always been known as the final frontier of geo-political defense over the course of its history and even in modern India as well because of our proximity to Pakistan.

Jaisalmer is situated in the heart of the Thar desert in the Indian subcontinent. We consider ourselves to be a desert kingdom existing long before the formation of the Indian republic in 1947. It is the ninth capital of the ages-old Bhati or Yadav dynasty. Interestingly, we are one of the few living deserts and forts of the world, as communities still live in various corners of the desert and around 300 families still reside inside the fort. We are famously known to be part of the old Silk Road as well as for the buoyant spirit of the people. Gazing into the history of this challenging promised land, I noticed its valor in fighting battles lasting more than a decade, and the stubbornness of its people in repeatedly re-establishing their roots throughout the course of its history.

The Bhati dynasty fought the Islamic invasion of the Indian peninsula for centuries before peacefully settling down in Jaisalmer. Since the inception of the Kingdom of Jaisalmer, we have successfully achieved harmony with Islam as well as the integration of people of various faiths. My father always mentioned a policy of the Jaisalmer princely state where Hindus respected Islamic faith by not consuming pork while the Muslims reciprocated by not eating beef.

This willingness to integrate comes in part from what it takes for a community of people to survive in an isolated desert kingdom. Governing people collectively to survive the harsh conditions of the desert was essential. Collective survival in the desert was far more important than caste, creed, or religion. We honor such governance policies of my ancestors as they are still practiced in modern Jaisalmer. Our harmonious polity still thrives in maintaining peace by taking inspiration from their ancestors.

Jaisalmer was one of the last major kingdoms to join the subsidiary alliance with the British. On December 11, 1818, Jaisalmer became a British protectorate in the Rajputana Agency. According to the treaty, the state paid no tributes to the British and was not required to send troops when requested. The state was given de-facto freedom in its foreign affairs. Throughout its history, Jaisalmer always maintained a distance from the rulers in Delhi and continued to stay independent. We preferred isolation over engagement as we feared our heaven in the desert would be destroyed by external factors.

Jaisalmer's determination to survive can be seen when the Silk Road began to slowly fade away due to the dismantling of land trade and the formation of ports with the development of maritime trade in the fifteenth century. We became nomadic raiders, looting caravans that stumbled upon the frontiers of the desert kingdom. Nevertheless, the polity of Jaisalmer has always lived sustainably through its governance policies and community-led social development. For instance, our water harvesting techniques and various old monuments were always built together, and even the king would come and work with his people to build such structures. These old monuments included check dams, wells, catchment areas, and the formation and preservation of water channels. In modern Jaisalmer, we still depend on these old monuments for our survival. Along with storing water, our agricultural practices also played a crucial role in the survival of this promised land. Because rain-fed agriculture was not possible, our water storage techniques were essential for a secure food and water supply.

Even during the partition of India, Jaisalmer almost had a smooth transition of people across the border as 40 percent of the erstwhile kingdom still exists in Pakistan. Although India is a modern republic, the people of Jaisalmer still have familial links across the border formed over centuries. It feels like a natural collective association of culture that has been able to cut across the colonial borders dividing people across the globe.

Jaisalmer being part of the ancient Silk Road has always been a hub for cultural patronage from diverse classes and communities. In the modern era, it's one of the oldest living forts of our time. The royal family over generations has been at the focal point of this patronage. The family's harmonious presence over the years has supported culture through ceremonies and rituals. The city is known for its folk musicians

16

as well as the yellow sandstone used in architecture and fine handcrafts, giving the city its nickname of The Golden City. It is an amalgamation of people from different beliefs and ways of thinking.

I find myself in a precarious position as the forty-fourth ceremonial Maharawal (King) of Jaisalmer in modern India. I believe community leaders all over the world have a crucial role to play in encouraging an ecosystem of harmony and collectiveness that in turn keeps people firmly rooted in local traditions. While this has undoubtedly led to a perpetuation of some hierarchies and social practices antithetical to modern forms of civic society, it has also kept the diversity of South Asia intact. The Jaisalmer I envisage is a combination of both—one where we are proud of and celebrate our culture while also adapting to the times and altering our consumption trends with a view towards the environment.

Being a student of politics has provided me with a stable base to equip myself to face the challenges of the world we live in. Life has taught me many lessons and I have overcome many obstacles along the way. There have been times when the future seemed bleak but having a strong will during every crisis has made me who I am as an individual. The willpower of an individual is developed over years through compassion and grace, with hope being a key underlying factor. Hope has been a central pillar in my own life, and it has been a central pillar in Jaisalmer's history as a community-driven polity.

Humanity needs a radical shift towards a stable global order, achievable only by transforming ourselves at the individual level to have a single, united voice for change. Here in 2022, humanity is at a tipping point in our history with an abundance of issues that vary politically, socially, economically, and spiritually, all of which have been exacerbated by the highly disruptive COVID-19 pandemic. Humanity has come a long way over the ages, yet we still find ourselves at this juncture where we ponder how and why we've lost direction in this beautiful voyage we call life. We have realized we are in dire need of a reset of our programming, including our infinite wants and desires.

This change should occur at the smallest scale by being a responsible civic citizen to a larger scale by making ethical decisions in our daily and professional lives. As individuals we perceive our surroundings at a personal, national, and global level. If we can make systematic changes at each of these levels, we will be remembered for not giving up and squarely facing the challenges of our time to build a positive future for generations to come.

Life is a precious gift. We are most alive when we are aware of each conscious moment. While sleeping is necessary for health, inattention in the waking state is time wasted. We truly live only when we make optimum use of our waking hours by being alert. If we are at home and thinking of the office, or at the office and thinking of home, intellectually we are not honoring the precious gift of life in the context of place. When we live in our regrets of the past or anxieties about the future, then emotionally we are not honoring or enjoying the gift of life in the context of time.

My hope lies in the firm belief that more and more people will see how the only way forward is through decisive *positive action* to build ourselves up as conscious humans at the individual level to achieve a collective state of being based on love and compassion. Where there is unity in community and shared humanity, there is hope.

United States

Chapter 2

Andrew Jackson Young, Jr.

Diplomat and Activist

Andrew Jackson Young was the pastor of a small country church when he faced down the Ku Klux Klan to organize a voter registration drive in southern Georgia. He became the leading negotiator for the national Civil Rights Movement, enduring death threats, beatings, and jail time to win for African Americans the rights of full citizenship they were promised by the Constitution—rights they had been long denied.

Alongside his friend, Martin Luther King, Jr., he marched through the most dramatic episodes of the great struggle, from the steps of the Lincoln Memorial to the streets of Birmingham and Selma, and finally to Memphis, where an assassin's bullet ended Dr. King's life.

Andrew fought on, winning election to the United States House of Representatives as the first African American to be elected to Congress. As a congressman, he supported a little-known former governor of Georgia in his long shot bid for the presidency, and when Jimmy Carter became President, he named Andrew to serve as his country's Ambassador to the United Nations.

Andrew also went on to serve two terms as Mayor of Atlanta. Once again, he proved himself an able negotiator, balancing the interests of the business community with the needs of the city's poorest citizens, completing the city's transformation from a battleground of the Civil Rights era to the proud showplace of the modern South. Half a century after the battles of the 1960s, Andrew Young remains an outspoken champion for the rights of all mankind.

* * * * *

What is hope? I won't try to define it, but it is something I've never been without. Hope is a heritage for me, and it has everything to do with generations of my family extending all the way back into slavery.

I grew up in New Orleans, which was and is a surprisingly well-integrated city. Our home was just a block off Canal Street. I remember there was an Irish grocery store on one corner, an Italian bar on another corner, the headquarters of the German American Bund (a German American Nazi organization) on the third corner, and a Chevrolet dealership around the fourth corner. My brother and I were the only African American children on the block, although there were other African American families in the area. By and large the neighborhood functioned in peace. But because it was in the center of town, kids from other neighborhoods who didn't know us would ride through our neighborhood on their bicycles. Sometimes they might throw things at us or call us names and so forth.

I was born in 1932, so I was four years old in 1936 when the Olympic games were held in Berlin. My father took me to watch the games on the *Fox Movietone News* newsreels played in movie theaters. We'd walk by the German American Bund, hearing people singing the "Deutschland Über Alles" (the German national anthem at the time) and seeing a huge swastika displayed out front. I asked my father what these people were doing. He said, "Now, you know from Sunday School how God created from one blood all the nations of the earth. But these folks don't want to believe that because they are white supremacists. They think white people are better than everybody else. White supremacy is a kind of sickness, but you don't have to pay any attention to them because you know better."

My father took me to watch newsreels of Berlin Olympics because he wanted me to see Jesse Owens, the famous Black athlete, run the 100-meter dash. Of course, he won, much to the dismay of Adolf Hitler with his view of Aryan supremacy. Hitler himself was supposed to award Owens the gold medal, but because he was angry a Black man had won the race, he and his stormtroopers left the arena as an insult to Owens. My father told me how Jesse Owens paid no mind at all to Hitler. He wasn't there to be received by Hitler, he was there to win gold medals in the Olympics for himself and his country. Owens focused on what he was there to do, not on Hitler's attitudes and behaviors. And because Owens didn't allow himself to get caught up in Hitler's antics, because he focused on his job and what he was there to do, he ended up winning four gold medals.

I appreciate my father instilling in me this sense of how important it is to keep your own mind together. He also wanted my brother and I to learn how to box so we could defend ourselves. My father always told us to never get angry in a fight. Anger would cloud our judgement and cause us to lose focus and not think clearly. The way he reminded us of this over and over was with the simple phrase, "Don't get mad, get smart." Staying calm even under duress or when being provoked was a lesson he taught us every day.

In the end, it wasn't that our father wanted us to fight. In fact, his fervent hope was that we would never have to fight. His perspective was that if we knew how to fight, we probably wouldn't have to. Why? Because by teaching us to be confident in our fighting skills, we could be in threatening situations and remain calm and not show fear. If we showed we were nervous or fearful, others would be more likely to pick a fight with us. He also figured if we ever did have to fight, we'd know how to do well enough that a couple well-placed blows would get the job done and people would then leave us alone.

Our initial training in boxing was by happenstance. My father was a big fan of the fights, and he was also a dentist. If he saw a boxer get his jaw or teeth hurt during a fight, he would let them know they could come by his office and he'd fix them up free

21

of charge. It was when these boxers were hanging around my father's dentistry office that they'd play with my brother and I, teaching us the basics of boxing. A couple of these boxers became good friends of the family, and we only lived about five or six blocks from the gymnasium where they trained. After getting their teeth fixed by my father, they'd take us back to the gymnasium with them and teach us more about training and boxing.

Many have wondered how all this focus on learning how to fight could lead me to my interest in Mahatma Gandhi's philosophy of nonviolent resistance as a tactic for social change. But to me, it was a seamless transition because I understood my father's philosophy—that by knowing how to fight, we would hopefully never have to do it. But Gandhi didn't say you'd never have to fight. There's the kind of fighting you do to defend yourself if you're being attacked or provoked. Gandhi accepted fighting in self-defense, a kind of defensive violence, when needed and he never condemned people for defending themselves.

What Gandhi always condemned was aggressive or offensive violence. He was clear you should never use offensive violence to provoke someone else to anger, bitterness, or violence. He also promoted the rejection of violence altogether, a nonviolence where you refuse to respond in violence even when being attacked. That's a higher level of consciousness you must grow into. For me, I rarely ever had to fight, but I also never backed down. My wife also had a lot to do with my interest in nonviolent tactics. She attended Manchester College, a Church of the Brethren school in Indiana where she took a course on New Testament Nonviolence. She knew a lot about it and was spiritually committed to changing the world without violence, which is one of the reasons I wanted to marry her.

My family went to church regularly. My mother was the superintendent of the Sunday School, and my father was a deacon. We were in church every Sunday for both Sunday School and the regular morning worship service, as well as every Wednesday for prayer meetings. My father also sang in the choir and went every Thursday for choir practice, and he'd take my brother and I with him. The church was only a couple blocks from where we lived, so we were there a lot of the time. I got along well with the people at church.

I was in the church nursery school where they taught us not only about the Bible, but also math, reading, and writing. That was my education up until I was six years old, which was the age a child became eligible to begin attending public school. I had learned so much from church school that when I went to public school, they placed me in the third grade because I already knew everything being taught in the first and second grades. While this was fine academically, it also meant my fellow classmates ranged in age from nine to twelve, and I was only six. I was the youngest and the smallest, but I always had confidence.

My grandmother played an important role in my life as well. By the time I was eight years old, she had lost her eyesight and it was up to me to read to her, both the newspaper and the Bible. She would discuss the Bible with me. During the last six years of her life, from age eighty to eighty-six, I listened to her complain and argue with God about how she had lived long enough and was ready to be done with this earthly realm. She'd say how she had five children of her own but took in another six along the way, meaning she had raised eleven children. It was as if she were stating her case to God in her prayers that it was time for her to go. After all, she'd done more than her share. She also didn't want her blindness to be a burden to others. I learned so much from her, and from reading the Bible and the newspaper to her. I loved her dearly. What this did was instill in me the hope that there is more than just this earthly life.

Interestingly, while some African Americans I've met along the way have reached a point of feeling hopeless about racial equality, not so for me, and not so for most African Americans in my view. For many of us, hope is something instilled in us through family that persists for generations. Back around the time leading up to the Louisiana Purchase in the early 1800s, Andrew Jackson came to New Orleans to form an army willing to defend New Orleans against Napoleon and the French. The way he enticed people to join this army was by handing out land to former slaves, indentured white people, and Native Americans—basically anyone who'd be willing to join this army in exchange for the land.

While I don't have any documented proof, my great-grandfather was a recipient of such land. Why else would he name one of his children Andrew Jackson Young? It was my grandfather's brother who was the first to get that name. Then my grandfather went on to name my father Andrew Jackson Young, which is the name my father gave to me and that I have now given to one of my children, and he's given that name to one of his children as well.

It's ironic this name persists in my family. After all, Andrew Jackson was not a role model. He owned as many as forty-four slaves and was brutal in his treatment of Native Americans for the most part. I should also note how the land my family received from Andrew Jackson wasn't good land. It was swampy land located about a hundred miles west of New Orleans. But as former slaves, they were very grateful to own any land at all.

My active political career has been inspired by my grandfather. He was born in 1860 before the Civil War. After the war, many Christian missionaries from the North came down South to help educate African Americans, especially those who had been caught up in slavery. I think he made the most of whatever education came his way and it served him well. By the 1920s he had formed a burial society, was the treasurer for a Masonic lodge, and managed the money of several other organizations such that he had bankrolled or managed millions of dollars. This was not something most former slaves achieved. The burial society was especially significant because everyone wanted to provide for a dignified burial for their loved ones, and my grandfather made a hugely successful business out of it.

After I was elected to the US Congress in 1973, I met a minister from New York who had grown up in Louisiana. He knew I was originally from Louisiana and wanted to know if I knew anything about "old man Frank Young," and I said he was my grandfather. This minister went on to say how proud my grandfather would be to see how far I've come. Then he added, "But you've still got a long way to go to catch up to him and all the progress he made." He was basically saying my grandfather had far more power and influence in his day from his business and money-management skills than I had as a freshman congressman!

My mother and her sister went to a missionary college for teachers in New Orleans. They were the first graduates of the school, and my mother was only sixteen when she graduated. My father went to the dentistry school of Howard University, and I also attended Howard. This is all to say how important education has been as a source of hope and empowerment in my family's life going right back to my grandfather and the education he received from northern missionaries.

I must also note how my life was deeply impacted by Dr. Martin Luther King, Junior, who I first met in 1957. He was already famous for his civil rights activities, and I was quite active myself. Sometimes when he was invited to speak somewhere in the local region, the people organizing the event didn't know if he'd be able to make it or not, so they usually had a backup speaker ready to go if needed. At a particular event in 1957, I was the backup and so he and I both showed up and met for the first time. What we soon discovered was that in addition to us both having recently become fathers, our wives had attended the same high school in Alabama! What's interesting is that we didn't spend a lot of time talking about the civil rights movement. We just

24

couldn't stop talking about these precious little baby daughters we both had. Several years later, however, I did accept his invitation to get involved with his Southern Christian Leadership Conference in Atlanta.

People often refer to me as a bridge-builder, and many wonder how I'm able to do it. After all this thing of building bridges between people who seem irreconcilably different or diametrically opposed to one another must be difficult. They want to know my secret, but it's really very simple: Treat everyone as a fellow human being deserving of basic dignity and respect. It's that simple! Wherever I go, I don't only speak to Black people, I speak to *all* people. And this was something I have done since I was growing up in New Orleans. When walking through my neighborhood back then, I would speak to everyone, even the Nazis. I don't mean long conversations or anything, I just mean greetings and so on. But what I was doing was recognizing each one of them as a person, as a fellow human being, which in turn forced them to recognize me as a person.

Whenever I speak to students, I always emphasize how they need to first learn how to be human. Part of that is treating their teachers with basic dignity and respect. After all, the teacher has a life they're living, a family to take care of, along with other responsibilities and obligations. When entering the classroom, a student should always greet their teacher by name, "Good morning" Mr. so-and-so or Mrs. so-and-so. This simple act of humanity makes all the difference, not just because it's a basic, decent human thing to do. There is a very pragmatic aspect to it is as well. When it comes time for grading students, it's always a far more subjective process than most people think. Treating a teacher like a human being deserving of dignity and respect could easily mean the difference between a C and a B or between a B and an A.

A lot of people who read or listen to MLK's *I Have a Dream* speech wonder how in the world things can still be as bad as they are today. Back then we were trying to redeem the soul of America from the triple-threat evils of racism, war, and poverty. We did make some excellent progress on all three fronts, but of course there is still much work to be done.

As my grandchildren grow older, I wonder what the most important thing from my life is that I want to tell them. Lately, I've settled on the story of getting beat up down in Florida back in the 1960s. Dr. King had sent me down to St. Augustine, Florida to try to stop the Black activists from continuing their marches and protests and demonstrations. Why would MLK want to do that? The reason was simple. Tensions had grown to the point that he knew violence could erupt at any moment and he didn't want the Black marchers to become the victims of serious violence. I went down there and explained the situation and that it was time to ease up a bit, but the Black folks there weren't having any of it. They wanted to continue their marches despite the potential for violence.

I decided the best thing I could do was to go ahead and lead these marches myself so if violence came it would be directed at me. During one march, there were a couple hundred known Ku Klux Klan members lining one side of the street, all of whom had been deputized by the sheriff. They were there to beat us up. I made sure all the marchers stayed on their side of the street, but I crossed over to the other side and sure enough they beat me up pretty good. I was unconscious for some amount of time, but when I came to, I caught up with the marchers and planned to do the same thing again. This time a big police officer stepped between me and the KKK men. The officer said to them this needed to stop before someone got killed. He told the Klansmen to let these people march through to their destination, which was the historic slave market site. We made it, but not before a few more of us were beat up.

This went on for another week in St. Augustine, and a lot of us were badly beaten several times. By the time the following Saturday came along, the Klansmen were frustrated they had not been successful in provoking us into violence. They decided they would have their own march into the Black community. They clearly wanted trouble. They were dressed in full KKK regalia, and probably had guns under their robes. I had no idea how the people would react to this provocation. As soon as the KKK marched into the Black community on the main street in Lincolnville, all the Black folks along the street began singing the hymn, "I Love Everybody in My Heart." It was so disarming that miraculously no violence took place. If the Black community at that moment had allowed themselves to be provoked to violence, it could have derailed the passage of the Voting Rights Act. By the grace of God, it passed in 1965.

When I look at the heritage of hope instilled in me from generations of my family passing it along, I also want hope to be a legacy I leave behind, not only within my own family but beyond. When people look at the state of the world today and feel overwhelmed by how much trouble still exists, I recall the simple phrase from my father that has become our family motto: "Don't get mad, get smart." Keep a calm, level head as you continue working toward your hopes and dreams for the world and progress will happen. If I may paraphrase something Deepak Chopra has said, we are not physical beings who have a few spiritual experiences, we are all spiritual beings who spend a short time in this physical world. In other words, we all share a common, enduring spirit of humanity. If you view life this way, it's not hard to maintain hope.

26

United Kingdom

Chapter 3

Dr. Jane Goodall

Primatologist and Anthropologist

Dr. Jane Goodall, DBE, Founder of the Jane Goodall Institute (JGI) and UN Messenger of Peace, is a world-renowned ethologist and activist inspiring greater understanding and action on behalf of the natural world.

Dr. Goodall is known for groundbreaking studies of wild chimpanzees in Gombe Stream National Park, Tanzania, which forever changed our understanding of our relationship to the rest of the animal kingdom. This transformative research continues today as the longest running wild chimpanzee study in the world. Jane's work builds on scientific innovations, growing a lifetime of advocacy including trailblazing efforts through her international organization the Jane Goodall Institute to advance community-led conservation, animal welfare, science, and youth empowerment through JGI's Roots & Shoots program.

Today, Jane continues to connect with worldwide audiences, despite the challenges of the pandemic, through "Virtual Jane," including remote lectures, recordings, and her podcast, the "Jane Goodall Hopecast." In 2021, Jane was the recipient of the Templeton Prize, and recently published her newest book, *The Book of Hope: A Survival Guide for Trying Times*.

Jane is a global icon, spreading hope and turning it into meaningful positive impact to create a better world for people, other animals, and the planet we share.

* * * * *

I have lived on this planet for almost ninety years, and I have seen much change. England declared war on Nazi Germany when I was five years old. Because everything was rationed, nothing was wasted. Those years taught me to take nothing for granted, including human life. I also learned a great deal about the two sides of human nature—kindness, love, and courage on the one hand; brutality and true evil (the Holocaust) on the other.

I was born loving animals. I learned about them from nature and books, and I was ten years old when I determined I would go to Africa, live with animals, and write books about them. "Impossible," people said. After all, Africa was far away, we had little money, and anyway I was just a girl. But my wonderful mother simply told me I would have to work hard, take advantage of every opportunity, and if I did not give up then I might find a way. I have shared her advice with many young people, and because I did go to Africa and lived with animals, I am often thanked with something like, "You taught me that because you did it, I can do it too."

I finally got to Africa when I was twenty-three years old. In those days, the cheapest way was by boat. The Suez Canal was closed due to a war between England and Egypt, and the first place I set foot on African soil was Cape Town, in South Africa. It was exciting, but then I saw all the signs in Afrikaans that translated as "Whites Only," and I witnessed first-hand the abomination of apartheid. I was not brought up to judge people by the colour of their skin and was glad to leave.

In Kenya, in 1957, people were still recovering from the Mau Mau uprising, when rebels from several tribes carried out guerrilla warfare against the administration, the white settlers, and any Kikuyu tribe members who were loyal to the government. In fact, the rebellion did not end until 1960, but the main fighting had just ended the year before I arrived. I heard about the many horrendous atrocities that had been committed, but at least this uprising would soon lead to the end of British colonial rule in Kenya, and the atmosphere was very different from that in South Africa.

It was during this visit to Kenya when I met Dr. Louis Leakey, who gave me the opportunity to study chimpanzees, the animals most closely related to humans, in Tanzania's Gombe national park. As they gradually lost their fear of me, I got to know the different individuals and something about their complex social structure and way of life. Most fascinating was how similar they were to us. I watched them kiss and embrace in greeting. I observed them using and even making tools. Eventually, I learned about their close and lasting family relationships, including the long childhood during which learning and the type of mothering plays such an important role. And I watched the swaggering competition between males for dominance. Chimpanzees are highly intelligent, able to solve problems, and they have emotions similar to ours: happiness, fear, anger, depression, and so on. In fact, like so many other animals, they are sentient and sapient beings.

I was sad to find that chimpanzees have a dark side and are capable of violent aggression. They are territorial, and community males regularly patrol their boundaries. If they see an individual of either sex from a neighbouring community, they chase and subject the "stranger" to a brutal gang attack, leaving the victim to die of the terrible wounds inflicted. The only exceptions are adolescent females who have not yet given birth—they are actively welcomed by patrolling males. While there are many aggressive incidents within the community, chimpanzees can also be very caring of each other and there are also many cases of true altruism, as when an adult male adopts an unrelated infant whose mother has died. Like us, chimpanzees can be violently aggressive but also gentle and nurturing.

The fossil record tells us that some six million years ago chimps and humans shared a common ancestor. And this is why Leakey, who spent his life searching for fossils of the earliest humans, wanted a study of chimpanzees. We can tell a lot about extinct animals from fossils, but behaviour does not fossilize. Leakey reasoned that if I saw behaviours in the chimpanzees similar to ours, then possibly they were inherited from a common ancestor and had been part of the behavioural repertoire of both chimpanzees and humans throughout our long, separate evolutionary journeys. This would help him better imagine how stone age humans probably behaved.

Because chimpanzees and humans both have this dark aggressive side, does this mean we humans have an innate predisposition for violence and war? Surely the answer must be yes. If we look around the world, we find examples of such behaviour everywhere. Does it mean violence and war is inevitable? Here I believe the answer is no.

The main difference between humans and chimpanzees is the explosive development of our intellect, probably triggered when we developed a spoken language. This meant we could teach others about things not present, make plans for the distant future, and get together to discuss problems and work out solutions. This also enabled us to formulate a moral code—a list of behaviours that are acceptable and those that are not. Not all cultures have the same list of rights and wrongs, but all have a moral code of some sort. Moreover, every major religion has the same Golden Rule: "Do to others as you would have them do to you." If only we all followed this rule, and applied it to our interactions with people, especially those from other cultures, and also to animals and to the natural world, what a peaceful world we would have! Instead, that other tendency we share with chimpanzees—the desire for power—works against a peaceful world.

Still, for the most part people can control their aggressive impulses. We may feel like beating someone up, but usually refrain from doing so, partly because we fear retribution, and partly because we've been taught it is better to solve a problem with words. Education undoubtedly plays a major role in shaping behaviour. Children can be taught that lying, stealing, and harming others is wrong. Unfortunately, they can also be taught it is okay to despise and even hate certain kinds of people, so that slavery, apartheid, discrimination, and genocide become okay.

We are living in grim times. There are armed conflicts in many parts of the world, terrorist attacks, demonstrations that turn violent, police brutality, and so on. Can we use our intellect to turn things around? First, we must understand the root causes of some of this violence, much of which stems from our disrespect of the natural world. There can be no lasting peace between people and nations until we learn to live in harmony with nature. The idea that there can be unlimited economic growth on a planet with finite natural resources and a growing human population is absurd.

It is important to realize we are a part of the natural world, and depend on it for food, clothing, clean air, and water—everything. And it is *healthy* ecosystems we depend on. During the years I spent in the rain forest, I learned how everything is interconnected, how each species has a role to play in the ecosystem. We are now in the midst of the sixth great extinction of plant and animal life. It is unique in that the main reason for it is our own relentless exploitation of nature, which has also led to climate change, which in turn is affecting many species. If they cannot adapt to changing conditions they will not survive. More ecosystems will collapse, endangering the lives of those people who depended on them.

Of course, the affluent are buffered from the worst effects of the problems which, to a large extent, they have caused by the desire for ever more material comforts and wealth. Is it surprising people get angry as the gap widens between the haves and have-nots, when the super-rich get tax breaks while the poor cannot even afford health care and struggle to feed their families? Too often in disadvantaged communities, children are deprived of a good education, which means they are less qualified for good jobs later. It is not surprising many lose hope and resort to alcohol, drugs, or crime. There is only just so much people can take, and eventually the worm turns. Sometimes this leads to social change, but too often demonstrations by desperate people are suppressed savagely by autocratic regimes.

It is vital to develop a new and sustainable relationship with the natural world. Fortunately, more people realize how important it is to change our ways. Groups are fighting the illegal wildlife trade, others working to protect and restore nature, to create corridors between wildlife habitats, allowing animals to move between them and thus preventing inbreeding. Rewilding programmes are working—often very successfully—to protect and restore biodiversity. There are more and more voices raised to end industrial farming and produce our food working with and not against nature. Regenerative agriculture, permaculture, and agroforestry are among the many successful efforts to restore life to degraded farmland. And there is a global move towards a plant-based diet.

Clearly, the alleviation of poverty is a key issue. Poor communities cut down the last trees in their desperation to find land for growing food or to make charcoal to sell. For the same reason they hunt the last animals—just to survive. The Jane Goodall Institute's method of holistic community-led conservation, Tacare (take care) was begun in the early 1990s to address the deforestation around the Gombe national park. Due to population growth, there were more people than the land could support, farmland was over-used, and people were struggling to survive. I realized then that

31

unless we helped people find ways of living without destroying the environment, we could not conserve chimpanzees or their habitat.

Major components of Tacare include microcredit opportunities for people to start small, environmentally sustainable businesses and improve health facilities, including access to family planning and scholarships enabling girls to have the chance of secondary education. People realize education is a way out of poverty and cannot afford to educate the 8–10 children per woman that used to be the norm. All around the world family size drops as women's education improves.

Today, Tacare operates throughout the chimpanzee range in Tanzania. Trees have returned to the bare hills as the villagers realize conserving the environment is for their own future and not just wildlife. Tacare now operates in six other countries around chimpanzee habitat and is just one of many community-based conservation programs around the world.

Roots & Shoots is the Jane Goodall Institute's environmental and humanitarian movement for young people of all ages. Each group chooses three hands-on projects to help people, animals, and the environment. The main message is that every individual matters, can make some impact on the planet every day, and can choose what sort of impact we make. The cumulative effect of thousands or millions of even small ethical choices—what we buy, eat, wear, how we interact with people and animals, and so on—will move us towards a better world. Because they are tackling what they care about, they are passionate, dedicated, and hard working—and they also influence their parents and grandparents.

We bring young people together (usually virtually) from different countries. We work with young people from diverse socioeconomic, cultural, and religious backgrounds. Whether they be Christians, Muslims, Buddhists, and so on, they discover that far more important than skin colour, language, culture, or religion is the fact we are all humans—we all share emotions such as happiness and sadness, frustration, and compassion. We all laugh and weep. We all feel pain. Many young people have said that in a gathering of Roots & Shoots members from different countries, they never feel any discrimination.

Young people are my greatest reason for hope, along with the human intellect, the resilience of nature, and the indomitable spirit that helps people tackle what seems impossible and never give up. The state of the world is indeed grim, but we have a window of time. We must get together and take action—*now*—before it is too late.

32

New Zealand

Chapter 4

Peter Hillary

Mountaineer and Philanthropist

Peter Hillary comes from one of the great families of mountaineering and has a history of world-class achievements in climbing. Like his father, the late Sir Edmund Hillary, who made the first ascent of Mt. Everest with his climbing partner Tenzing Norgay in 1953, Peter has summited Everest and forged a new route to the South Pole.

The names Everest and Hillary are forever linked and will always be associated with high adventure. Peter Hillary is an accomplished mountaineer, speaker, and expedition leader. He raises funds for Himalayan Foundations around the world and is a partner in

Edmund Hillary clothing which produces premium heritage clothing. Peter has led a life of high adventure since his father took him climbing at the age of seven. His philosophy has always been to live life to its fullest.

* * * * *

So much of life gets tossed at you when you least expect it.

In 2015 on the steep ridgeline above the little village of Khunde, we paused at the three memorial chortens at 4,100 metres built by the villagers for my father, mother, and younger sister. It occurred to me that for the first time I was up there in the Himalayas with a group of people who had all known them. This had never happened before. As we gazed out towards the bulk of Everest and down at the little village hospital my parents had built, this connection with the past and my "precious ones" felt particularly special.

Back in 1975 the Hillary family was living in Nepal to help my father build his biggest hospital at the important village of Paphlu five days trek south of where we were at Khunde. My mother Louise (43) and younger sister Belinda (16) boarded a small plane to fly into the mountains to join Dad at the building site. But the New Zealand pilot disregarded the standard safety procedures and pushed the throttle to maximum power, lifting the plane into the air above Kathmandu. It was only then that he realised the control guards were still attached to the ailerons. He lost control of the aircraft and it crashed into a paddy field north of the Kathmandu runway near the great stupa of Bodhnath. No one survived and the Hillarys lost half of our family, our hearts forever broken, and our lives forever changed. Chance events change everything and take the trajectory of life in new, unanticipated directions.

But here I was years later, in the company of old friends; we trekked on. Group photographs were arranged as much for a rest along the trail as for a photographic record, and they were always punctuated with "Where's Hamish?" as our camera-shy amigo was rounded up, grinning happily for a round of high-altitude digital vainglory. "So how far is today's trek, Peter?" Of course, all my estimates were lampooned for outrageous optimism so, "We will double that," they would say and then inquire about how much climbing was involved to reach the next village. "Today there is a net altitude gain of zero," I replied. "Yeah, right, except we have to complete an 800-metre descent and then two 400-metre ascents after lunch!"

We all mastered the road rules of "give way to yaks" and the synchronised cross-ing procedures for suspension bridges above Himalayan cataracts—you don't want to meet a yak in the middle of a 100-metre suspension foot-bridge! We all adopted our own versions of the "Himalayan plod," a pace that allows your heart and lungs to operate in an RPM range suitable for your age, fitness, and the lofty altitudes.

This all happened seven years ago when I organised a group of my old collegians to trek through the Himalayas past the schools and hospitals my father, Ed Hillary, had built and then up valley to Everest Basecamp at an altitude of 5,360 metres (17,600 feet). The great form of the world's highest mountain was our beacon, and it occupied the northern horizon as the stories of climbing the mountain were frequent topics around hot cups of tea in the trekking lodges. And, of course, the greatest story of them all was the first ascent by my father and Tenzing Norgay during the 1953 British Mt. Everest Expedition where they ascended to where no one had gone before.

But the truth is that in our own small ways we are all going where no one has gone before. The challenges of outdoor adventure put everything else in our lives into perspective. It transforms a hot shower, a comfortable bed, and simple food into the luxury they are.

I have climbed Everest a couple of times and made five attempts on different routes on the mountain among my more than fifty expeditions to mountains around the world. I work with the foundations my father helped establish to run education, health, and environmental programmes in the Himalayas around the foot of Mt. Everest. And like my father in 1953 I found that the sting-in-the-tail of an Everest climb comes when you least expect it—just below the summit. It's a vertical step in the ridge now called the Hillary Step that guards access to the top.

And this is the hallmark of any adventure or undertaking: Often the biggest challenges come when you least expect them. And so it was for us when twelve sixty-year-old men decided to go on a reunion trek to Everest Basecamp in Nepal, where there are no roads and few of the amenities of our affluent western lives. This was a chance to rekindle friendships and share in an adventure in the lofty Himalayas, delving behind our aging physiognomies for the teenage cohorts we knew so many years before. Incredibly, the men I trekked with were the personalities and idealisms of the boys I had known long ago, only now their older, wiser, more experienced selves were over-laid on the youthful personalities of boyhood.

For two weeks we trekked from my father's airstrip at Lukla (which he built in 1964) into the "high Himal," as Dad always referred to it with a smile, staying with people I have known all my life, and sometimes in their own homes. Of course, despite being a bunch of old school friends with receding hairlines and bulging waistlines, there were plenty of high jinks. On Phil Barron's birthday there was a cake and speeches and the singing of the old school song, "O floreat semper," and plenty of jocular aspersions caste.

When Guy Haddleton and I stayed at my "Sherpa aunt's" house, he composed a skit that was filmed by Russell Tills of Guy remonstrating to camera that he had paid for a single room upgrade and here was his ensuite, a hole in the floor of an outhouse with leaf litter for a flush and a wooden pole to assist aging knees regain their vertical composure! Oh yes, we laughed a lot. And we encouraged each other on along the narrow footpaths as we headed up valley at a methodical ascent rate to enhance our acclimatisation.

It was the 25th of April and after a dawn service honouring the ANZAC-war-dead from World War I (which is an annual event in Australia and New Zealand) at the little hamlet of Lobuche at 4,900 metres when we trudged up valley in lightly falling snow. We arrived at Gorak Shep just three kilometres south of Everest Basecamp (EBC) and stopped at one of the five tea shops there to quaff hot drinks and eat some food. It was just before midday and the usual banter was there between us when all hell broke loose. The dry-stone building started shaking violently from side to side and while some dived beneath tables I knew that stone buildings were best vacated and I roared, "Everyone outside!"

This was a huge earthquake (we learned later it was 7.9 on the Richter scale) and it felt as if the whole Himalaya was being shaken and in danger of coming apart. When we rushed outside the little teashop at 5,100 metres and stood together in stunned silence as gently falling snow landed upon us, the violent shaking stopped. There was silence. And then in the distance we heard the roar of avalanches pouring off the mountains above us, around us, like "a hundred freight trains." Looking to the north to where Everest Basecamp was and the great Khumbu Glacier, I could see the sharp form of the lateral moraine and suddenly a great boiling cloud of avalanche blast came over the moraine and straight towards us across the lateral moraine valley at what I estimated was probably 100 knots. I knew what to do so I called to the old collegians to "get back in the building!" To which someone mumbled, "First you tell us to get out and now you tell us to get inside again!" I was sure that this catastrophic event did not bode well for the climbers at EBC.

What we lived through then was five days of hell.

At EBC a huge block of ice had released from 800 metres above the camp and on impact exploded into an enormous aerosol avalanche, producing a blast of air and ice particles so severe it devastated the lower portion of the camp. Twenty-one people died, a hundred were injured, and the camp was largely destroyed. That was the same avalanche blast that had come down the glacier and hit us at Gorak Shep.

So, within a couple of hours trek of our goal at Everest Basecamp, I turned the old collegians around and in the gloom of low cloud and lightly falling snow we trudged down valley past destroyed villages and trekkers lodges.

By now we were on a mission to get out of the mountains. The two weeks together and the violence of the earthquake had knitted us into a very cohesive group. Eventually, some communications were repaired, and we were able to call home, as well as our contacts in Kathmandu. The news was bad. Over 10,000 people had been killed and millions of homes damaged. People in Kathmandu were too afraid to sleep indoors with the ongoing aftershocks and instead lived outside on the streets and fields beneath large blue tarpaulins.

Compared to this news, the next two evenings for us were upbeat affairs. How fortunate were we? There were rousing speeches while sitting around yak dung fires in damaged accommodations and a heightened sense of the good life despite the quake, the destruction, and the loss of life. That first night at the village of Dingboche, Greg Kay most eloquently summarised our experiences with positivity and a touching nod to the camaraderie of the dozen. It was a special moment. This had been a big undertaking for him, and he was probably the one who found the relentless ascents on the Himalayan trails the hardest. But it was a journey he had looked forward to with such enthusiasm.

At the badly damaged Tengboche Monastery, we spent the night in the restaurant of a wrecked hotel. As luck would have it, we were there with my old friend Jamling Tenzing (Tenzing Norgay's son), who was guiding a group of young Indian women to Everest Basecamp. Like everyone else, he was reviewing what he would do after the earthquake. That evening we all shared a marvellously light-hearted time together— the Tenzing party of young Indians and the Hillary party of old collegians—inspired by the uncertainty of our reality and the sheer wonder of being happy and contented when happiness and contentment had vanished for so many around us. As he had done once before, Greg came up to me and asked, "Have I shown you a photo of my little granddaughter?" and proffered a picture of a beautiful little girl. It was a touching gesture amid the mayhem in which we now lived.

Then at 6am on the 27ᵗʰ of April we awoke to find Greg couldn't be roused. He lay motionless in his sleeping bag while three of our number attempted to resuscitate him, but it was to no avail. It seemed he must have died from a heart attack or stroke an hour or two before. We were all stunned. Speechless. Heartbroken. This compounded upon the horror of the quake's devastation and left us all in a discombobulated state of confusion and sorrow. The loss of Greg was a terrible and personal blow for all of us. His absence haunted us as we did what we had to do to transport him to Lukla and to contact his family. As darkness approached that day, a helicopter landed in the meadow in front of the ruined monastery at Tengboche and shuttled Greg's body down valley to Lukla with his close friends, John Reyburn and Michael Caughey.

The following day the rest of us trekked down valley to the village of Monzo deep in the Dhud Kosi Valley, passing groves of flowering rhododendrons, then descended the switch-backed Namche Hill with a growing sense of purpose. To my horror, as we looked down on the Dhud Kosi River I saw some of our duffle bags floating in the river and later learned our porter Narayan Katwal was also in the water, and Nepalese porters can't swim. We had lost another! Narayan, or Nikon as we nicknamed him, was a marvellously enthusiastic character and famous with us for rescuing Phil Barron's camera from a teashop up valley. We never did find out how he had fallen into the river, but then the Himalayas themselves seemed to be falling down around us. There were many huge boulders that had come down the mountainsides and across the tracks where we walked, so our journey and our prospects were chaotic and ill-defined. While our sirdar Pasang Temba filed a police report on the accident, we all had an early and subdued night. It felt like our world was coming asunder.

On the fifth day of our trials, we trekked to Lukla Airstrip with some light rain causing us to don parkas and umbrellas for the last part of the trek. After lunch we went to the earthquake damaged heliport building beside the runway to retrieve Greg's body. He lay, white-shrouded, within the three remaining walls of the heliport office with two other bodies tied in red and blue tarpaulins (one labelled *unknown*) that had been brought by helicopter from EBC. We carried him outside past an injured Sherpa climber in a stretcher and beneath the rotating blades of a helicopter onto the slippery mud and rock tracks of Lukla village and up the hillside to a ridge above the little town. A Buddhist monk led us up the track with a silk karta-scarf symbolically drawing Greg on up the path to the next life and to an airy cremation site with views (once the rain stopped) to the north to the Himalayas and west to the setting sun. Beneath a parade of umbrellas, we old collegians said farewell to Greg as the smoke lifted into the clearing Himalayan sky.

38

And so we returned home to the deep sadness of the family of Greg Kay and to his grieving friends. Why did he go on this journey? But the truth is he wanted to go; he was excited to go. This was a whole new challenge and Greg liked challenges. Of course, none of us would have agreed to trek to Everest Basecamp (or anywhere else for that matter) if we knew there would be a 7.9 earthquake followed by the five days from hell that we lived through, but of course you never know what lies ahead with most things in life. Perhaps that is just as well because we would end up living in a state of foreboding and fear.

On our trek together we lived so richly. Through the smoke of the yak dung fires, the energised conversations, the anticipation of what lay ahead at EBC, or even as we planned our evacuation from the mountains and how we would get ourselves home after the earthquake, we were living fully and none of us will ever forget it. We who returned are changed men. And we still congregate as the old collegians.

Life is a gift and an opportunity, and it is riddled with uncertainty. While this may seem gratuitous when people have lost their lives, the truth is they would want us to make the most of our lives, especially when they cannot. They would want us to make the most of it, every day. We live in times of persuasive uncertainty—earthquakes, forest fires, a COVID-19 pandemic, detestable human conflicts and cruelty, and the creeping spectre of a changing climate with the potential to make everything that has gone before look relatively minor. And yet in all of this we must seek out the joy in life and living. We need to be proactive and make changes for the common good. Who knows what the world will be like as the pandemic restrictions are eased and the much-discussed "normalcy" may be five or more years away, if it's even possible, because the future will confound all expectations.

On the 18th of May 2021 during the pandemic's second wave in Nepal, I receive an email from our accountant Baween Tandukar in Kathmandu. In it he described how his mother died of COVID-19, then his thirty-four-year-old cousin (a father with young children), and then his wife's aunt. This was a family being ravaged by the virus and tossed into despair. I literally wept as I read his message. It is true that chance events change everything and take the trajectory of life in new unanticipated directions. In the end, it's how you deal with it that matters. That is all that matters.

This is why we are going back to Mt. Everest. Next year a third generation of Hillarys will head to the mountain (with their father in support) to sample the exhilaration of the summit and the legacy of what it was like to be first.

Curaçao (The Netherlands)

Chapter 5

Dr. Byron Martina

Scientist and Virologist

Dr. Byron Martina is the head of Artemis One Health Research Institute and CEO of Artemis Bio-support in the Netherlands. Between 2008 and 2018 he was head of the group "exotic viruses" of the Erasmus Medical Center Rotterdam. During this time, he was also head of the WHO reference Centre for arboviruses and hemorrhagic fevers.

Dr. Martina spent his career studying the mechanisms leading to viral diseases and translating that knowledge in development of effective intervention strategies. He was one of the virologists at the forefront in the fight against COVID-19 in The Netherlands. As he puts it, "I know there is a long way to go for diseases like AIDS, but the difference between the impossible and the possible lies in man's determination."

Recently, Dr. Martina lost his wife to metastatic breast cancer, a battle they lost after six long years. He has now dedicated his work towards finding a vaccine for cancer so that families do not have to suffer. He was left with a little girl to raise alone, along with a determination to make the world a better place for future generations.

* * * * *

My interest in viruses started at the age of twelve when I heard about the Human Immunodeficiency Virus (HIV) for the first time. The fascinating questions researchers had about how the virus causes immune deficiency and where did it come from caught my attention. I started reading a lot about viruses, especially HIV and the viruses that could cause leukemia (HTLV), and soon I realized I wanted to become a virologist. Inspired by Robert Gallo, I also wanted to help in identifying and combating disease-causing viruses.

As a virologist I have been educated to expect the worst, meaning the emergence of new viruses able to cause a serious viral pandemic (a global spread of an infectious disease at a particular time). Most pandemics are caused by viruses that jump from animals into humans. For instance, consumption of or close contact with exotic animals like bats has been associated with emergence of several "new viruses." But an increasing world population, which is associated with human encroachment on wildlife habitats, also increases the encounter of humans and wildlife and therefore certainly increases the chance of viruses jumping to humans.

As soon as I started my training as a virologist in the department of virology at the Erasmus Medical Center Rotterdam in the Netherlands, my professor, Dr. Albert Osterhaus (a renowned virologist who I read a lot about long before I started my training), was already expecting the next influenza virus pandemic. "It is not a matter of *if*, but *when* we will experience the next influenza pandemic" was his frequently used statement. He was using the Spanish flu pandemic, which resulted in 50–100 million deaths, as the model argument for why the world should be prepared for the next pandemic.

It is intriguing that despite the history of infectious (viral) diseases, being prepared for a pandemic was not a priority for most governments. I think this lack of importance was caused by the different phases of infectious disease perspectives. First there was a phase in which viruses such as smallpox or polio were responsible for high morbidity and mortality, resulting in significant attention for developing and using vaccines, which eventually resulted in the eradication of smallpox from the face of the earth.

The second phase was characterized by the feeling among experts that infectious diseases were not a problem anymore, a feeling propagated by the eradication of smallpox and the successful use of antibiotics. However, soon thereafter several viruses emerged, including HIV, which led to phase three, in which infectious diseases were again considered important public health threats. And yet the alertness that a serious pandemic could occur decreased as the interval between pandemics could take decades.

To date, infectious diseases still have an impact on public health systems and economies worldwide, affecting especially the vulnerable populations living in resource-poor countries. History has taught us how pandemics may decimate societies, influence outcomes of wars, and may even wipe out entire populations. One advantage of past and recent pandemics is how they stimulated innovations in biomedical sciences (including rapid development of drugs and new generations of vaccines).

Despite all the innovations, solutions to most viral disease problems (neglected diseases) remain something that benefit the wealthy countries, and if infectious agents (viruses) do not pose a threat to the rich countries, not much will be done for the poor. This is due to the great inequality in pharmaceutical research, in that "health research" is determined by the market for treatment and not the burden of disease. This is beginning to change, however, because now it is clear that viruses do not respect borders of countries and do not need a passport. With the extensive travel occurring daily, viruses can spread from one country to the other in matter of days.

When we care for our fellow human beings the death toll caused by any virus should not be relevant; helping to solve the problem should be the focus. For instance, there are viruses that may kill up to 60,000 individuals per year, a relatively "small" problem, especially if the infections are restricted to resource-poor countries. However, that number is equivalent to one person dying every nine minutes. To further put this number into perspective, it is the equivalent of a full 747 airplane crashing every other day. Consider the crash of Malaysia Airlines Flight 17 on July 21, 2014, which is vivid in the memories of everybody worldwide. In the Netherlands, the minister of foreign affairs at the time (Frans Timmermans) expressed the emotions many were feeling during a speech at the United Nations Security Council:

We are here to discuss a tragedy: the downing of a commercial airliner and the death of 298 innocent people. Men, women and a staggering number of children lost their lives on their way to their holiday destinations, homes, loved ones or international obligations such as the important HIV/AIDS conference in Australia. Since Thursday, I have been thinking how horrible must have been the final moments of their lives, when they knew the plane was going down. Did they lock hands with their loved ones, did they hold their children close to their hearts, did they look each other in the eyes, one final time, in a wordless goodbye? We will never know.

This was without any doubt one of the most horrible tragedies against mankind and the case of neglected viruses (such as rabies) is no different: we need one such crash every other day for a year to reach the 60,000. Timmermans delivered an emotional speech, which was widely praised by the international community. Don't we owe it to the people who cannot fight any deadly virus because they do not have the resources to help them in the battle?

I have the hope and evidence this is changing by using the innovations in the fight against neglected diseases as exemplified by the rapid development and implementation of vaccines against Ebola in Africa. Although it may seem we are not making big leaps forward in dealing with neglected viruses, it is important to focus on the good things happening and work to expand the successes. As stated by Maxwell Maltz, "Close scrutiny will show that most 'crisis situations' are opportunities to either advance, or stay where you are."

In 2020, the world had to deal with a devastating viral disease, the SARS coronavirus. When the virus hit Europe and the Americas, it became clear we were dealing with a serious pandemic, as evidenced by the total collapse of health infrastructures. Coronavirus victims accumulated in the corridors of hospitals, with many patients waiting for several days for a bed. The mortality rate even when several supportive treatments were applied was high. Different measures were implemented worldwide in a desperate attempt to control the disease and save lives.

As a virologist, I felt obliged to use my skills and knowledge to help fight this killer virus. This was done in collaboration with many scientists all around the world who came together in solidarity with one common goal—fight the virus and free the world of this devastating disease. The pandemic not only brought together the scientific community, but also non-scientific community. It brought our values of

44

solidarity and fraternity to the fore with the understanding that no one is safe until we are all safe.

"Hope is being able to see that there is light despite all of the darkness."

~ Desmond Tutu ~

The above is not a cliché; it is true that hope (having an expectation that something good will happen in the future) is powerful. It can inspire us to do what may be seen as impossible and therefore provide the strength to carry on during difficult times. During the severe measures implemented by different governments, many people felt depressed and hopeless. I felt it was imperative to stay positive (that a solution will be found) and kind (to adhere to the measures to protect the vulnerable population).

I am naturally optimistic and found ways to build the resilience needed to go through the difficult times we were facing. However, some of those who were depressed asked me, why bother trying to be hopeful when things are so overwhelmingly bad? The message of being kind and staying hopeful during the crisis was a key message put forth by many leaders. Clearly, during the COVID-19 pandemic many people felt it was impossible to maintain any sense of hopefulness or optimism about the future. It was important to find ways to keep hopeful. While I felt the desperation during lock-downs and all the other heavy measures, I also found a way to help those who did not see a light at the end of the tunnel.

During the pandemic, which caused a lot of stress by itself, we were dealing with another situation as a family. My partner had been fighting metastatic breast cancer, also known as advanced breast cancer. The cancer spread to her lungs, liver, and brain. When she was diagnosed, she looked at me and said, "Now I have to rein-vent my purpose of existence." In addition to living a new normal imposed on us by COVID-19, she was also living a "new normal" due to the cancer. Life was never the same again after the diagnosis. What is normal will constantly change and evolve into a "new normal." As time goes on, we begin to feel better, gaining strength and deter-mination to keep fighting. Every day we needed to revisit and re-evaluate priorities in life.

Something you hear constantly from cancer patients is how the diagnosis of cancer changes your perception of time. Cancer and dying become one and you start living one day at a time. Her character changed in some ways, for instance she changed from a very patient person to impatient, and she became easily frustrated. But one thing that didn't change was her optimism, combative attitude, and hope for a better tomorrow, including the hope that new medicines would become available to keep her both positive and combative. This helped her cope with the uncertainties and stress of the COVID-19 pandemic. Unfortunately, she passed away May 2, 2021, six years after the initial diagnosis.

While quality of life is very important for people living with a terminal disease, the measures implemented to protect all those vulnerable people (like herself) also took away a quality of life from her. Enjoying each day to the maximum was no longer possible during the pandemic. As both of us are naturally optimistic people, we sat down one day and asked one another how to create a picture of meaningful goals that expands to a sense of surviving and staying positive? The factors we identified are the ones I used to help people through the difficult times of COVID-19. Some of the things that helped us to see the possibilities, to keep a positive attitude, and stay combative, waiting for the better times to come included the following:

1. Get involved in a cause that interests you by volunteering your time. I have been actively working to provide urgent medical support to members of the community throughout the COVID-19 pandemic. My partner was helping with fundraising for more research on cancer and she was participating in online support groups. Volunteering is a great way to become more hopeful.
2. Start doing things you love to do and enjoy life. In our case we focused on simple things like cooking, dancing, taking a nature walk, listening to our favorite music, and so on. Doing things you love will give your day a sense of worth. Especially during the lockdowns, it helped us and many others to forget the bad times caused by the pandemic.
3. Stay optimistic by not stressing out on the bad things or worst-case scenarios and focus on what is positive and successful in your life, such as family and friends. When negative thoughts come up, try to reframe them. It is easier said than done, but it is imperative to find your own way to reframe negative thoughts to prevent becoming depressed.

Dr. E. Alison Holman, a Professor at the University of California, Irvine, has noted the following about this difficult time:

> The Coronavirus pandemic has become an unfolding, chronic, collective trauma that has ushered in an era of profound uncertainty and fear about the future. As an ambiguous, invisible threat, it has laid bare our illusory assumptions that the future is knowable, controllable, and guaranteed, and replaced them with a future that feels unsafe and uncertain,

a combination sure to trigger stress and anxiety. Add to that the compounding traumas of an economic crisis, systemic anti-black racism, and climate-related disasters, and you have a perfect storm for people feeling like they are living in a time warp.

Almost all prisoners incarcerated for a long time or people who have experienced the horrors of war will face psychological and emotional issues that can show up many years later. The same holds true for some victims of the lockdowns used to deal with the pandemic. People felt robbed of their freedom, friends, family, and a social life. While there was hope that a vaccine, other kinds of medicines, or intervention strategies would become available and bring an end to the pandemic, it seemed far away. Many people were unable to focus on that hope and were instead trapped in the negativity of the pandemic. I believe it is crucial for professionals to share a perspective of hope more often during a crisis. I want to finish by saying we should remind ourselves as often as possible how *it's not the load that breaks you down, it's the way you carry it.*

United Kingdom

Chapter 6

Khaled El Mayet

Solutions Consultant

Khaled grew up in the UK being half-English and half-Libyan. He was proud of being both, but couldn't fully identify with either one, which made him especially sensitive to judging people on who they are not where they come from. When Khaled saw the humanitarian crisis in Ukraine, he remembered the precious words his mother spoke to him just before she passed away: "Do what you can to show that love is greater than hate." He felt a moral obligation to do whatever he could to help, which was to send ambulances.

Khaled had played a small part in a similar mission in 2011 when two ambulances were driven to North Africa from the UK in response to the humanitarian crisis caused by the Arab spring. When he started an online fundraising page for the Ukraine, his goal was to take several ambulances to the Poland-Ukraine border to give to paramedics who could use them to save lives. This initiative has now facilitated the delivery of fourteen ambulances, four neonatal incubators, fourteen defibrillators, and more than four tons of medical supplies.

* * * * *

I call my letter *Ten Sticks: A Story of Hope*.

I was born in England in the 1980s to a Libyan father and English mother, and although I was proud of both heritages, I never truly identified as either. As such, I have never put much thought or consideration into where someone comes from, or indeed what religion they follow, as I see people as either being good or bad or, as is the case with most people, a mix of the two.

I believe we should judge people by their actions rather than their words or their cultural or religious origins. J.K. Rowling summed this up well in her fourth Harry Potter book with the quote "It matters not what someone is born, but what they grow up to be."

My father is a man who has experienced much of what life can offer, having seen the best of life and, indeed, the worst of it. I have learned so much from my father. His love and mentorship have given me the ability to be strong when needed, to use my intellect and experience to judge a situation or person for what they are, and to base my decisions on logic driven by unwavering principles (you will likely never meet a man as fearless or principled as my father).

My mother, and I pray her soul is at peace, taught me other lessons. She was the most selfless person I have ever met and was someone who always saw the good in people even when it was hidden away behind an outwardly negative appearance. Her love was truly powerful and taught me to be kind and soft, to have empathy for humanity, to understand how everyone has their own problems (often hidden due to ego or embarrassment), and to try and appreciate how not all actions are driven by what I might initially assume.

I lost my mother, Oline El Mayet, to Cancer in 2010. She died in my arms having battled the illness for nearly four years (having initially only been given three

50

months to live when first diagnosed). She fought through the pain, not motivated by self-preservation, but because she did not want to leave her children alone to face the world. Her only dream at that stage in her life was to have grandchildren to love and teach; a dream that unfortunately did not come true whilst she was still alive.

The penultimate thing my mother ever said to me as I held her in my arms, was to "Do what you can to show that love is greater than hate." Straight after that, she told me she loved me and then fell asleep for the last time. It comforted me to know she was at peace and without pain for the first time in four years, yet it was without doubt the hardest thing I have ever had to accept. I realised for the first time in my life that no amount of money, friends, or popularity mattered. All that matters in the last moments of life is true love.

I chose to dedicate the rest of my life to fulfilling her charge to me, to *do what I can to show that love is greater than hate.*

In 2011, when the Arab Spring caused a major humanitarian crisis, not only to one nationality but to a large part of an entire region, my family dedicated most of their time to helping save as many people they could, with the sole purpose of helping those who so desperately needed it.

It was my father who came up with the idea of buying two ambulances and taking them to North Africa, having heard from friends on the ground they were desperately needed. My brother and I helped him as best we could to make it a reality; with my brother leading the convoy across Europe while I supported the organisation from "mission control" back in England. During this time, I was lobbying several governments, predominantly through the media, to have the no-fly zone introduced as we knew this would save many innocent civilian lives. To that effect, both missions were successful and although we will never know the true impact of our efforts in 2011, I am confident they played a part in making at least some people's lives better.

Now let's fast forward to February 2022. My daughter was only eight years old and had effectively lost the last two years of her childhood to the global novel coronavirus pandemic. Most of us took for granted in our youth the simple idea of being able to play with our friends, going to school, and generally having a natural and normal upbringing. For two years this was not possible for children all around the world with them always having to worry not only about touching their friends but also worrying about touching anything their friends had touched.

The last thing we needed, when things were finally starting to look optimistic from a pandemic perspective, was a war with the potential to escalate into a global crisis.

Having a keen interest in history, the comparisons to WWII, the Cuban Missile Crisis, and the Cold War in general, were all too clear. Concern was growing around the world about what we might experience over the course of our lifetime. As well as being a keen historian, I am also a keen consumer of well-written literature. JRR Tolkien summed it up well, in *The Lord of the Rings*, when Frodo expressed to Gandalf, "I wish it need not have happened in my time," to which Gandalf replied, "And so do all who live to see such times. But that is not for them to decide. All we have to decide is what to do with the time that is given us."

In that line from Tolkien, there is hope—hope that at least some people will do whatever they can to help others in need; hope that humanity is better than it is worse; hope that love is greater than hate.

On the first day of March 2022, I sat on my sofa in the Cotswolds, England, watching the news and seeing the horrific price being paid for the political games driven by what is, in reality, a tiny number of people. That price was paid most highly by the innocent civilian population of Ukraine, and they paid with death, physical and psychological torment, and the end of the world as they knew it.

Normal everyday people, with little interest in global politics and the affairs of the world's power brokers, who just days earlier may have been worrying about what to wear on a first date, how they would get their work done on time, or whether they might get the job offer or promotion at work they were hoping for, are now worrying about how they will survive and keep their children from being killed in the most horrific of ways imaginable. This is not something being looked back on through the historical lens of a documentary, it is happening before our eyes in the world we all call home.

With my eight-year-old daughter, who is the only thing that truly matters to me in my life (as she is the only thing I am completely responsible for beyond myself), I cannot even begin to comprehend the fear parents in Ukraine must be experiencing. Even if they manage to save their children's lives, just the idea of my daughter knowing the feeling of such fear and the trauma it must cause is enough to bring tears to my eyes.

So, as I sat there watching the news, what I saw was my mother in my arms asking me to do what I can to show how love is greater than hate.

Inspired by what my father had done in 2011 and my mother's dying wish, I set up a JustGiving page and started to raise money to buy at least one (but ideally three) ambulances I could fill with medical supplies and drive 1,400 miles across Europe to the Poland-Ukraine border where I would give them to people who could take them into Ukraine and save innocent lives.

If my daughter was to ever need a stranger's help, I hope someone will help her. But how can I hope for that if I, in turn, could not offer the same hope to others?

The initiative picked up momentum quickly and was widely covered by national and international media, even being referenced by US Secretary of State Antony Blinken in an official White House press release. There has been incredible support from people like Ivor Ichikowitz who, through his family foundation, funded two ambulances and supported the effort in many other ways.

With that momentum and support, I have so far managed to buy and deliver ten ambulances, with additional pledges to fund the purchase of another six ambulances. The initial fundraising was £30,000 on the JustGiving page. To date, I have raised more than £200,000 and counting.

On March 15, 2022, only fourteen days after coming up with the idea, a team of thirteen volunteers, led by me driving one of the ambulances, took a convoy of six ambulances across Europe and successfully delivered these vehicles to an amazing organisation called Global Outreach Doctors that had paramedic responders waiting to risk their lives by driving these vehicles into Ukraine. It was through Adria Dunn's Vine Network, a group of amazing people who collectively do so much to help people across the world and indeed shares its name with this book, that I met both Ivor Ichikowitz and Andrew Lustig of Global Outreach Doctors.

One of the stories from this first mission, which inspired the name of this letter, is from when we were at the ferry port in Dover, England as we were about to cross over to France. A Brazilian lorry driver saw our ambulances and came over and asked if they were going to Ukraine. When I confirmed, he gave me fifty Euros and asked me to buy my team some food and drinks. When asked why he did that he said, "If you take one stick, it is easy to break. If you take three to five sticks it is more difficult. But if you take ten sticks together, it is impossible to break... and we the world are the ten sticks standing together to help people that need it."

The desire to help does not end here. I am now also leading an appeal for neonatal incubators and related medical supplies. The psychological stress of the war has resulted in a significant increase in premature births and the shortage of incubators is resulting in lives being lost. Innocent babies who are fighting for their lives from the moment they are born need this vital medical equipment. Without it, they have little to no chance of surviving.

Hopefully, the work I have done, and the work of the hundreds of amazing people who have supported me, has resulted in lives being saved... and I hope actions such as mine are providing hope to people who will never know my name even as I will never know theirs.

For anyone who reads this... please help me to do what my mother asked me to do.

All it takes is to get up and do one thing today, and indeed every day, no matter how small, to help someone, and in so doing you are helping me spread my mother Oline's message that love is greater than hate and providing hope to people who are in desperate need of your support and love.

India

Chapter 7

Gurudev Sri Sri Ravi Shankar
Spiritual and Humanitarian Leader

Gurudev Sri Sri Ravi Shankar is a humanitarian, spiritual leader, and ambassador of peace and human values. Through his life and work, Gurudev has inspired millions around the world with a vision of a stress-free, violence-free world.

He has designed programs that provide techniques to live a deeper and joyous life. Gurudev founded The Art of Living in 1981, an organisation that today functions in more than 170 countries. He has also established many non-profit organizations that recognize and enrich human identity beyond the boundaries of gender, race, nationality, and religion.

Gurudev is engaged in bridging religious, social, ideological, and economic divides in society by revitalising the ancient Indian ideal of *Vasudhaiva Kutumbakam* (One World Family). He reminds us that diverse traditions and cultures are all rooted in the shared human values of peace, compassion, truth, belongingness, and non-violence.

Apart from enriching and transforming individual lives and giving people a direct experience of inner peace, Gurudev has provided a refreshing framework for peace negotiations globally. From Kashmir, Assam, and Bihar in India, to Colombia, Kosovo, Iraq and Syria, and Cote d'Ivoire, Gurudev's programs have had documented impacts on people involved in armed conflicts, persuading them to pursue the path of peace. His engagements and mediation efforts played a vital role in ensuring a peaceful end to the long-standing Ayodhya conflict in India.

Gurudev's simple message that love and wisdom can prevail over hatred and distress stands as a harbinger of hope in a world besieged with stress and conflict.

* * * * *

A key component of the wisdom we impart in the Art of Living is this: *Opposite values are complementary*. It's natural to experience ups and downs in life. When people forget this inevitable fact, life becomes like a yo-yo and even small events sink one to despair. An awareness of this principle brings forth the strength to stay centred in the face of contrasting circumstances.

Though people wish for a problem-free life, such a life, even if it were possible, would be dull and boring. Human life is shaped by experiences both positive and not-so-positive. Good times bring a sense of expansion while challenging times make us stronger and wiser. Each of these enrich the grand tapestry of life.

When one faces situations that demand stretching beyond one's perceived capabilities, the tendency is to give in to fear and anxiety. When negative events such as pandemics, disasters, violence, or corruption rattle the mind, people tend to lose hope. However, it is during such times one must hold on to hope. Research suggests when one is hopeful, other positive emotions, such as courage, confidence, and happiness follow, enabling one to take proactive action. Although it is paradoxical to tell someone to be hopeful when nothing seems to be going right, that is the time to nurture hope and act on it.

The world has witnessed a phase where nothing seems to be in control. During this critical juncture, it is the job of leaders to instil hope and courage in people. To give you an example, let me share what occurred during the three-day World Cultural Festival we hosted in 2016 in Delhi to celebrate thirty-five years of the Art of Living. This mega festival showcased live performances by more than 36,000 artists from across the globe and brought together more than 3.5 million people over three days. The opening day was greeted by a sudden and heavy downpour that lashed Delhi. Everybody from the performers, organisers, guests, and the audience was drenched! Our people had all but lost hope as the forecast predicted further thunderstorms.

The main organising team came to me, urging us to shift the venue to an indoor stadium. They reasoned that as the ground had become very wet and muddy and rainwater would have seeped into the giant LED screens, there were chances of short-circuits.

I could see the shadow of worry on their faces as they tried to convince me to shift the festival to an indoor stadium, one that would accommodate only 15,000 people. I held a different point of view and insisted they keep to the same venue. This was because hundreds of thousands had travelled from across the globe to attend this event and would have been extremely disappointed at being left out. During the Art of Living, we are usually very democratic and act on consensus, but on this occasion I put my foot down. In a few minutes, the mood changed from despair and despondency to a certain buoyancy and readiness to face any challenge that may arise. From then on, it was a great show and thankfully Nature cooperated fully.

During these challenging times, when people are in the grip of anxiety and fear, we need to increase the hope, enthusiasm, and happiness quotient. What will help in staying optimistic is attending to our inner energy or the vital force, which we refer to in Indian philosophy as "prana" or the "life force" energy. The quality of this energy determines whether one will sink or swim when faced with a critical situation.

You cannot expect to be brimming with hope when your life force is diminished. On the other hand, when it is high, you will stay positive no matter what. Similarly, a chattering mind depletes the life force and wears down the body, mind, and intellect. On the reverse, being centred and still can have the opposite effect of making one more energised and focused. A person who has learnt the skill of managing their energy will always remain optimistic and be able to negotiate the direst of situations.

To conserve *prana* and retain a positive mindset, it's necessary to take up some measures to still the mind. So how does one keep one's *prana* at an optimal level? One of the best ways is a combination of yogic practices such as *pranayama* or breathing techniques and meditation. Meditation is one of the most effective and natural ways of stilling the mind. Inculcating it, along with prayer and *pranayama* as part of your daily routine can do wonders in uplifting your mood and staying positive.

These are the very tools the Art of Living introduced to US war veterans returning from conflict zones in Iraq, Afghanistan, and other such places. Under our Welcome Home Troops initiative, these soldiers were taught meditation and *Sudarshan Kriya*, a rhythmic breathing technique which is a cornerstone of Art of Living programs. These techniques have been widely acknowledged for having transformed the lives of hundreds of American soldiers traumatised by high-casualty conflicts.

A spiritual outlook, or a life infused with wisdom, enhances your capacity to deal with the trials and tribulations one faces while also enjoying life to its fullest. As the saying goes, *every adversity is a blessing in disguise*. Know that whatever happens, happens for the good. Although it's hard to believe this when things are not going well, it is so. A seemingly negative happening may end up with a positive consequence like in the following story:

> The king of a small kingdom had a passion for hunting. Every Sunday, he would go to the forest to hunt, accompanied by his able and loyal General. As a matter of routine, every Saturday evening he would sharpen his tools to use the following day. On one such Saturday evening, while handling his tools, his fingers were cut. The General, who was with him and in the habit of passing comments, remarked, "Whatever happens, happens for the best!"
>
> The king, who was in pain, was furious. "How can my General be so casual about my suffering?" he fumed and decided to put the General behind bars for a couple of days! The General cheerfully accepted the punishment as he was sure something good would present itself even in the punishment!
>
> The next day, the king went hunting without the General. As it happened, he lost his way and wandered into the territory of a neighbouring kingdom where he was captured by a group of tribals who were preparing for a sacrificial ritual. Unfortunately for the king, the tribe believed he had been sent to them by their God for sacrifice and they began

checking to see whether he was fit to be sacrificed. This tribe had a rule, though, that anything less than perfect and complete cannot be offered in sacrifice. When they saw the cut fingers of the king, they rejected him as unfit and set him free. The king was saved!

At that moment the king realised the wisdom behind the General's comment. As soon as he returned to his kingdom, he freed the General, acknowledging he had indeed been right. "If my fingers had not been cut, I would have been sacrificed today, but I cannot fathom what good there was in my imprisoning you!" he said.

With a smile, the General said, "Had I not been imprisoned, I would have been with you and I would have been the one sacrificed in place of you!"

Have faith that no matter how it seems in the moment, only the best will happen to you. You are never given a problem you cannot handle. There is an energy always caring for you and guiding you. When you trust it, fear vanishes, gives way to love, and allows your innate strength to come to the surface.

Another thing we must remember is the changing nature of the world. If good days don't stay forever, then bad days will not stay forever either. Realise everything here, including our lives, is ephemeral.

Throughout human history, mankind has faced many challenges and has displayed resilience again and again. This realisation will kindle valour in you. Focussing on strength further enhances it. Remember, life is bigger than all your gains and losses. Seeing life from a larger perspective and understanding the laws under which it operates makes us wiser and more skilful in dealing with difficult situations.

Another way to enliven the spirit is to be useful to people around you. Look at those who are less fortunate than you and engage in some service activity. Not only will your hopelessness evaporate, but you will become a source of hope for others. And there are endless ways of reaching out to people who are in need.

Amidst its devastating trials, the current global health pandemic has ignited the desire for serving those in distress, for collaborating for the maximum good, and to fight the crisis with solidarity and togetherness. Many rigid boundaries have broken. As a service organisation, we ourselves conducted programs throughout the globe to help healthcare and frontline workers who were reeling from unprecedented pressure and exhaustion.

Recount how many times you have faced a hopeless situation and sailed through it. Instead of complaining about problems, start becoming aware of and grateful for the courage that helped you face the challenges of life. Gratitude endows us with growth and abundance while blame games and complaints shrink us further. Worrying and panicking don't help but hurt. When worried and stressed, the body's natural resilience drops and immunity suffers, making us even more vulnerable.

Science says that when we panic, the amygdala or *chintamani*, the emotional management mechanism of the brain, gets hijacked, thus compromising our decision-making and judgment abilities. What creates panic is our fear of losing control of our own lives and the events around them. But realise that in fact, there is very little of which we are in control. Let me share the story of a Gujarati family I met in England about thirty-five years ago. At one point in time, they were the wealthiest family in Uganda with enough money to last the next four generations.

When Uganda's ruler, President Idi Amin, threw out all the Asians from the country, they had to run for their lives, fleeing with just a suitcase in hand. This experience made them realise nothing was in their control. One can become a pauper or a prince overnight. It dawned on them how they had taken life for granted. With hard work, humility, and renewed hope, they built their fortune again in the UK. Even if you lose everything, if you have the confidence to recreate everything again, that is a mark of success. The resilience to be able to rise again from the ashes is one of the most beautiful qualities of the human spirit. Until you give up, there is always a possibility of something extraordinary unfolding. A big vision of life brings the strength to take on challenges and make the impossible possible.

Take the case of our interventions in the Colombian peace process in South America and the Ayodhya dispute in India. I was in Colombia in 2015 to receive the country's highest civilian award, during which I met with President Juan Manuel Santos. In our discussion, he shared his deep concern about the violence the country had been facing for the last fifty years due to civil unrest. The wide chasm between the FARC guerrillas, the Colombian government, and the public looked impossible to bridge. Many attempts to broker peace had failed. I offered to try and help in what looked to be a hopeless situation.

I sent some of our local Art of Living volunteers to reach out to the FARC leaders and convey my desire to meet with them. A few days later a meeting was arranged in Havana. What transpired over the next few days is a testimony to the power of hope. In our conversations, I introduced them to the Gandhian principle of *Ahimsa* or non-violence and succeeded in persuading them to adopt this ideal in the pursuit of their goals. We discussed and debated at length, and finally they were convinced and motivated to declare a unilateral ceasefire, which eventually led to the signing of the Colombian peace accord.

A similar development took place during a mediation process to resolve the raging 500-year-old Ayodhya Ram temple-Babri Masjid dispute in India. It is the belief and faith of Hindus that Ayodhya, a city in the northern state of Uttar Pradesh, was the birthplace of one of their most revered deities, Lord Rama. An ancient Rama temple was destroyed, and a mosque built over it by Babar, the Mughal emperor who conquered India in 1528. Communal tensions around the issue have prevailed ever since.

Despite the vested interests trying to derail the mediation process, we persisted in continuing our talks with all the stakeholders. Everybody believed the Sunni Waqf Board, the main Muslim body in the conflict, would never agree to concede the land for building a Rama temple where the existing Mosque stood and shift the Mosque to the five-acre plot of land outside the would-be temple complex. But eventually, they did! Not only that, but the entire Muslim community accepted the settlement without any protest. It was nothing short of a miracle! The conflict that had been dragging on for centuries in which both the Hindu and Muslim communities had daggers drawn, was resolved peacefully.

Life is a beautiful mystery to be wondered at and not something that can be understood in its entirety by the logical mind. Your reasoning is based on the limited experiences and knowledge you have. Creation is so much vaster and dynamic.

Living the mystery of life to its fullest is the way of the wise. Accept it and embrace it. When we shut off the mystery or the wonder in life, we not only curtail our growth but also unknowingly make life mechanical. Just as there is no fun in watching a game whose result is already known, life would also be very boring and mechanical if everything were known.

The way to grow is to focus on the positive. If you are trying to get rid of darkness, your attention is on the darkness. But if you turn towards the light, the darkness automatically disappears. Move away from fighting with the shadows and instead focus on the light. Drop the memory of the dark times and move on. A bright future lies ahead, and we have a lot to do. Bring joy and be joyful.

Saudi Arabia

Chapter 8

HRH Princess Reema Bandar Al Saud
Ambassador to the United States

HRH Princess Reema Bandar Al Saud was appointed Ambassador to the United States on February 23, 2019, by the Custodian of the Two Holy Mosques King Salman. She is the first woman in the country's history to serve in this role.

From 2007 until 2015, Princess Reema was the CEO of Alfa International Company Limited, a luxury retail company. In 2013 she founded Alf Khair, a social enterprise aimed at enabling financial self-sufficiency for Saudi women. In 2016, Princess Reema began a career of public service as Vice President of Women's Affairs at the General Sports Authority and then served as Deputy of Development and Planning. In 2018, she was appointed President of the Mass Participation Federation, making her the first woman to lead a multi-sports federation in the Kingdom.

Princess Reema received a BA in Museum Studies from George Washington University and an honorary doctorate from Marymount University. She is a founding member of Zahra Breast Cancer Awareness Association. She has served as a member of the World Bank's advisory council for the Women Entrepreneurs Finance Initiative since 2017. She is a member of the International Olympic Committee (IOC) Women in Sports Commission and the IOC Brisbane 2032 Coordination Commission.

HRH serves as Chairman of the Executive Committee of the Fashion Commission at the Ministry of Culture, and as Honorary Chairman of the Saudi Special Olympics. Princess Reema is a member of the Voting Council for the RBG Awards. She also serves as a Board Member for Panthera and the Future Investment Initiative.

* * * * *

To the women of Saudi Arabia, their families, and friends, and to those around the world who have dreams and aspirations; to the men and boys who have supported their mothers, their wives, their sisters, and daughters, I see you. I hear you. I know what it is like to dream, and I want your dreams to be your inspiration, to help you work through your frustration. I want your hopes to be a motivator and catalyst for change. Change that will shape your life and the lives of others.

I grew up the child of a diplomatic family living between my home country and the United States while my father served as Ambassador. A daughter of Saudi Arabia, I was shaped by our traditions and motivated by our promise and our enormous potential. Ours is a culture founded on tribal principles of hospitality, warmness, honor, and friendship.

My father, Bandar bin Sultan Al Saud, served as the Kingdom of Saudi Arabia's Ambassador to the United States for more than two decades. His work as the bridge between the Kingdom of Saudi Arabia and the United States was more than just his work; it was the mission and the passion of our whole family. As a father, he supported me and my brothers and sister in our ambitions. He taught us not to stop at first impressions. He challenged us to look further and see ourselves in others. He showed us how to seek out commonalities and view the world from the experiences and perspectives of others. That's diplomacy.

But more than diplomacy, that is the test of our humanity. Can we put our own interests aside to understand the interests of our neighbors? Can we value empathy and compassion as much as we value personal or national success and accomplishment?

In my nation, I have seen the compassion and kindness of people every day. The kind that truly inspires hope and change. The kind that is true to our values as a people and a nation and the kind that pushes me every day to serve to the best of my ability.

I am often introduced as the first female serving as Ambassador for my country. And while that may be true, it omits the women who have paved the way for me—the women who I know and whom I have never met who inspired me and endured more hardship so I wouldn't have to. Those who led their communities.

Our vision of the future, our hopes for the future, they depended on change.

When women were first entering the workforce in larger numbers, I led one of the largest international retail firms in the Kingdom. I saw the door opening for women. I appreciated the importance of the moment, for those women and their daughters, and so I was committed to ensuring the successful introduction and assimilation of women into the workforce of my company.

I heard from the employees. I heard their grievances but also their aspirations. I worked to help open a daycare for women because we understood how the barriers to entering the workforce were real but so were the opportunities for a solution—not just opening the door, but keeping it open, being able to walk through it, and being successful once inside.

I also did it not just for the success of my company—and I never doubted women would provide our workplace an advantage—but to validate the larger societal decision to fundamentally transform the public and private workforce through the integration and inclusion of women. As CEO, I saw how many of the girls and women I worked with did not manage or have access to their finances. I founded Alf Khair, a social enterprise organization focused on providing women the tools for financial literacy and self-sufficiency. A woman who is empowered to make financial decisions is

65

a woman who has independence. Self-sufficient women raise sons who support women's inclusion and daughters who know they can achieve their aspirations.

Many women enrolled in our financial literacy courses. They may be the first in their family to get the necessary tools for self-sufficiency, but they will not be the last. The skills we invest in and equip our daughters with today are the real, lasting impact of hope.

The women I have met throughout each chapter of my life and my career have inspired me, challenged me, and helped guide me down my path. I mean women like Dr. Suad Amer, a woman who wasn't knocked down by grief or loss, but instead used it to better serve her community. She founded Zahra Association after losing her mother to a battle with cancer.

After realizing the lack of resources for women in the Kingdom for breast cancer, Dr. Amer took action. I joined forces with her and other women to bring hope to the women of my country suffering from breast cancer, as well as to bring awareness to our population. We launched 10KSA to encourage women's health throughout the Kingdom because a woman in charge of her health is an empowered woman. We broke a record for the largest gathering in a human awareness ribbon, standing together in solidarity with our sisters who are living through breast cancer, and those we lost. Women leading their health initiatives showcase the essential nature of representation. It ensures that women don't only have a seat at the table, but that their voices are heard.

Access to sports and physical activity is a gateway to wider, more far-reaching change. I served as the Deputy Director of Saudi Arabia's General Sports Authority and the first woman President of the Mass Participation Federation. In those positions, my job was to increase access to sports and physical activity for underserved communities—primarily young girls and women. Until then, sports were a realm for men. Few women participated in or even watched sports. Young women were not encouraged as athletes. There were no women's soccer leagues, no women athletes in the Olympics. In many schools, there wasn't even physical fitness for young girls.

As someone who helped increase women's access to sports, I can tell you how this change was about far more than just playing football at school or watching a game in a stadium. This change was about inclusion. This change was a confirmation of worth and value. Access to and participation in sports empowered women to explore and develop their potential, cultivate their confidence, and become more self-assured and reliant. And it more fully integrated women into their communities.

You see, this is the interesting thing about change. At the time, its significance might be hard to see. But once it takes hold, once its full effects become apparent, even the smallest change can be transformational. Girls growing up today in the Kingdom are living a better life, and the daughters of the next generation will know their dreams and aspirations can become a reality.

In this process of development and the unprecedented transformation now taking place, I learned how change is not to be discouraged or feared, because change makes us stronger. Change brings us closer together. Change allows our creativity and ingenuity to build a better world. I learned how change is hope but I have also learned how the people of our nation are resilient and motivated. Nothing has ever been as clear to me as this. Why? Because I see how we can only have hope when there is the potential and possibility for change.

My father taught me this from his time as ambassador. Diplomacy stagnates if the relationship between nations cannot adjust, adapt, accommodate, and change when needed. My mother taught me this as a woman—a woman with dreams and ambitions in a world where those dreams are not always prioritized; a world where women had to work longer and harder because the ceiling above them sought to limit and contain them. With ambition and vision, change is possible.

Both my parents taught me that the seeds of hope—personally, professionally, societally—are change. For women in my own country, we have seen the power of change. In Saudi Arabia, we have witnessed more change in the past seven years than in the previous eighty years for women and the society.

As an individual, I have tried to embrace change and channel it to improve the lives of those around me. There are no guarantees. If you reach for the stars, you still might never touch them. But there's no way find out unless you try. And the magic is in what you experience along the way, what you see, who you meet, and what you learn. I have tried to let this happen throughout my life. Instead of resisting change, I did my best to welcome it, accept it, remake myself as a reflection of that change, and encourage others to do the same. It's what my father did. It's what my mother did. Following in their path, it's what I have attempted to do.

Change is hard, and it can take time. Often, it feels like it takes too much time. But once it happens, once change begins, it must continue, it must be accepted, and it must lead to positive outcomes because change is hope. In a young nation (75% of the Kingdom's population is under the age of 35), hope is the one ingredient essential to the future.

Without hope, there is no reason to strive.
Without hope, there is no reason to dream.
Without hope, there is no reason to sacrifice.

Does hope allow change, or does change enable hope? I'm not sure it matters. They're intertwined like two sides of the same coin. There is not one without the other. With women moving towards equality and equity, the hopes of a nation have fueled near-constant change and continued the path of the inspirational women who have come before us.

Every generation has its trials. This is true globally and it is something we all have in common. Our collective hopes must be united in action and change. If we can do that, I have no doubt our future is bright. I have seen so much change in my lifetime, including changes many thought were all but impossible, that my confidence in what we can now do, what we can achieve, defies uncertainty and has no reservation.

When we have hope, there will be change.
Where there is change, there will be continued hope.

To my sisters and daughters in Saudi Arabia and around the world I say this: Believe in yourselves, believe in what we can do together, believe in the world we can inspire and create.

I believe in you.

United States

Chapter 9

Brad Bandy

Pastor and Refugee Advocate

Thirteen years ago, Brad Bandy and his wife Kim founded The Spero Project, a non-profit organization based in Oklahoma City that welcomes resettled refugees by connecting new neighbors to the people, resources, and learning opportunities that make Oklahoma City a place of belonging. As the Director of Community Development, Brad acts as an advocate for the resettled community, resourcing and supporting leaders as they work on behalf of their communities (locally and globally) and facilitating collaboration among diverse refugee populations.

Prior to Spero, Brad's humanitarian efforts led him to Southeast Asia, Central America, The Balkans, and East Africa. His music career has also taken him across four continents as a professional drummer and percussionist. But it was right back at home where he discovered the "wonder of welcome" among new neighbors and friends from all over the world.

In the "wonder of welcome," no one owns the table, and no one is the guest. Instead, each space is being formed as a new community, made whole by all who are present in equal measure. Brad envisions a world of mutual flourishing and believes there are no strangers. He knows this is possible because, through their sacrificial hospitality, those the world has termed "refugees" have never once let him be a stranger himself.

* * * * *

Breathing in rhythm was the key. Hands above my head, laying on my back, I would will myself to transform my erratic gasping into deeper, steadier breaths. My chest would continue to tighten, my throat would itch, and it felt like I was trying to breathe through a tiny straw. Sometimes one of my parents would sit with me in the middle of the night while I struggled through an extreme asthma attack. Often, I'd lay by myself because I didn't want to bother my dad who would need to wake up for work long before daylight.

I had incredible, loving parents, but our whole family was robbed of all forms of stability, including economic, by erratic and progressive mental illness. So, while ultimately an inhaler would make all the difference, sometimes we didn't have enough medicine to last through the month. I can't imagine how stressful it was for my father to work as hard as he did and still not be able to provide such a crucial aspect of my care. Many nights I felt scared and alone. I felt like I was a burden to my family.

One night, with an attack coming on that seemed too serious to regulate on my own, a memory flashed before me. Our elderly neighbor, Gladys, invited me into her house for some lemonade after I mowed her lawn earlier that summer and I had noticed an inhaler on her kitchen table. It sat next to a stack of bills and a stained coffee cup with a picture of a kitten on it playing with a ball of string. It was risky to use my energy and my breath to try to walk up the street and around the corner, but it was also risky to go without medicine. I'd been in an ambulances and hospital rooms before and been told I was "almost a few minutes too late" more than once, so I knew the stakes.

Pitch black while the rest of the neighborhood was sleeping, I moved up the street as quickly as I could toward the still, dark house where Gladys lived. I had slipped on my favorite shoes (Vans) and can still remember the spot where a hole had worn through to the ball of my foot. I stood on her porch, hands on my hips and heaving short breaths. A few minutes after I rang the bell, the faint yellow porch light came on and she met me at the door in her pink robe and slippers. After I puffed her inhaler, I managed to squeak out a "thank you" as she guided me to her kitchen table and hugged me for what seemed like forever. Looking back, I think I was only there for about fifteen minutes.

That was the night Gladys saved my life, and the story would repeat itself many times through the years. Each time I walked down the street with trepidation, I would force my steps toward the beacon of her house. An indescribable hope rose every time I rounded the corner and saw her porch's yellow glow, letting me know help was only seconds away. Over time, she started leaving the light on for me. This image became a symbol of hope for me.

In the years since these memories, I have been honored to know and learn from some of the world's most hopeful people—those with stories so hard it's difficult to imagine, and yet who survived. Our world has termed them *refugees*, but I call them brother, sister, mentor, colleague, and friend, and they have never once let me be a stranger. We share tea and coffee, food and recipes, grief and joy.

Through my work with The Spero Project, a non-governmental organization my wife and I founded to partner with the resettled refugee community of Oklahoma City, I've experienced the weaving together of so many stories of hope. Here, no one owns the table, no one is the guest. Rather, each space is being formed as a new community, made whole by all who are present in equal measure. It is a place of mutual flourishing where there are no strangers, for our stories will not allow there to be. It is here where we are moved by hope and our hope depends on each other.

A dear friend and colleague of mine, Sang, grew up in the beautiful mountains of Chin State in Burma. One of her favorite memories as a child were afternoon walks with her grandfather through the jungle to a nearby waterfall, swimming with her siblings and cousins, and making use of the natural elements for entertainment. But against the backdrop of this community, idyllic in landscape and full of incredible people, a

71

civil war raged. As the military began to target the region near her home, her family had to make the agonizing choice to flee their ancestral lands. What once was a joyous experience, walking through the jungle, became the most frightening time in her life.

After many years of knowing Sang and her family, I learned about their journey of displacement that began when Sang was thirteen years old. She and her family would have to take their sandals off as they ran through the jungle at night because any noise created would put their lives in danger. Small bands of families and friends would pool their resources to find an experienced guide, and she shared how the group they fled with included newborn babies and elderly grandparents alike, each group member hoping to make it to safety with every family member who started the journey with them.

Once they reached relative safety in Malaysia, Sang and her sixteen-year-old sister were arrested and detained when trying to buy shampoo one night just outside their apartment on the sidewalk below. Their crime was being undocumented while they tried to register with the UN office for refugees. The two were taken to a camp outside this city and held there for a month until her father and his Chin community in Malaysia were able to save enough money to pay for her release. Sang and her sister walked back to Malaysia barefoot again, this time because the camp took her shoes from her. She describes the most memorable moment being when she waded barefoot across an unfamiliar river to meet her father on the other side. The first thing he did when they got back was buy her a pair of sandals at a convenience store. Her eyes filled with tears, and she laughed, embarrassed maybe. "I don't even know why I'm crying," she said. "They're just sandals." But they weren't just sandals. They were a symbol of her father's love, restoring her dignity and reassuring her safety.

As Sang has shared with me through the years, she's mentored me in the defiant hope of walking toward a future that isn't guaranteed. As I've listened to her, I've thought of my childhood walking toward safety at Gladys's house so many nights, of feeling my shoes give way under my feet. It's a point of connection from which even more communal hope can grow. It's impossible for me to state just how much Sang has taught me through the years. Her drive, care for her neighbors, her joy, and her belief in good things to come have been formative in my own journey. Our stories of hope are intertwined, and they both tell me that hope builds on movement. Hope always moves. Even resting it is still in motion.

Often, I might know individuals for years or decades before I hear about their story of displacement and resettlement if I ever heard the details at all. These stories are so personal, and no one owes me an explanation of their journey. But my friend

Marcel was eager to share early in our relationship. I think he shared because I asked with genuine respect and curiosity. An asylum seeker from Cameroon, he wanted Oklahomans to understand just what that meant.

He walked at night. Marcel and his companions stood staring at the edge of a thick, dark forest they would later learn is called the Darien Gap. It is one of the most dangerous migration routes of displaced people in the world. He was forced to this stretch of trackless earth after being targeted by rebels in a cruel civil war at home. There was no option for him to stay in Cameroon and live. Knowing he could never go home was what made him continue through the grueling physical and psychological challenges despite the danger, the darkness, the vipers, and the bodies on the path of those who didn't survive the journey.

Marcel tells me about the "torches," solar-charging lights whose existence truly determine life or death for those holding them. Just as important at the torches was community. No one can make this journey successfully alone and Marcel, like all the other sojourners, was part of a small group of six and part of a larger group of around seventy-five who stayed together at different levels of support.

"You cannot travel alone. You won't make it. You will not be able to overcome the tremendous challenges you will unknowingly face. People die out there. I saw it many times," he told me. They made a pact. "We *all* go, or we don't go."

I'll never forget his retelling of the torches circling up when it was time to set up camp for the night. Everyone with a torch would gather and lean the torches together to shine upward. This would give those who had become separated a chance to make it back to the group before sleeping, following the faint white glow.

As I imagine how it must have felt to be someone who saw the group of lights, a beacon toward which to travel for safety, I flash to the profound relief I would feel when Gladys's porch light switched on. Marcel and I share a similar memory of our icons of hope, of others shining their light for us. He has taught me the meaning of true community, sacrifice, and love for my neighbor. Our journeys toward hope are intertwined and they both tell me that hope is communal.

In one of my first meals together with Anna and her family, I overestimated my spice tolerance (not an uncommon occurrence through the years). Anna, her husband, and her children laughed at me as my mistake became more and more clear to me. My eyes watered and I began to cough as Anna calmly gathered a handful of cornmeal, motioning for me to open my mouth. She dumped it in and motioned to me to chew it, rinse with water, and repeat. It worked like magic!

It was across this same table that I learned about Anna's journey, about her entrepreneurship and incredible work caring for women and children in her home country of the Democratic Republic of Congo and in countries where they lived after violence displaced them. It was around the table that she made me eat more plates of food than I thought I could consume. She always worried I was too skinny. And it was around this table that she got to know my family as her own.

When we met, my mother and father had both recently passed away and Anna mothered me, without the tool of a shared language, across a kitchen table in ways I could never repay. It felt like she had adopted me. I felt comfortable with her family. We poked fun at each other and laughed a lot.

Our son was one year old at the time. "Why only one baby?" she asked, her palms facing upward, head cocked to the side. "No good," she said. She was mother to seven children and found it strange and perhaps cruel to only have one if you could have more. They'd be lonely, she said.

"It's a matter of economics," I said jokingly. I told her that on her farm back home your kids make you money, but here they only cost you money! We laughed so much about that over the years. She was the first person we told when my wife became pregnant with our daughter. She yelled, clapped her hands, and squeezed us tight as we jumped up and down. It was pure joy. Children were a gift from God she would say.

She was like this with anyone she knew. When a coworker of Anna's (a mutual friend of ours) found out her mother in Iraq had died, Anna spent days sitting in silence with her. Without a shared language, verbal comfort had no place. Instead, Anna's presence across the kitchen table reminded our friend she was not alone in a way more profound than words could convey.

Anna is no longer with us, and I miss her deeply. I miss her wisdom and the way she called her sons' names. I miss learning new layers about her faith in God and her care for her community every time her family told me a story. I miss her larger-than-life laugh that filled an apartment suddenly. And I miss what she taught me about the table, about creating space for others to be themselves. Sometimes I think about Gladys's kitchen table and how it represented relief and safety and rest. And the memory is so much like what I experienced at Anna's table. Relief. Safety. Rest.

Anna was one of the most hopeful people I've ever met in my life. She inspired me in every way, but none more so than in the idea of holding a hope full of joy. Our stories of hope are intertwined. And they both tell me hope is belonging.

Every time a new neighbor joins our city through resettlement, I marvel at how our city grows in depth, wisdom, character, and hope. Please know I would never wish displacement and resettlement on any individual, and it's my deepest desire that no person would ever have to leave their home except by choice. Although we are in a world where this is not yet true, it's my honor to join my story with those around me, to anchor our hope in each other's lives. I never want to consume these stories or struggles simply for my own gain or for "life lessons," but as my neighbors have taught me, the things that have entered my life must cause me to move in defiant hope. They must cause me to work toward justice for all, and a world where we live in a community of belonging.

To Sang, Marcel, Anna, Gladys, and so many more neighbors and friends who have shaped me, may our hope continue to be anchored together. And to you I say this: Please remember to leave the light on. It could save someone's life, including your own.

France

Chapter 10

eL Seed

Artist and Farmer

eL Seed is a contemporary artist who uses the wisdom of writers, poets, and philosophers from around the world to convey messages of peace and to underline the commonalities of human existence. He uses his art as an echo of the stories of the communities he meets around the world. His artwork is a way of building a link between people everywhere. Whenever he works within a community, he spends a long time learning and researching to find the best art installation to summarize the voice of the community.

His work has appeared all over the world, including on the façade of L'Institut du Monde Arabe in Paris, in the favelas of Rio di

Janeiro, the demilitarized zone (DMZ) between North and South Korea, the slums of Cape Town, and in the heart of Cairo's garbage collectors' neighborhood.

In 2013, he collaborated with Louis Vuitton on their famous *Foulards d'Artistes* project. In 2015, he was recognized as one of the year's TED Fellows for advocating peaceful expression and social progress through his work. He was named a Global Thinker in 2016 by *Foreign Policy* for his *Perception* project in Cairo, for which he also won the International Award for Public Art from the Institute of Public Art in 2019. In 2017, he won the UNESCO Sharjah prize for Arab Culture. In 2017, he won the UNESCO Sharjah Prize for Arab Culture. In 2021, the World Economic Forum included him on their list of Young Global Leaders for his vision and influence in driving positive change in the world.

* * * * *

The past two years have shown us our ability to become "super-heroes." We all started wearing masks, covering our faces, not hiding our identity but showing our common superpower, our shared humanity.

Doing good without showing our faces, not for the praise, but with humility, out of sight, secretly. We all heard so many beautiful stories of people showing endless generosity and care towards people they barely knew. Our humanity was back.

We expressed compassion towards each other and realized our common vulnerability. Fear and hope were our shared emotions. We all feared the present, not able to project ourselves. The balance slowly shifted towards hope and took over our spectrum of emotions. Fear and despair weren't there and as we thought about how the world would be different after the pandemic, we all forgot at some point what we had been through.

Hope and fear need balance indeed. Fear teaches us what we're afraid of losing while hope, once we know what we're afraid of losing, helps us to keep it safe and preserved.

It is interesting to note how the Arabic word for human being is *insan*, which is derived from the word *nasiya*, which means *to forget*.

78

Indeed, as human beings, we tend to forget. We try to erase from our memories these times where we doubted, where we felt weak and not in control anymore. We all hoped for a different world, a post-pandemic one, as we kept hearing for the past two years. We are humans, and this is our essence. We forget but doing good is within all of us. A small gesture could be worth the world to someone else.

Ten years ago, I was painting in Melbourne when a little girl called Hadya interrupted me. She was eight years old. She asked me if we could talk in private. She pulled me by my hand, and we sat on some stairs in front of the mural. We talked for few minutes about what it means to be an artist and then she said, "I love animals and I love nature. When I grow up, I want to be an artist like you."

She asked me if I had a pen with me. I handed one to her. On a little blue piece of paper, she wrote her name and the date. 19/10/1200, meaning October 19, 2012. She then looked up at me and said, "Please keep this piece of paper so you always remember me."

The seriousness in her tone of voice for such a seemingly trivial gesture intrigued me at that moment. I took the piece of paper, folded it in four, and put it inside my wallet.

The little blue piece of paper stayed in my wallet for years. I forgot about it, as much as Hadya probably forgot about me. Things are worth the value you give them. I could have thrown it out or lost the piece of paper right after I met Hadya, but it stayed preserved, hidden in my wallet, waiting for me to find it again.

A few years ago, while I was reorganizing my wallet, I found this little blue piece of paper, folded in four, with Hadya's childish writing and the beautiful mistake on the date. At first, I wondered why I kept this piece of paper. We didn't speak for more than ten minutes. Why did I put it in my wallet, an object that carries your most precious belongings when you are outside of your home? I could have put it in my pocket and thrown it in the garbage the same day, but I didn't. Why did I unconsciously give value to this encounter? Her confidence intrigued me. She ordered me indirectly to keep the paper, as if something would happen. Since this day, I kept posting about my story with Hadya every year on October 19, asking my community to help me find Hadya. Years passed and unfortunately there was no trace of Hadya.

In 2021, I had an interview on a YouTube show where the host asked me about Hadya. I told him about the story and my quest to find her. Weeks passed and then I received a message from a woman from Melbourne screaming of joy in her writing.

She had found Hadya. Actually, she didn't even look for her. She was her daughter's friend. She put us in touch.

Hadya is now a young adult. She just turned eighteen and we have been in touch for almost a year now. She doesn't call herself an artist, but she loves drawing manga. Our first Zoom call happened in July 2021, and I felt as if I'd found my long-lost child when she logged in. We are now working on an art project together.

Radwa Ashour, the Egyptian writer said, "Time does not disclose its secrets to humanity." But it reveals them at the right time, I guess. Why did I keep the piece of paper? Why did Hadya give it to me? Maybe she will be the greatest artist of her generation and I hold her first autograph.

I see the little blue piece of paper as her own letter of hope. She came to me with the innocence of a child, hoping a random stranger would keep a tiny piece of paper given to him in the streets of Melbourne. She hoped for it, and it happened. She pushed me to keep my promise, as absurd as it could be. What were the chances she would remember the story of this little blue piece of paper? She was so happy and surprised that I kept it. I showed her a selfie of us I took in 2012 when we met. She was shocked to see this whole story was real.

The young Hadya taught us all a lesson. Do not underestimate the impact you can have on people's lives, or the impact other people can have on you. Honor your promises, for something beautiful might come out of it.

Today I realize the power of the little blue piece of paper. It taught me how important it is to give value to the people you meet and how even insignificant encounters can have a deep impact.

As an artist, I wanted, at the beginning of my journey, to leave something behind, to leave a trace. So, I traveled all around the world, met people, and discovered cultures. I wanted to leave a trace in people's lives. Soon enough, I realized the people I met were the ones leaving something in my life. It wasn't about me anymore. It was about the people I met.

I feel all my art projects are about instilling hope, showing people their value. A man once told me how sometimes you need somebody from outside to tell you how beautiful you are. He is right. We rarely see our own beauty or at least in the reflection of other people's perception.

French novelist Andre Malraux said, "Art is the shortest path between one human being to another one." I believe art is the most powerful tool to bring people, cultures, and generations together. All my projects and mainly this moment with Hadya made me realize the social responsibility artists carry. Our role is to make people dream, hope, and look at the world from a different perspective.

A few years ago, I decided to do a neighborhood project in Cairo focused on the garbage collectors. The goal of the project was to question the level of judgment and misconception society can unconsciously have about a community based on their differences. In the Mokattam Mountain neighborhood of Cairo, the Coptic community of Zaraeeb have collected the trash of the city for decades. They developed the most efficient and highly profitable recycling system in the world. Still, the place is perceived as dirty, marginalized, and segregated. To bring light to this community, I decided to create an anamorphic piece that would cover the entire neighborhood, only visible from a certain vantage point of the mountain.

At the beginning of each project, there is little interaction with the community. People don't understand the purpose of what I am doing. But soon enough, bonds are created. The first building I painted was the house of Uncle Ibrahim. He was such an enthusiastic person. He was always singing and making jokes, and his daughters and sons saved me from his bull, which tried to attack me on the fourth floor! Indeed, the garbage collectors of Cairo house their animals in their buildings. They use their animals to recycle the organic waste.

Uncle Ibrahim was always hanging out on the balcony and talking to me while I was painting. I remember him saying how he hadn't gone to the mountain in ten years and how he never takes a day off. He said if he stopped working, who would stop the garbage? But surprisingly, at the end of the project, he did come all the way to the mountain to look at the piece. He was really proud to see his house painted. He said it was a project of peace and unity that brought people together. His perception towards the project changed, and my perception towards the community changed also, including towards what they do. All the garbage everyone is disgusted by is not theirs. They just work with it. They don't live in the garbage—they make a living from the garbage.

There were times when I doubted myself and wondered what the real purpose was of the whole project. It was not about beautifying a place by bringing art to it. It was about switching perception and opening a dialogue on the connection we have with communities we don't know. Day after day, the calligraphy circle was taking shape, and we were always excited to go back on the mountain to look at the piece. Standing exactly at the same place every day made me realize the symbolism behind this ana-morphic piece. If you want to see the real image of somebody, maybe you need to change your angle.

The interaction with the community during this project gave me hope in human beings. We are inextricably bound together, intertwined by our shared humanity. I was carrying the little blue of paper from Hadya in my wallet while I was doing this project. Her letter of hope was spreading the beautiful energy of her innocence, her dreams, and her hope. I pray this energy reaches you.

United Kingdom

Chapter 11

Clare Mountbatten,
Marchioness of Milford Haven

Philanthropist, Author, Polo Player

Clare Milford Haven is a Trustee and co–Founder of James' Place, set up in memory of her eldest son James, who died at age 21 in December 2006. James' Place Liverpool was opened by HRH The Duke of Cambridge in June 2018, and James' Place London opened in May 2022. These are the first centres of their kind in the UK, offering free one-on-one therapeutic help and support to men who are experiencing a suicidal crisis, in an environment that has been designed to feel masculine, warm and welcoming.

Clare lives on a farm in the West Sussex/Hampshire borders with her husband George and their four children. Previously a freelance writer, including a hectic eight-year stint as Social Editor of Tatler, Clare has recently published her first children's book, *The Magic Sandcastle*. Clare is a keen and competitive polo player and has represented England internationally three times, in Mexico, Chile, and Austria.

* * * * *

"Hope lies in dreams, in imagination, and in the courage of those who dare to make dreams into reality."

~ Jonas Salk ~

One of the most powerful books I have ever read is *Man's Search for Meaning* by Viktor Frankl, an Austrian prisoner of war, incarcerated at Auschwitz during World War II. His mother, brother, and pregnant wife were all killed in the death camps. He lost everything except one thing, the freedom to choose how to respond to any situation. As he put it, "You cannot control what happens to you in life, but you can always control what you will feel and do about what happens to you."

Frankl firmly believed we could find hope in even the darkest of places and our motivation for life comes from meaning. Frankl hypothesised that when we do not have meaning or purpose in our lives, then our mental health begins to deteriorate. He knew he had to have hope or he would perish in the appalling conditions he experienced in Auschwitz: "The thought of suicide was entertained by nearly everyone, if only for a brief time. It was born out of the hopelessness of the situation...."

Frankl found hope in watching the tree in the yard as it changed during the different seasons, looking at the mountains from the hideously overcrowded trains, and thinking about when he would see his wife and family again even though he didn't know if they were dead or alive. These small things were all he had to cling to, and the only sources of joy that gave him a glimmer of hope in the most horrific of situations. That Frankl could find meaning out of his unimaginable suffering is a testament to his extraordinary mental strength.

His words were particularly helpful to me in the aftermath of the death of my eldest son James in 2006. Ten days after a minor operation, my twenty-one-year-old son took

84

his own life after a rapid decline. It left us all reeling and changed our lives forever. He had become fixated that the operation had left him impotent, or in his words, "no longer the man I used to be." He had quickly lost all hope. He did seek help from the National Health Service, but his search was fruitless, and he descended into an abyss of depression and acute anxiety. His decision to end his life is something I will never fully come to terms with, and it has challenged my own innate positivity and optimism.

After James died, I also could not see a way forward without him. I could not envisage our family unit without its key member. We were now fragmented, shattered even. I prayed things would get better for us, but in the days following his tragic and untimely death, I was clutching at hope. It eluded me, as did peace. I realised if you have no hope, you feel there is nothing to live for. Hope is key to our feelings of optimism and positivity. Hope helps us to look to the future. When hope goes, so do any thoughts of the future.

Having read Viktor Frankl's words, I realised surviving the trauma without lasting collateral damage meant regaining hope for myself, my family, my friends, and James' network of friends too. I became acutely aware of the role I played as a mother, wife, sister, daughter, aunt, friend. Everyone was looking at me to see how I was coping and conducting myself. It was as if they were looking at me for permission as to how they could go forward with their lives.

With this realisation, I braced myself and began putting one foot in front of the other to live a new life, one without James, but also a life that could have meaning and purpose, that could help to make sense of what had happened.

Eighteen months after James died, we set up a charitable foundation in his name. We wanted to fund projects to help prevent other suicides and families going through what we were enduring. For ten years we researched, learnt, and lobbied for anything that would help reduce the appalling statistics of male suicide. It was an immense and painful learning curve, at times hugely frustrating, but at other times extremely rewarding.

In 2018 we opened James' Place in Liverpool, a centre where men devoid of hope could come and get their hope back again. We created a calm place that values, respects, and nurtures all adult males over the age of eighteen who are in suicidal crisis. We opened another one this year, in May 2022. Once again, His Royal Highness, The Duke of Cambridge, came to support us at our launch and said, "The one take-away for me is the idea that there is a solution…I think men sometimes get so lost in the detail, they forget the bigger picture, and being able to have that bit of support that can move them forward and there is hope and a brighter future."

During the past four years, we have seen and helped over 1,000 men in suicidal crisis. Men who have made plans to die, to leave their families and loved ones have been brought back from the brink of despair and given another chance to live a life of optimism and hope. The therapeutic relationship between the men who come in through our doors and their therapists is key. We are asking men to trust us when they have lost all hope. We are saying to them that, if they engage with us, we can help them to find hope again. That is the promise we make to them. Our strap line is very clear: "Preventing Suicide. Providing Hope".

I am often asked how I managed to get up in the mornings after James died so suddenly. My reply is that I had to get up as I still had a life I wanted to live, however much pain I was in. I had to keep going for myself, my family, and my friends. I will freely admit there were times when I could find no peace and questioned my existence without my eldest son. I especially remember the first Christmas Day, only ten days after James left us. I found it impossible to be remotely festive. I knew I had to go through the motions of the day, but it was like a slow torture. I remember lying on my bed in the afternoon and just wanting to find some respite from the emotional pain I was feeling. I felt it was wrong to call a friend because it was Christmas Day, and I didn't want to disturb anyone or upset anyone else's day. It was probably the closest I came to feeling I had lost all hope, but somehow I got through it.

How have I found hope in my life since those dark days? I have been surprised at how much nature and animals have played a role in this. I used to walk up to the church where James is buried and marvel at the way I suddenly saw nature in a heightened way. During the half-hour walk, I would notice the beads of water on the leaves of the trees as if they were in glorious technicolour. I would hear the birds singing and it was like a symphony. My senses were somehow enhanced to the things I had previously taken for granted.

I live on a farm with plenty of animals and in springtime we have lambs, foals, and more recently a litter of nine Labrador puppies. I have found such joy in nurturing these small, vulnerable souls. You will find me early in the morning sitting in the middle of a field and bottle-feeding a lamb rejected by its mother. I feel totally at peace with the world. I listen to the birdsong, I feel the early morning sun on my face, and it feels so good to be alive. These small animals give me immense hope as much as they give me unconditional love. They need me as much as I need them. It is a totally

86

symbiotic relationship and I feel hugely blessed and privileged to have these creatures in my life.

Likewise, I have found immense hope through sport, which plays a big part in my life. I have been playing competitive polo for the past 23 years. It is a sport I am passionate about and have worked hard to make it possible for me to continue playing over the years by gaining the sponsorship of two global brands. My son James also played polo and was captain of his school's team. He was equally passionate about the sport, and we played together many times. After the game, we would analyse our performance, both as individual players and as a team, on our way home in the car. If we had won, we would put music on full blast and sing all the way home. If we lost, the atmosphere in the car was more subdued…

After James died, I could not see myself ever playing polo ever again. It felt wrong to play without him, even worse to enjoy myself. However, my sponsors had paid me and therefore I felt obliged to play, even though it didn't sit well with me. They gently cajoled me into it. It was the best thing they could have done. I came off the field after my first game back feeling emotional but elated. The endorphins had kicked in and, for the first time in months, I felt alive again.

I have continued to play ever since. I call it my aggressive meditation. It focuses my mind on something else for an hour or more. I don't think about James or any of the sadness. I don't have time to. I just focus on hitting a white ball and scoring a goal. I think about how I can best contribute to my team. I love being part of a team and always promote collaboration.

Family and close friendships also bring me hope. Those moments when we are all together as a family unit make everyone feel safe and secure. The laughter that comes from being with people we know well, even those we haven't seen for some time, warms the heart. And then there are those people who come into our lives and shine a light where there was darkness, people who we never anticipated meeting, providing us with a different perspective, another angle, a fresh way of looking at things.

With this in mind, I am reminded how this November I will be a grandmother for the first time! This fills me with immense hope and joy. My second son and my daughter-in-law are expecting their first baby. It will enhance our lives enormously, and I look forward to greeting this little creature into our world. I have no idea how it will feel. This is my first time! But I know it is going to be a very positive and life-changing experience.

Thinking back to my childhood, my hopes were more superficial and more selfish, such as "I hope Father Christmas will bring me something this year," or at school, "I hope I will pass my exams and get picked for the netball team." As I grew older, my hopes became more desires, such as "I hope he loves me," and "I hope I will get married, have children, and live happily ever after." More recently my hopes are more universal, as in "I hope for world peace and a rapid end to the war in Ukraine, and to reverse global warming".

But I also realise hope on its own is not enough. We also must pray and do so with conviction. If we truly believe in something, we must visualise it happening and keep it constantly in our thoughts and prayers because if hope doesn't become reality, there is always disappointment. Hope is not certain. It's a wish, a whim, a dream. It may or may not be or happen. But we must grasp hope with both hands and hang on tightly to it, because without hope our lives become meaningless.

Mexico

Chapter 12

Leon Rocco Feldman Birigner

Student

Leon Rocco was born in Mexico City and is currently attending the fifth grade at the American School Foundation. His biggest passion is soccer, and he is great at it! He plans to take it to the professional level. Even though Leon Rocco was born in Mexico City, his family ancestry goes back to Hungary, Romania, Brazil, and Colombia, which helps explain his eclectic personality.

Ever since Leon Rocco was a toddler, you could see he was compassionate towards others. By age eight he had already begun his philanthropic career. When the pandemic started (March 2020) Leon Rocco could only think of the less fortunate children on the streets. He was sad that these poor children were forced to sell sweets to earn money for food and had no choice but to work unprotected from the virus.

He decided to start a campaign to raise funds to buy protective gear for these children. It started with facemasks and hand sanitizer, then expanded to distributing food packs. During this time, he was able to help more than 2,000 children and started his own non-profit called Ninos Ayudando Ninos (Children helping Children). Together with Cocinamos Mexico he was able to distribute food and protective gear packs personalized with beautiful positive messages and drawings to the most vulnerable population in marginalized areas of Mexico City. Rocco truly believes if you plant seeds within our youth they will grow into a beautiful harvest to create a prosperous future.

* * * * *

Grownups always say children are the future of the world, and this is as true as the fact that my favorite food is pizza, but it is also a cliché. I would like to modify it in your minds because while we are the *future* of the world, even more importantly we are the *present* as well, and if we start acting now and making a difference in our present, we *will* have a better and brighter future.

The pandemic changed our lives, and probably the lives of every human being and animal around the globe, maybe even plants and the air we breathe. We all felt vulnerable, scared, and even depressed. But it also brought with it many positive things, like being able to spend lots of time with our families. Animals were free to wander around and the planet had the opportunity to breathe freely. The skies were clear again, whereas before on some days you could not see past the mountains because of the pollution. Whales and manta rays played and jumped fearlessly close to the coastlines, and some of us were lucky enough to witness this. So many people around the world were fortunate to see and acknowledge there was something different happening all around us, and this I believe brought hope and changed our vision of many things, in even amid such dark days.

What did the pandemic bring to you? For me, the pandemic was a turning point in my life.

90

It all started in March 2020 when I was eight years old. My mom had just come back from the supermarket, it was already past my bedtime, it was dark, and it was raining. It was a sad night. We were already in lockdown. My mom had a really sad face and decided to share with us the story of what she had just witnessed.

Outside the supermarket was a boy I always refer to as *niño marzipan* (marzipan boy). He was maybe nine years old at the time and was selling marzipans in the street. Just so you know, in Mexico there are a lot of people selling all types of things in the streets. This is their way of earning money. She decided to give him some money and the boy took it and gave her the marzipans. My mom told him to keep the marzipans so he could sell them the next day and make more money and to go home since it was already late at night. The boy didn't seem happy about this and insisted she should take the marzipans, but she didn't. As she was walking away, she realized he was asking her to please take the marzipans since he could not go back home until all were sold. She went back and asked him if this was the reason and he said yes. She bought all the marzipans he had left. Finally, the boy headed home with a smile in his face. He had finally finished his workday.

When my mom finished the story, I had so many questions. Why is a nine-year-old boy selling sweets in the street? Why so late? Where were his parents? Why is he not home with his family protecting himself form the virus we were all so scared of? For the first time I learned and understood how this was the only way some families had to make a living. I was so sad. I had to do something! How could I help these children? My brother and best friend Milo, who was four years old at the time, had a fantastic idea. "Why don't we bring them all home?" But, of course, we couldn't really do that. There had to be something else I could do.

I went to my room and couldn't stop crying. I had such an emptiness in my stomach even though I had just finished dinner and my heart was hurting. I felt so fortunate and felt so much need to help these children who were not as fortunate as me to be able to stay home and try to escape the scary virus. I could see in my mind not only marzipan boy, but many other children being scared. And then, just like that I had the idea—one that would end up helping more than 2,000 children.

I could not take them off the streets, but if they had to stay in the streets, I could help them do so as safely as possible. I had to do a whole fundraising campaign to buy the items I wanted to put in protection kits for these marzipan children who are forced to stay in the streets and work long hours to help feed their families. I could at least help protect them from the virus with face masks and hand sanitizer. I did a video and my family helped me share it online. It started reaching so many people who connected to this cause and the help started pouring in.

We began making kits with hand sanitizer and face masks inside a paper bag with a message of hope and a drawing on the outside of the bag for every kid. I asked many of my friends from school to help me draw them. Later, a milk company heard about my campaign and reached out to me, and we were able to include milk in the kit, and then later we even stared adding food. It was so exciting to see people getting involved and making the project so much bigger!

I personally went with my family and other adults who were making a difference in people's lives to deliver the kits and delicious warm meals. I understood then how simple things so common we don't even think about them can make such a difference in somebody's life, like a hot meal on your table. Cocinamos Mexico did this through-out the pandemic and I was fortunate to help. There are so many things we take for granted or don't see anything special about, such as being able to choose between scrambled eggs or waffles or cereal for breakfast. Meanwhile, many children are lucky if they can have tortillas and beans, an many don't even get that.

So many children started connecting to the campaign. My cousin Leah, who is like my older sister and a role model who was thirteen years old at the time, started braid-ing beautiful bracelets and making tie-dyed tee-shirts to sell and raise money for the cause. Andrea, her best friend, made videos to help us spread the word about the campaign. My cousin Ayla did amazing weekly slime classes, and my friend Maika did origami classes, both on Zoom to raise funds. These are only a few examples of how children started getting involved. That is when Mariana Hanukinuki noticed us! She called me and talked to my mom because she visualized a much bigger project than just this campaign we were doing, a project that wouldn't end with the pandemic. This is when Niños Ayudando Niños (Children Helping Children) was born and it's the best idea ever!

Children have so many ideas on how we can make this a better world. Most of the time these stay just as ideas, or at least stay as ideas until we make them happen when we become adults. Even though they can be great ideas, we children don't have the means to make them happen. But if we get the support and help of adults, then this is where the magic can start to happen.

"Whoever saves one life saves the world entire."

~ paraphrased from the Talmud ~

Niños Ayudando Niños is a non-governmental organization directed by me that invites all the children of the world to be part of it, to share their ideas about how to make a difference in the world and help improve the life of any human being. It is a place for brainstorming and a place where adults listen to us and help us get our ideas out there in the world. It's about planting seeds of hope in all children to become a harvest in the future of incredible leaders and citizens of the world.

Imagine how something as simple as nutrition can affect the future of a child. If they have anemia, their brain will not develop properly and will not be able to learn as much as it could. This immediately affects their future and their possibilities to get out of poverty and fulfill their dreams. Something as basic as this could change their life and their future. This to me is mind-blowing. We need to start changing the present to have the best future. Together we will construct day-by-day a beautiful future—one full of possibilities and full of hope.

I think this pandemic has affected all of us and has been very hard. So many people have lost close friends, family, and pets. But many people also never lost hope, and one of those people is me. I never lost hope for these children, and with the help of my family, friends, and many others, we were able to help more than 2,000 children and raised more than $250,000 Mexican pesos. So, if a little eight-year-old kid never lost hope and started something this big, so can you!

"A thousand candles can be lit from the flame of one candle, and the life of
the candle will not be shortened. Happiness can be spread
without diminishing that of yourself."

~ The Buddha ~

Democratic Republic of the Congo

Chapter 13

Eric Rutingabo Muhizi

Motivational Speaker

Eric Rutingabo Muhizi is a refugee from Katanga, Democratic Republic of the Congo. He was born to two phenomenal parents, Muhizi Asheri and Anne Nyirazaninka. At the age of three, he and his six other siblings (Brigitte, Innocent, Franck, David, Niyo, and Peter) were forced to flee their country due to multiple civil wars. His family migrated to Burundi in 2001 to seek a better life. In 2004, his family migrated to Uganda after seeing the genocide in the Gatumba camp. After four refuge processes, ye maintaining faith and hope, God answered his prayers. In 2008, his whole family was granted a visa from the United Nations High Commissioner for Refugees to migrate to the United States of America.

Eric is currently a senior at the University of Central Oklahoma, pursuing an Industrial Safety Professional degree. As of today, he helps people in his community as a leader and advocate for international students at his school and back home. With God's grace, he would love to give back to his home country because he knows how it feels to walk in their shoes. His goal is to build an organization for people in need, whether they are refugees, orphans, widows, and so on. He has a desire for them to grow with love, happiness, hope, and the belief they can achieve anything they set their minds to.

* * * * *

What is childhood? When you hear the term *childhood*, what is the first thing you automatically think of? Is it where you spent time with your friends? Where you got to make mistakes and be told it's okay? Celebrating birthdays with your friends and relatives? Going on a field trip with school or family? Or is it where you got to enjoy time on a playground? What *is* childhood?

Well, here is mine. I believe I was born with the gift of retaining information at a very early age. At two years old, I could name most of the capital cities of African countries and this is one of my favorite memories. I have utilized this advantage against my siblings to entertain guests, and it really bothered them a lot. My parents would brag to guests how their son was the smartest with a very high memory capacity to recall anything you might tell him. The look on my brothers' faces was always one of being stunned and offended.

My father would always say *mwana wanje* (my child), *one day you will rule the nations.* My second-favorite memory my father told me about was how I was very excited at two-and-a-half years of age when he tried to teach me how to milk a dairy cow. It was a complicated task to snag the cow and tie it up without letting go of the rope. My brothers were there as well. It was just one of those happy moments of family that made a deep impression on me. Little did I know my so-called childhood would soon come to an abrupt end.

On the evening of August 14, 1998, the atmosphere in the neighborhood transformed as the government officials whom we interacted with and looked up to as our guardians and protectors on daily basis changed. Their facial and physical expressions changed as evening approached. On regular days we would play, brag, and connect with them in the community as normal citizens. On that day, however, the government army began surrounding the village, not to protect it, but to ensure anyone who tried to escape would be captured.

This is the day my childhood was taken away from me. As evening fell, the governmental official started attacking people in the community, pushing them toward the center of the village where their headquarters were located and where my family lived. When my brothers and I were outside, the governmental military began telling us to stay inside the house as the whole place was surrounded so no one could escape. A few hours later we started hearing gunshots and our father yelled *nimuze muzu twatewe* (come inside, we are under attack)! We ran inside the house, and we were told to stay in one room.

We heard much more gunfire and to us it sounded like raindrops. We really thought it was beginning to rain. The sound of rain was always loud in the hut houses with a roof made of corrugated steel roof panels as the raindrops pelted the corrugated silver steel like it was being torpedoed. Then we heard soldiers were pounding on our door and yelling *nfungura murango* (open the door)! My father did not have any other choice but to open the door. They took my father and mother (Muhizi and Anna), my siblings (Bridget, Innocent, Frank, David, and Niyo), and I was left behind because I had fallen asleep and everyone thought someone else had grabbed me in the confusion and chaos.

Soldiers came back to steal all our belongings and they found me sleeping and they threw me outside. I made my way to one of the disabled grandmothers in the community who couldn't leave her home due to her health conditions. I spent a night with her, and she told me to hide behind a chair in case soldiers came searching. A few moments later soldiers made their way inside the house and started firing bullets at the granny. They tried to shoot granny five times but because of God's protection, none of those bullets hit her. After witnessing this, she told me to go look for others. As I was exiting the house, one of the soldiers saw me and caught me.

On that night, my parents thought I must be dead. I had no idea if my parents and siblings who had been taken from me were alive or not. I was gripped by fear. I started praying to ask God to forgive me for whatever reason made those soldiers attack us. I don't know why I didn't get shot on the spot. Perhaps they didn't want to waste a bullet on a two-and-a-half-year-old child. I was just a little boy, after all, so how could I possibly survive? It must have been a minute or two that I stood there, expecting to die, but it felt like an eternity. One soldier grabbed me and took me to a men's facility and threw me through the window as if I were a ball. When my father saw me being cast through the window, he described it as the most shocked and exciting moment of his lifetime. To this day when we discuss it, I can still visualize all his emotions. Later, I was transferred to where my mom and other sibling were being held.

People from different villages were forced out of their homes, gathered in a huge empty field where they had brought hundreds to thousands of people. They were surrounded by soldiers and the plan was to count to three and start shooting everyone (remember, these are the same soldiers who we viewed as our guardian protectors). The commander who was in charge began counting from one to three, but when he reached two, he stopped counting. He stated to his army he wanted to separate males, females, young adults, children, and infants from each other, so he could have statistical numbers specifying who was killed to report to their superior officers.

On that day thousands of people were captured from all the surrounding villages. They began isolating men from women, boys who were eighteen years and older were taken with older men to a local church facility where they were held captive while women and younger children were distributed in different classrooms in a local primary school facility as prisoners. Those classrooms were small, but my bothers said they held hundreds of people in one classroom. There was no remaining space for even children to lay down. They spent the entire night standing.

On the morning of Saturday August 15, they put everyone in a queue, separating children and their mothers based on age. Children who were ten years and under stayed with their mothers, boys who were between eleven and seventeen years old were placed in a different room. On Sunday August 16, the soldiers gathered those older children and took them to collect firewood. The plan was to slaughter all the younger children and burn them with firewood they had just collected. Imagine collecting wood knowing that they were going to burn us with. It is like digging your own grave.

Everything was well-planned and Tuesday was the day to execute all people in captivity as they were still waiting for trucks full of knives, machetes, other weapons, and military reinforcements. Tuesday August 18 around 5am guns were fired, and people broke through the prisons and started running towards the forest. We spent about a week-and-a-half in the forest, hoping this was temporary and would soon come to an end. We ate whatever was available, including wildlife. On that Tuesday, more than 100 people lost their lives. Once the situation calmed down, we came back to our houses hoping life would go back to normal. Instead, a few days later things escalated, leading us to flee our homes and head to Kalemi, which was approximately

180 kilometers (112 miles) away from us, and we traveled on foot to get there. A lot of lives were lost throughout the journey. Many families were separated, not knowing if they would survive.

You might be wondering what caused the war. The It was a conflict between politically affiliated entities that had nothing to do with us regular citizens. Mobutu Sese-Seko had been the President of the Democratic Republic of the Congo (DRC) from 1949–1997, but the opposition revolutionary Laurent Desire Kabila tried to overthrow the sitting president by force. He and other politically affiliated parties signed treaties contingent upon defeating the regime. Kabila indeed was able to overthrow Mobutu.

Upon Laurent Desire Kabila becoming president, however, things didn't go according to how they had planned with those who helped him, and conflicts between them commenced. Among those who assisted him during his revolutionary journey, there were some from Rwanda who looked like those of our tribes (Banyamulenge) based on facial structural descriptions. Based on whatever disagreements they had with Rwandese, Kabila went on national television and encouraged everyone to kill anyone who looked Rwandan and anyone who was Tutsi or looked Tutsi. That is what started the war in our village. They killed our people just because of our appearance.

Upon our arrival in Kalemi, we quickly realized it wasn't safe there either as the war broke out throughout the entire country. We kept fleeing from place to place hoping to find a safe area we could call a new home. We found ourselves in a refugee camp in Bujumbura, Burundi under the United Nations High Commissioner for Refugees (UNHCR). We lived in Burundi from 2000 to 2004. We attended basic school within the camp. We enjoyed playing drums, soccer, and other activities during the time we lived in Burundi.

In 2003, another war broke out in Congo which caused more people to flee to another camp in Burundi called Gatumba camp. It was in the west of Burundi near the DRC border. On August 13, 2004, Gatumba camp was attacked, and many people were killed.

This is the day that every Munyamulenge (my tribe's name) person will never forget. A force of armed combatant rebels massacred 166 people and wounded more than 300. It is one of the largest civilian massacres ever carried out in Burundi. After seeing our people die on that day, my family decided to seek safety by fleeing to Uganda. Upon arriving in Kampala, we reported in at the police station, hoping to find a safe shelter where we could get some rest, but things didn't go according to plan. We ended up spending three nights sleeping in abandoned buses. After those three nights, we were told to move to another camp called Cyaka-2. We only stayed there for a few days due to rebels who were threatening to murder my family. They told us to leave the camp or they would murder us just like what happened in Gatumba camp.

When we returned to Kampala (Uganda) we went to a refugee agency and told them how our family was threatened in the camp and how they were going to kill us. The refugee agency decided not to help us. We had nowhere to go. My family and I became homeless as of September 27, 2004, living under a mango tree for three months. The tree was a on higher elevated ground and there was a high school below it. I recall seeing kids of my age playing outside and I would run towards them because I wanted to play among them, but they would call me all sorts of names because I had no home to live in. I questioned God so much and I would ask my parents hundreds of questions about why our lives were that way.

I remember one day sitting down with my father and having a conversation. He told me to look in the sky and tell him what I saw. I said all I saw was an airplane. His response was, "One day we will be able to sit in one of those planes and will be in the United States of America." After all that we went through, my father had faith, hope, and belief that one day God would open doors. While living under a mango tree, my parents met a man named Pastor Jackson who helped our family with housing and paid our rent for nine months, but he passed away few years later (may he rest in peace). We waited patiently for our refugee case process to move forward. We hoped and believed God would one day find us a better, safer place to call a new home.

When US officials finally reviewed our case, we were accepted to settle in the state of Oklahoma. With all requirements fulfilled, we were granted a refugee status Visa to the United States of America in September 2008.

We landed in Oklahoma on September 19, 2008 and were welcomed by the Refugee Resettlement Agency. Fast forward a month later and I had met many people. Among them was Brad Bandy, with whom our family connected deeply. He had established The Spero Project and allowed me to be part of it, serving with a group of friends who became like a family to me. From that moment I knew Oklahoma was truly my new home. I attended Taft Middle School and Northwest Classen High School. I am currently a senior at the University of Central Oklahoma, pursuing a degree in Industrial Safety along with Certified Safety Professional Certification.

I learned a tremendous amount from my parents, and one of the many things they taught me is to give back to the community. This is something I deeply value and respect as someone who came from nothing because I know how it feels to walk in their shoes. My goal is to build an organization for people in need whether they are refugees, orphans, or widows. I want them to grow with love, faith, happiness, hope, and the belief they can achieve anything they set their mind to.

I dedicate this letter to my mother (Anna) who we lost in 2018. It is because of her and for her I continue hoping to inspire, uplift, and restore faith in those who are going through hardships. Although I went through a hard time, I never missed a single meal. My mother made sure we had food on the table. It's unfortunate today she is no longer with us to witness the man I have become. May she rest in peace.

Mongolia

Chapter 14

Oyungerel Tsedevdamba and Ider-Od Bat-Erdene

Mother (Politician, Writer, and Human Rights Activist) and Son (Technology Entrepreneur and Standup Comedian)

Oyungerel is an author of thirteen books. Her most well-known work is *The Green-Eyed Lama*, a historical novel co-authored with Jeffrey Falt, has been in the top 10 bestseller's list every month since its release in March 2008. She is also a well-known human rights activist, having proposed, advocated, and eventually played a leading role in adopting laws to de-criminalize libel and abolish the death penalty in Mongolia. Oyungerel received a master's degree from Stanford University in International Policy Studies where she was a Fulbright Fellow. In 2012 she won election to Mongolia's Parliament and was appointed Minister of Culture, Sports, and Tourism.

Ider-Od is also an internet persona with more than 570,000 followers on Instagram and 680,000 followers on Facebook. His YouTube channel podcast is one of Mongolia's most viewed and has 180,000 subscribers. Ider-Od is well-known a stand-up comedian in Mongolia. His biggest solo show had an audience of 1,500 people and was sold to Mongolia's most popular steaming platform, Ori. He co-established a language school called FARO Education located in central Ulaanbaatar, as well as a successful online language learning app business called Hippocards, which has received more than 1.3 million downloads and has 20K daily active users.

* * * * *

November 1986, Sverdlovsk (currently Yekaterinburg), USSR

I am walking on the sidewalk of a busy, snowy central street just after learning I am pregnant. I'm a student from the communist People's Republic of Mongolia studying planning economy in the Soviet Union. I don't know if I will have a girl or a boy. For the first time in my life I am noticing babies and hearing their little voices as I walk. A Russian boy of three or four years of age walks by me with his mom. He asks his mother, "Where is our house? Is it far?" Maybe the child inside my belly asks the same question of me. "Where is our house?" This is a strange new feeling, to have a conversation with a baby I don't know at all but accept as my very own immediately and tenderly by instinct.

"My child," I say to my new baby while walking. "Your house is far away from here. We can reach your home after five nights of a long train ride and a two-hour flight. In fact, we don't have our own house yet. Maybe one day your dad and I will build a house. No one sells apartments in Mongolia. It's illegal. So, we can't possibly buy one. We can just build our small house on a piece of land if the state distributes one to us. It might take a few years, though. All apartments belong to the state, which means your father and I will only have one if the state distributes it to us after we serve the state for several years."

I go on to explain, "Luckily, my dad, your grandpa, has been working for the state for many years and his is one of only 316 apartments existing in our town of Muren. And it is connected to the grid! I hope your dad and I will have my father's permission to stay with him in his two-room apartment during our first years of marriage. If my dad doesn't agree, your father will have to find someone else's apartment or a room for rent. So, you shouldn't have any high expectations until we have our own apartment. We'll be alright wherever we can find a room to stay because the three of us will be together, my darling."

April 27, 1990, Davaadorj Square, Muren, Mongolia

When I took my three-year-old son, Ider-Od Bat-Erdene, to the Davaadorj Square meeting, it seemed like everyone in our town of 40,000 had gathered there. I took my son to the front so he would not be squeezed by the crowd. My son sat down and pulled off his grey shoes. The main star of the gathering, a young teacher from Ulaanbaatar, didn't notice my son was making some of the crowd laugh by wiggling his bare feet. The teacher was busy talking about a multiparty system, democracy, freedom, and a market economy, things he said Mongolia desperately needed. On my way home after the meeting, my son finally asked me, "Who was that man, mom?"

"My son, his name is Zorig. He is very famous. He's one of the leaders of the Democratic Union of Mongolia." That was my short answer to my little son. But inside, I wanted to pour more answers to him: My son, Zorig came to our town and stayed at our neighbor's apartment for a couple of days to support hunger-strikers who are demanding free elections with newly established political parties in Mongolia. If his movement for democracy reaches its goal, you and I might have our own house! We might get the right to own a piece of land or other private property. We might even have our own businesses and we might have freedom to travel! As of now, you must have state permission to travel between towns or go abroad. Maybe learning English will be permitted too. It is exciting to hear him speak, and I am so hopeful for this upcoming change called *democracy*! And look how many thousands of people are united just to listen to these ideas!

July 1993, Sheremetyevo International Airport, Moscow, Russian Federation

I am waiting for my son and dad with excitement. This is a historic moment for my dad, who is sixty-one years old and arriving in a foreign country for the first time. He's been taking care of my son while I studied business administration and market economics at a year-long program of the newly established International Business School of Moscow. When the passengers emerge, I don't see my guests. Then a Russian officer brought my seven-year-old son and asked me to translate for my father at an immigration point. The first word my son yells is, "Mom, they gave me free lunch in an airplane!" Then he is worried, "Why aren't they letting grandpa come out?"

"My son, let's find out," I say, walking with him to the immigration point where my father was standing in his thick red *deel* and Mongol boots, and pointed Mongol hat. A Russian officer demands I translate dad's documents. "Foreign Passport" was written in Mongolian on the red cover of my dad's passport. Everything inside the passport was also written in Mongolian and it was issued by a policeman back in Muren town.

"Where is his visa to enter the Russian Federation?" the officer asked. I translated the question to my dad. He showed a white paper stapled into his passport. The paper was signed by the same policeman back in Muren. Handwritten on it in Mongolian words was "Tsedevdamba Luvsan is permitted to travel to the Russian Federation. Signed by (the policeman's signature), Muren town policeman."

When I translated all that, the two Russian officers watching us laugh out loud. Not only had my father never traveled abroad, but also Muren's local government officers of Mongolia hadn't learned anything about how a visa is issued or who should be issuing it. No one knew anything about the tourist travel of a free citizen. Even the officials in the Ministries in Ulaanbaatar knew nothing beyond how to request a study visa. Thanks to their help, I obtained my own visa to Russia. Otherwise, I would have arrived in Russia with the same foolish document.

As we continue the translation of the confusing document, my son's innocent and endlessly curious look attracted a Russian officer's attention. "Alright, if your father is bringing your curious little son to attend your graduation, we will help you. But next time, make sure this Mongol hero has a proper Russian visa!" A stamp was placed on my dad's Mongolian "Foreign Passport." With a big smile on his face, my dad, my son, and I finally united at the Russian border.

September 10, 1996, Sukhbaatar Square, Ulaanbaatar, Mongolia

As an assistant to the Vice Speaker of the Mongolian Parliament, I'd come to Ulaanbaatar's central square to help my boss, Elbegdorj Tsakhia, but I was emotionally overwhelmed by the gathering. Thousands of people were holding old photographs, God images, and praying beads. They were crying and praying while listening to the State Apology and the Law on Rehabilitation of Political Purge Victims announced by my boss. They were the people who were still connected to their roots, those who were repressed by the government as "counter-revolutionaries."

I realized I was the only one who was not united with my own roots. I knew nothing about my ancestors, their stories were never told to me. If my son asked me who my grandparents and their parents were and what they did in life, I had no answer other than they were nomadic herders. When I came home, the evening news showed the Sukhbaatar Square gathering. My son, while taking care of his two-year-old sister, immediately asked, "Is there anyone from my family who will be rehabilitated?"

"I don't know," I stumbled trying to my son's innocent question. "I will find out. I promise…" Inside, I felt shame. I promised myself I would not only find out my ancestors' stories but would also write a book in their memory if they were politically purged during communism. Disconnected from my past, being unable to unite as a family by knowing their story was a scary thing to realize. I didn't know if there was anyone left in the family who could recount those times to me.

But my son had his own inquiry. "Mother, is it true my dad died in an airplane crash?" he asked that night.

"I knew I would have to explain this one day. Maybe you are now old enough to listen to your dad's story," I began. "I always told you your father exists but has been far away. It is true that his soul is always with us. He watches you grow and hopes you will be a good person. He was a very talented painter, wrestler, guitar player, and the liveliest human being. One day, when you were just three months old, he had to fly to Renchinlhumbe soum for his work. He was a good pilot. His colleague was a good pilot too. But his plane was very old, produced in Poland thirty years earlier, and had not been properly maintained in a long time. The clouds that day obscured much in the sky when the plane passed through the highest mountains in the west of Lake Khuvsgul…"

Tears ran down my son's face. "My poor father," he murmured like an adult. "I want to know more about him. I want to achieve success on his behalf."

Two promises, two sets of tearful eyes, both in connection with our past. We began our search for knowledge and success together. We both yearned to unite with our past and both wanted a happier future for us together.

107

December 2001, Apartment #54, Ulaanbaatar, Mongolia

My son is curious. He had already started studying English, his school is specialized in Math, and he speaks with me freely at any time. He approaches my newly purchased computer and asks many questions about anything I am doing on it.

"Mother, what are you doing now?"

"I'm applying to a school, on the internet," I reply.

Unsurprisingly, he asks, "What is the internet?"

"It is like I write a letter and click this button and then a second later someone in America can read my letter," I explain.

"In a second? In just a second?"

"Yes!" I exclaim and proudly showed him how to dial-up from home and get connected to the world.

"I want to learn how to use the internet!" my son shouts in excitement.

"The computer will be free after I finish my application, son! Wait and do your homework first."

Of course, my son's curiosity was un-stoppable. Technology opened a door for me to study in the West and lit a brand-new spark in my son's eyes.

Thanksgiving, 2006, New Haven, Connecticut, USA

Our family gathered to celebrate Thanksgiving—Jeff, his two daughters and their husbands, my daughter and son, and me. This is a first-time gathering of our mixed family of Mongolians and Americans. While I was studying through the Yale World Fellows Program, my son arrived from Lawrence, Kansas where he was a student at Kansas University for the feast of Thanksgiving. He first saw America in 2003 when I attended Stanford University. Following all the food and celebration, my son and I had a little private chat.

108

"Mother, what are you going to do when you go to Mongolia?" he asks. "Whatever you do, good luck with your book with Jeff."

"I have so many things to do," I said. "The more I learn, the more I realize how much we are divided and how much we have to do to unite people and create equal opportunities and hopes everywhere."

"Why did you name your book *The Green-Eyed Lama*? Why is eye color so important?"

"Don't you know, son, that in Mongolia there is prejudice against green eyes? No one likes green eyes. But they are beautiful despite all the prejudice in the literature of the Communist period. If I am to write, I'd better change these prejudices while telling a story about our purged ancestors."

"Isn't it strange? Here in America, we live among the most colorful people. No one cares who has green or black or blue eyes." My son said happily, but then he lowered his voice. "But sometimes I notice my narrow eyes are little bit un-favored. I try not to notice and prefer to joke about it when it is too noticeable."

"You'd better address that issue," I tell him. "And not only for yourself but also for the many others with narrow eyes."

Naturally, he asked, "How?"

"I don't know but start by believing you have been given one of the beautiful complexions of humanity."

"Really? Are you saying it's beautiful because you are my mother?"

"No," I insist. "I am saying it because I see it. When I was sixteen, I fell in love with your dad as soon as he looked at me with his narrow eyes. They are captivating and beautiful."

"Yes, there are so many differences, mom. I am one of the different ones, thought I never thought about it when I lived in our country."

"That means your world has become bigger, son! But we have way more things in common if we give a thought about it. We all talk, we all sing and dance and love."

"Yes, we all joke and laugh!" my son smiled.

November 2021, Ulaanbaatar, Mongolia

Winter's long season of cold has begun in Ulaanbaatar. My son is traveling in Los Angeles to do a comedy show for Mongolians in California and explore his possible entry onto the American stage. Just seven years ago he and his friends founded the first stand-up comedy club in Mongolia, which became incredibly popular.

He and I chat every day via several internet tools. The technologies for communication developed so rapidly I sometimes forget there was a time in my own life when we wrote letters on paper! We share our ideas and dreams, and sometimes I forget I am talking to my son. He is more a friend than a son these days.

Both my son and I managed to do our explorations into our past. I and my husband Jeff co-wrote two historic novels, both of which became best-sellers in Mongolia. My son's journey to explore his father's story took him to aerospace engineering, then to MIAT-Mongolian Airlines. Then he found his own calling—helping people to unite, to communicate, and to understand each other for a better future together. He does it through comedy, technology, education, and business.

Miraculously, this is my calling too, although I do mine little a differently—through public education, political party outreach, breaking taboos, and writing.

That little human being who called me mother for the first time is now my strong ally, and my friend in dreams of hope for the future where all are united in our common humanity.

Afghanistan

Chapter 15

Dr. Mina Ehsan Leghari
Politician and Activist

Dr. Mina Ehsan Leghari hails from Afghanistan and migrated along with her family from Kabul, after the Soviet invasion. Her family traveled to Pakistan en route to Delhi and stayed there for a year. Due to deteriorating political conditions in Afghanistan, the entire family moved to Germany via London as refugees. Her family finally settled in the East Bay are of California, USA. She graduated from San Francisco State University with a master's degree in International Relations and married Jaffar Khan Leghari, a prominent figure of Pakistan's leading political family. After leaving school they permanently relocated to Pakistan.

Over the years, Dr. Leghari has played a significant role in local and national political activities along with her husband. She was a Member of the National Assembly (MNA) in the General Musharraf era and worked as their Chairperson of Tourism. Dr. Leghari has also been a prominent supporter of all social activities in South Punjab as a voice for women's empowerment, education, and social issues. She even selected the area of South Punjab for her research thesis in order to provide an all-encompassing academic work on the area.

Dr. Leghari is keen to bring about change and awareness among the masses in general and in the people of Southern Punjab in particular. She has been invited to the Universities of Pakistan as an expert on Afghanistan and South Punjab issues and also on the traumas of migration. Her views and political experiences are highly valued by the Pakistani academic and student communities.

* * * * *

My Dear World! Let me tell you a story:

Once upon a time there was a little girl who lived in Afghanistan. She was the apple of her parents' eyes and loved playing with her cousins her hometown Kabul. Unfortunately, her country was attacked by the monsters of war, death, and poverty. She had to run for her life and leave behind all her belongings and loved ones. She left her country with tears and a heavy heart, travelling to a faraway land where she worked hard to begin a new life and adjust to cultural differences in her new home while still retaining her royal charm, dignity, and individuality.

She lived the life of an ordinary girl and followed the path of education and empowerment. Soon she met her prince charming who hailed from a neighboring land of her native country. They married and she became a queen in a new land with new people. But it was not their happily-ever-after because in the lands of her prince she had to put up a fight against the monsters of illiteracy, poverty, corruption, and demonic traditions. She struggled hard against all these demons. She did not believe in happily-ever-after only for her own self or her family. She dreamed of a happily-ever-after for the whole world. While she was busy fighting the monsters in one country, yet another kind of monster appeared called COVID-19. It began mercilessly killing people all around the world. The Afghani girl believes in the unity of humanity to fight against demons like this pandemic, and many other demons such as wars, corruption, and hatred.

Let us meet this little Afghani girl today who has survived war, migration, corruption, floods, earthquakes, and one of the worst pandemics of our times.

I am Mina Ehsan Laghari, that little Afghani girl. It has been fifty-two years since I started my life's journey on planet Earth. It began in a metropolitan city of Kabul, Afghanistan. I was born into a large, traditional Afghan family. My father's family belongs to a large tribe from Qandhar but settled in Kabul and was blessed with the modernity of the city. My maternal family hails from both Afghan and Iraqi origins. My maternal family has the privilege of being a descendent of the great Sufi Saint Sheikh Abdul Qadir Jailani from Baghdad.

In Afghanistan, the only life I knew was the love of my family, having fun with my cousins, and enjoying the best of life any nine-year-old could ever imagine. I was not aware of politics, financial issues, or life in general. All I knew was the blessing of having wonderful people in my life who loved me. We lived in large homes near to our close relatives' houses. I ate well, went to the best school Malalai, dressed beautifully, and travelled to the other parts of Afghanistan, especially Jalalabad, a village two hours away from Kabul.

We even used to go to India during our winter holidays, driving through Pakistan. My exposure to the world was limited to my own little version of life with my family in Afghanistan. I used to enjoy climbing the mountain next to our home in Kabul or exploring the desert in Jalalabad. I loved nature and felt it was the best source of energy for me, though at that age one does not know why we do things because we don't reflect deeply on how our behavior shapes our personality. There was no television to occupy our time, so we had ample time to be outdoors. Every evening our street would be flooded with my cousins where we would cycle, play hide-and-seek, or simply hang out on the private road that became our personal playground. We were like a school of fish, all these cousins almost all in the same age group, moving about together.

On Fridays, our caretakers might take us to the city Park or famous cinema houses to watch Indian movies, and occasionally we were allowed to join the adults of the family for a drive to the hill stations of Kabul, Paghman, and Qargha. Those nine years in Afghanistan were like a fairytale, until it was all wrecked by the demon of war.

Then came a day in 1978 that began like any other with getting ready and going to school but became a day unlike any other around 2 pm when bombs began falling on my beloved city. We school children were petrified. Our teachers were also confused and baffled. The explosions echoed all around the city. The principal came to usher me my cousins out of the school, where my dad and uncles were waiting to walk us home. Little did I know it was the last time I would ever set foot in that school, or the last time I would see any of those friends and teachers.

The sky was filled with bomber planes, the streets were choked with tanks and troops marching about. My father had to quickly escape the country to preserve his life. A month later my mother left with me, my brother, and one aunt. I cried all during the journey to Jalalabad and on to Peshawar. We had left all my cousins behind. Eventually we made it to India and reunited with my father in Delhi. I enjoyed being in India, but only because I thought we would soon return home, but it was not to be. After the bloody coup, it was only a matter of time until Russia would invade my home country. We could not return home.

After much travelling in secret, my father had decided somewhere in the West would be best for us now that more and more countries were opening their doors to Afghan refugees. We eventually arrived in London, then went to Germany to wait for our refugee visa for San Francisco. The city of Frankfurt was full of Afghans, many friends and luckily some of my family members. Suddenly life was normal only because I had my family there. It was that strength of love that made me get through life.

I fell in love with San Francisco the moment we landed there, especially because I had my aunts with me, and soon the city became a permanent home to millions of Afghans. I started school, worked very hard, grew up, and adjusted to the Western life. I tried to coexist without losing my cultural identity. I studied and worked like everyone in America and continued with my life. The day I earned my master's degree at age twenty-five was the very day my Prince Charming proposed to me. I accepted without thinking how it would cause a monumental shift away from becoming the career woman I had envisioned.

My new husband was a well-established man of the most powerful families in Pakistan, of a large and prestigious tribe deeply with much political power. This didn't really sink in until I accompanied him to Pakistan, my new home. I was received as a

114

royalty in Pakistan. I was a queen both of my husband's heart and of the people of his area. It was a blessing to share my life with a man who also believed in his purpose in life. I soon gave birth to a beautiful baby girl who quickly became the main focus of my attention.

And yet within a few years I found myself becoming a mother to many in my new home. You see, I had fallen deeply in love with my corner of Pakistan, with the beautiful simplicity of the people and their love my husband and me. I began focusing more of my attention on our village of Choti Zarine, part of South Punjab, and its surrounding rural communities. I found myself meeting so many people who did not receive a lot from life, which made me appreciate the privileges with which I has been blessed.

I realized that to fully embrace my new life in Pakistan meant becoming a politician and social activist myself. Following my husband's example, I made it my mission to serve the public and bring social and economic development to my area. An important part of the example my husband set was never accepting bribes or commissions as was the way of most Pakistani politicians. We did not exploit people for our own financial gain. Instead, we had our own non-governmental organization funded by our own estate and through which we brought about positive, much-needed change.

I was able to abolish the practice "Kala Kar" in our area. It is a form of punishment for a girl who tries to marry the man of her choice. Her own family either murders her or sells her off to the people of other tribes, mainly in the mountains. It was not easy to change deeply embedded traditions as these, but sometimes it is imperative to make bold decisions. Initially, I was greatly criticized by the elders, and while some may still discreetly practice the custom, it continues to become less and less common. This is hope embodied in social progress.

I was also blessed with the opportunity to open small literacy school where many women would come for a few hours to learn how to read. These women had the enthusiasm of young children. The most memorable incident was a lady breast-feeding her newborn while two other toddlers were lying next to her as she was reading her first sentence to us. It is moments like this that make life worth living. The power of emancipation from illiteracy was glowing in her face. As she read, we all wept. It was hope in the form of women's empowerment.

During my journey, I have had many teachers who helped me realize the true value of life, the beauty of life that can only be experienced when you help other people in need.

In the fifty-two years of my life so far, I have seen and experienced many difficult things, including war and migration. I have survived two earthquakes, one in San Francisco in 1989 and another in Islamabad in 2006 in which my apartment collapsed, though I was fortunate enough not to be home when it happened. There were floods in 2010, 2015, and 2016 in which I saw people and their livelihoods being washed away in front of my eyes while standing by helplessly. In 2020 a plague of locusts destroyed the crops that would have fed millions. And most recently a global pandemic continues to ravage humanity. But it is also in that same fragile humanity where I see hope because of what we all have in common. We all suffer. We all share the same color of blood. While our countries, cultures, and languages may differ, we still all share the same human identity. Our shared humanity is our hope.

I have travelled the world, and yet I have seen no significant difference in anyone, so what is it that holds us back from unconditional love and respect for the world and all its people? We seek knowledge to control and to destroy. Is this really the way to live? Can we really claim to have learned anything? I am a student of Sufism and have come to understand through its beautiful teachings that life is not complicated except when we make it so.

I feel hurt if a person in Yemen is suffering. It gives me immense pain if someone is murdered in America. I suffer if someone in Brazil is hurting. I feel miserable if Afghans are homeless. I suffer because I love this world and every person in it. I want to be a human who feels for the universal life. This world is alive and it is up to us to protect it, to give it what we can, and to differentiate between right and wrong. I hope to see a better tomorrow because I have hope in us, in people who are instrumental as we can be teachers for others and still remain a student of life. The most important institution is life itself. Before chasing degrees we need to understand ourselves. Let these hard times of this pandemic be a lesson that guides us to humanity, humility, and empathy for each other. Let it help us to learn how to heal each other and provide solace beyond the boundaries of nation, race, and color.

I have witnessed the resilience of human beings, be it the West or East. I have seen many who had no idea where their next meal would come from, and yet they had hope. I believe we all can be and should be hopeful in life. This is our Earth and our life. The one who lives is the one who has shared, and the one who has shared is the one who is eternal. Grateful for every moment of my life, the journey continues. It is meant for sharing my blessings with more people. What I hope for is a happily-ever-after for the entire world.

Armenia

Chapter 16

Dr. Armen Arzumanyan

Deputy Minister of Economy

Dr. Armen Arzumanyan is a public and political figure, currently serving as Armenia's Deputy Minister of Economy. He received his master's degree with honors in economics from the Armenian Agricultural Academy. He went on to conduct research at the M. Kotanyan Institute of Economics in the National Academy of Sciences of the Republic of Armenia and earned his PhD in economics in 2012.

Armen previously served as the Deputy Minister of Transport, Communication, and Information Technologies of the Republic of Armenia in 2018–2019. He is the Chair of the Board of Export

117

Insurance Agency of Armenia and the Founder and President of Institute of Nations, Development Foundation for International Relations, Political, Economic, and Social Affairs.

He was a founder of FinStab, a business development and management company that is the parent firm of more than ten companies operating in different industries. He is an author of numerous analytical and research publications, a visiting lecturer of Economic Diplomacy, Business Communications, and Negotiations at the Public Administration Academy of the Republic of Armenia, International Scientific-Educational Center of the National Academy of Sciences of the Republic of Armenia, and other educational institutions.

* * * * *

It is September 27, 2020, in Artsakh. A soldier lies next to a burning tank, teeth clenched in pain. This is Narek. He wants to move toward a friend who is a little further away, but he cannot. He shouts, "Hayk!" There is no reply. "Hayk!" he calls again in a worried voice. Hayk is moaning weakly. Narek breathes a sigh of relief.

"You sigh as if you were sick with COVID," Hayk mumbles.

They laugh, then fall silent again. Narek cannot move. He can't feel his legs. "I hope ours arrive first. What if they are late?" Silence. "Hayk, do you have a grenade?"

Hayk guesses his thought and says, "Let's say I do. It is not your matter."

"Well, you know…" Narek begins, but trails off without saying it.

Hayk stiffens and says, "No I don't know. This war is about *life*, and the grenade has an addressee. Get up."

"I cannot. I can't feel my legs," Narek replies matter-of-factly.

Hayk gets up. He can barely walk over to Narek and kneels at his side. Narek tries to see himself in the eyes of his friend, but Hayk closes his eyes. It's horrible to see. Narek's feet are gone. He quickly removes his belt and Narek's to serve as tourniquets and bandages the bleeding wounds as best he can and says, "Don't go anywhere, I'll be back soon."

118

Narek's eyes are heavy, but he smiles a little and says, "Don't go far."

Hayk runs to look for other friends, but in vain. He cannot find them anywhere. There is no time for him to even to realize how much pain he himself is in. Narek is waiting for him. He believes he will save him, he *must* save him…

One year has passed since the end of the war between Armenia and Azerbaijan.

I am sitting next to my childhood friend, Narek. We have lived our lives together. We have passed the paths of our childhood together. We have passed the paths of adulthood together. We still have a long way to go together, but we cannot do anything else as before. From now on, I will be the one who supports Narek.

My name is Armen Arzumanyan, son of Artak. I was born in Armenia, a country whose people have lived for thousands of years and whose history is marked by centuries of struggle to preserve their right to exist on this planet.

I was born into a family rooted in our land and long-standing identity, each generation of which has left its name in the rich register of Armenian science and culture. There was my father, Artak Arzumanyan, awarded the posthumous Medal of Courage and one of the brightest names in the history of Armenian television, and before him my scholarly grandfather Sevak Arzumanyan. The noble blood of my family runs in my veins. I bear responsibility for my family, my generation, my nation, Armenians all over the world, and all those living on this planet, regardless of nationality, for whom the highest value is Human.

Rooted in the soil of my land, living on my own land, I still have a big home called planet Earth, where I travel to get to know as much as possible, learn about nature, people, customs, trying to connect the world with the world. And in order to connect with the world and all in it, we need mutual love and responsibility for people, the world around us, for what is possible, and even for what seems impossible for us.

"In the morning, when you wake up and tidy yourself up, you have to take care of your planet with the same care," said the famous hero, Antoine de Saint-Exupery. What are we doing for our planet? Instead of trying to tidy it up, we "wrap up" these sorrows and send them into space, thinking that they will never return.

We often get angry, not realizing that this can be destructive. We forget how a drop of kindness, given to each of us, can save the world. We often think more about how

119

to rule the world than about saving it. We want to discover the universe, and we are proud of the achievements of science, forgetting they often happen to the detriment of humanity and to the detriment of the very planet that affords us the unique opportunity to live.

Our planet is a living organism, and each of us is one of its cells. If we do not realize this in time and do not take care of the health of our soul, mind, conscience, and body, then one day the Earth will get sick just like a person will get sick with unhealthy cells. And maybe that's why our planet got sick and infected with a pandemic, համաճարակի, Համավարակ, 大流行, pandemia, пандемия, 감염병세계적유행, pandémie, پاندمی, パンデミック, pandeeminen, პანდემია, , цар тахал, πανδημία, pandemiczny.

The global pandemic, announced in hundreds of languages around the world, has invaded the daily lives of people in known and unknown parts of the planet, forcing them to stop the crazy race of life, to stop and consider the most important value of all—human life.

Planet Earth is our home. It may sound somewhat primitive or strange under ordinary circumstances, but when our planet is faced with a problem, each of us feels it on our own skin, and for each of us it becomes ours. For millennia catastrophes have haunted humanity from time to time Thinking about it can make a person feel as if the door to his house is not at the entrance to the building, but in space, on the way to Earth. It's a feeling of somehow being a detached observer watching what's unfolding even while being in the midst of it.

The pandemic has forced us to get to know ourselves, to understand whether we love our neighbors so much that we risk being close to them, and to test whether we treat someone who is in trouble the way we would like to be treated. The novel coronavirus rejected the constructed inequality of crowned heads and ordinary people, reminding them once again of the equality of human origin and nature.

Nature still supports the equal sign. Unfortunately, people still forget about the equal right to exist. My country has experienced two disasters: an epidemic and a war—a war *during* the epidemic. This war was a fight for identity, a fight for justice, the absence of which harmed the planet. This battle was fought by Armenian soldiers, some of whom were infected with COVID-19 but preferred the battlefield to a hospital ward. Years will pass, and when the world gets rid of the pains of the pandemic, it may

120

remember how tiny little Armenia for forty-four days fought for the values that have provided the momentum of my country for millennia.

A nineteen-year-old soldier was lying next to Narek and Hayk in the Stepanakert hospital. He was seriously injured and doctors fought to keep him alive. When his blue eyes were fixed on the ceiling, it seemed he was trying to throw dreams into the sky, for at least there they could have life. He was a student. He was going to become an actor. He decided to make a film about life in the army after the army. Reality turned into a violent film in which he played his first and last role. When he regained consciousness, he asked the assembled doctors to tell his relatives to send balloons into the sky from time to time if he dies…

As the New Year 2021 approached, there were no decorated trees or festive lights in the squares of the Republic of Armenia. Instead, on New Year's Eve, thousands of kite-like balloons flew into the sky. They ascended carrying our love to our heroes in heaven. Armenian families celebrated the arrival of 2021 in Yerablur, which became a sanctuary and a new Tsitsernakaberd (genocide memorial). Small Christmas trees, decorated with their favorite sweets, were placed next to the heroes' graves along with greeting cards expressing the hope and desire to meet again one day. The pain was too much to be in a festive mood, and even New Year's Day could not ease it.

Every Armenian living anywhere in the world felt this pain. This means there are points in the world where feelings and emotions are the same, and if we connect these points, we get a small planet where people live and think the same way. I want that on New Year's Eve. I want all the Armenians of the whole world to not lose their fairy tale. I want not a single child in the world to lose the hand that puts gifts under their pillow. I want all New Year's letters to reach their addressees. I want humanity to live without such horrible wars, so that doctors and soldiers do not have to save lives at the cost of their lives.

I love life and appreciate every day given to me. I live my share of life trying to leave something to this world, trying to create new opportunities for the life of next gener- ations, and to make this world a home for everyone. I try to connect the world and its people, preserving my identity and respecting the identity of all people who consider themselves citizens of the world, people of the planet. As a member of a large family on planet Earth, I love to celebrate most holidays with my family around the world. Yet the challenges we face are real. Millions of people did not think after so many desires for health and success that planet Earth could get sick, or that success could elude billions of people.

121

But I continue to believe and to hope. I believe for all people whose faith has been destroyed by pain. I believe for soldiers who have been in the forest for nearly eighty days under siege, hoping for their salvation, believing they will one day embrace their mothers again. And thanks to this faith, they were saved and returned home, where parents who did not know about the fate of their children received the strength to live for months on the expectation of a miracle. I believe in miracles, and although a year has passed since the war, I hope many of our missing soldiers will yet return home.

My country was the first to adopt Christianity as a state religion. As a supporter of the Christian faith, I am convinced the world is built upon and supported by the pillars of hope, faith, and love. To ensure it is not one day destroyed, we must strengthen these pillars every day with faith in the Creator of the world, love for people, and hope for the shining of new lights on planet Earth. I believe this hope has strength. I believe hope is the axis of planet earth. Without it, the planet will stop rotating.

Gandzasar Church is overcrowded. This is Narek's wedding. In the darkness of war, Narek found his light. Ani is Narek's nurse who never went far from his bed day or night on difficult days. Narek is in a wheelchair. He cannot walk, but he will live ready to fly like an eagle. Hayk, who took Narek off the battlefield and took him to the first car he met, promised at the most difficult moment he would save him, that he would still dance at his friend's wedding and be the godfather of the children. Hayk kept his promise and is now launching pigeons over the bride and groom. He launches pigeons, but he knows the truth: No matter how many pigeons you may launch, it is still the eagles that bring peace.

United Kingdom

Chapter 17

Sayed Ali Abbas Razawi
Chief Imam

His Grace, Imam Dr. Sayed Razawi, is a British scholar and religious leader with a research interest in Islamic philosophy, mysticism, and comparative religion. He is the Chief Imam and Director General of the Scottish Ahlul Bayt Society (SABS). He is also an associate at Harvard Divinity School, as well as being an honorary Visiting Scholar at the University of Strathclyde.

Nationally, Imam Sayed Razawi has served as an advisor on the United Kingdom's Independent Sharia Review commissioned by Theresa May and participates as a member of the Oxfam GB Zakat

* * * * *

My Dearest Friend,

With the heavens opening up late in September and the drops of rain being heard on this blessed night, so I begin to write this letter of hope to you. Know that my purpose is not to write a philosophical exposition or an academic commentary. Today I sit here watching the world and it's challenges—where we as people have perhaps witnessed so much in the last few years that some have become desensitised to death. At times many seem oblivious to the urgency of reversing an environmental catastrophe threatening to destroy the very planet of which we are custodians for future generations to come.

Ironic as it may appear, as a collective having experienced so much pain and suffering, we seem to have reserved ourselves to a gloomy fate where we feel nothing can be done. It was in the last century when the world experienced revolutionaries such as Mahatama Gandhi, Martin Luther King Jr., Lady Diana, and Mother Teresa (now a Saint). It is worth mentioning that the term *revolution* comes from the Latin *revolutio*, which means *a turn around*. In essence, when I use the word *revolution* or *revolutionary*, what I mean are those individuals who were *able to turn* or *revolve* the hearts of people. In doing so, they changed the course of human history by making profound contributions to society.

Perhaps this is what we are missing today—individuals or a collective who have an ability to bring positive change through influencing the hearts of people. I always felt that by changing hearts, you are in fact lighting a candle of hope in the darkness of confusion. Though currently such individuals are a rarity, when I see the likes of Greta Thunberg or even Malala Yousafzai, it does give me hope that a younger generation of charismatic leaders are firmly on their journeys to bringing about global change. This doesn't mean, however, that hope for me isn't also coupled with anxiety. Having witnessed great leaders corrupted, I do find myself wondering how our new generation of influencers will keep themselves grounded. What was apparent in the likes of Lady Diana and Mother Teresa, whose lives and times I have been privileged to have lived through, was a sense of selfless service, or more precisely, an ability to empathize with the other. After all, I find changing human beings only comes through love and empathy. So, I have found myself asking, is there really hope in our times? Can I as an individual make any real difference?

I, in fact, did find answers to these questions. However, the answers came not through global influencers, but when I experienced day-to-day interactions between people. Not everyone gets an opportunity to work on a global level, but each one of us does get a chance to treat those we come into contact with on a daily basis with love and compassion. It is the Golden Rule in action that has given me much hope. When we start treating others in the way we would like to be treated, change begins. It is equivalent to lighting a candle of hope. What I would like to share with you, though, is not just a metaphor but an actual story. It is a story of when I was unexpectedly gifted candles to light. One may be forgiven for asking what significance, if any at all, does this have to do with hope. Well, hope is very personal, and in this case was extremely symbolic as well.

It was on an afternoon in the summer of 2020, corresponding with the toughest lockdown in British history, that through the comfort of our homes a group of members from the Incorporated Trades of Edinburgh were having a conversation about religious festivals of light and how best to contribute to them. Whilst the discussion advanced, I remembered how on the night of Ashura (Ashura being the day when Imām Hussain, the grandson of the Prophet of Islam, was martyred with his family and friends in the land of Karbala), traditionally candles were lit as a sign of hope and rebirth. In fact, even to this day children in Karbala light small candles, which are then allowed to float across the river Euphrates. In the darkness of night, it is stunning to witness.

When my turn to speak came, I mentioned this tradition and how I would like to light a candle in each major city of Scotland as a commitment from my community to peace and hope. Very kindly, Ian Robertson, a devout Christian who was Deacon Convener of the Trades and a candlemaker himself, promised to have candles ready for me, which both he and the Deacon of the Candlemakers proceeded to make by hand. These candles were special because they were made of beeswax. Why does that make them special? The answer is again found rooted in religious symbolism.

Not only are beeswax candles meant to be longer lasting, but from an environmental perspective they are cleaner, brighter, and drip-free, as well as (at least in our case) free from chemical products. Supposedly, beeswax candles also purify the air and were once the preferred type of candle type for the church, nobility, and royalty. You may be forgiven for thinking I own shares in a beeswax candle company.

This is not the case, of course, but the reason I mention these points is because there is something pure in tradition. As the Deacon Convenor of Trades explained, it was traditionally thought that bees procreate through immaculate conception, thus the beeswax was deemed a fitting substance from which to make candles. The candle, after all, represented the body of Christ. The wax symbolised the humanity of Christ and the wick represented his soul. As the candle burnt, it was a sign of absolute sacrifice. When I was presented with the candles, I was told they were made by hand. What immediately came to mind were two mystical concepts: The first was the importance of light in faith. The second concept, found in the Qur'ān, is that God made Adam with his two hands. In a dialogue with Satan, God said, "What prevents you from prostrating yourself to one whom I have created with My own two hands…"

These two hands are symbolic of several ideas, one being that the two are representative of the physical and spiritual sides of humanity. Indeed, one dimension of man is his physical nature, but the other is the sacredness found deep inside.

Encapsulated in these candles for me was Adam as a hope in creation, despite his flaws.

It was after I had come to understand the story behind the making of traditional candles that I spontaneously decided it would be important for me to light a candle in Babylon, a biblical land known to the Abrahamic family, but also a land of hope. As I was going to Iraq, I thought it important to light candles at the birthplace of Abraham, as well as at the Sacred tombs in Najaf and Karbala.

My purpose had changed and now these candles became a symbol of hope, and a sacred light in the darkness of uncertainty. How apt was it that I would light candles made by devout Christians at the burial places of men who not only symbolise humanity but were figures of resilience and fortitude? There was, however, something missing. I knew to truly gain from this action of lighting these candles required me to also have these candles blessed by others. The excitement on the face of my Jewish friends was visible as I mentioned Babylon and Ur—and there it was, hope. Suddenly,

126

a sense of belonging, togetherness, and family started to grow in me. I went on to tell my story to Dharmic leaders. Indeed, I saw excitement in their eyes, too. I asked them to pray for hope and they did. Armed with hope and the prayers of holy men and women, it was a moment of immense hope brought about by goodwill and loving thy neighbour.

What was more interesting for me when I got to Babylon was a renewed understanding of how *resilience* is the very thing that binds the Abrahamic faiths—an ability to survive even the worst of tribulations. Through a strong belief in the promise of God and a will to succeed, Abraham overcame Nimrod, Moses parted the sea, Jesus healed a nation, and Muhammad saved desert dwellers by teaching them how to become a civilisation. Abraham's people came to know God through resilience and perseverance. It's strange that when I read about faiths, be it Judaism, Christianity, or Islam, the journey seems to have the same ingredients: a struggle, one patriarch, and a shared message. Perhaps I have oversimplified it, but stripping away the scholarly debate reveals the essence of a surprisingly simple message: Obey the one God and serve His creation, or in the words of Jesus, "Thou shalt love the Lord thy God with all thy heart, and with all thy soul, and with all thy mind. This is the first and great commandment. And the second is like unto it, Thou shalt love thy neighbour as thyself."

It should come as no surprise that the Qur'ān in its own language says something similar: "Worship God and associate none with Him, and to your parents do good, and to relatives, orphans, the needy, the neighbour, the stranger, the companion at your side, the traveler…"

As I lit the candles, I came to realize how this story did not begin in Edinburgh or even in the United Kingdom. It began approximately two thousand, six hundred years ago, in the land of Babylon, where a people found themselves exiled after the destruction of the first Temple by Nebuchadnezzar in 586 BCE. You may well ask, what an event from so long ago has to do with my candle? It was as if the land of Babylon was saying to me that it was here a nation learnt to survive through deep trust and hope in God. From being a Temple religion, they became a mobile one, as once again the promise of God gave birth to a theology of resilience, "I will be their God, and they shall be my people" (Ezekiel 37:27). Babylon may not be our promised land, but it had given hope to nations, and today it has given hope to me.

My story is very personal, but as a faith leader I have come to appreciate how faith and hope are a state of mind and being. This state can come from what may be perceived as small acts of generosity and kindness, yet even such small acts are seismic in changing hearts. If I may conclude by saying, in each of us lies a *revolutionary*. We can all change hearts and therefore redirect the course of our collective history. All it requires is empathy and loving thy neighbour.

Ethiopia

Chapter 18

Prince Ermias Sale Selassie

Consultant

Prince Ermias Sahle-Selassie Haile-Selassie is a grandson of Ethiopia's Emperor Haile Selassie. He was born in Ethiopia in 1960 and studied at the Old Ride Preparatory School and Haileybury College in England. He completed undergraduate studies at the University of California Santa Barbara and post-graduate studies at the Fletcher School of Law and Diplomacy.

When a communist revolution overthrew his grandfather's government in 1974, Prince Ermias remained in exile for many years. In 1993, his uncle, emperor-in-exile Amha Selassie I, named Prince Ermias to be the President of the Ethiopian Crown Council, the representative of the Ethiopian crown during periods of inter-regnum. Over the last twenty years, Prince Ermias has returned frequently to Ethiopia, working to preserve his country's cultural heritage and restore the Ethiopian crown as a constitutional monarchy.

Prince Ermias focuses on economic, cultural, and philanthropic issues. He campaigns to attract foreign investment to Ethiopia, with a particular focus on impact investment. In recent years he has met with Pope Francis I, addressed the Swedish parliament, and led an official visit to Jamaica to commemorate the 50th anniversary of Emperor Haile Selassie I's visit in 1966. He has been particularly engaged in interfaith dialogue to bring peace and stability to his country. He has fundraised for clean-water technology through the Water Initiative for Africa, collaborated with international donors to preserve and digitize Ethiopian manuscripts, and secured twenty-five full college scholarships for Ethiopian students at La Roche College in Pittsburgh, Pennsylvania, USA.

* * * * *

This year has been an amazing one filled with unexpected challenges and reflections. When I was asked to write a chapter in this book of hope, it made sense to me, especially in these uncertain times when we are all questioning so much in our lives and around the world.

Pondering the subject matter also made me realize how it is quite difficult at times to have a clear line between our own personal experiences and the world in general. Whether it is history, our present, or our future, life in my personal experience is a dynamic filled with mystery and challenges. What transports us through these labyrinths is a mixture of hope and faith. What makes the journey so uplifting and personal is who we choose to travel with on the great adventure of life.

I am blessed and grateful to be able to contribute my small reflection about hope and what it has meant for me personally. As many interpretations as it may conjure for me, hope is founded in spirituality, from which it radiates love, personal warmth, a common humanity grounded in tolerance, and a consciousness grounded in wholehearted service. This concept, despite all its challenges, is one that allows us to reach our own spiritual fulfilment. It is one that has no place for judgment but one that embraces our own frailties and seeks the best in each of us.

Ethiopia is a country founded on hope. Nearly three thousand years ago, the Queen of Sheba (Ethiopia's *Nigist Saba*) left her home in search of wisdom. Her hope bore unexpected fruit through a union with King Solomon and the birth of their son, Menelik, the founder of Ethiopia's Solomonic dynasty. Menelik himself left his father and their home in Jerusalem as an act of hope, believing he and his closest friends (Ethiopia's future leaders) could build a better home, a better land, and a better faith than their fathers. That daring spirit is still alive in Ethiopia and its diaspora today, and it fills me with hope for my country's future. Our children too will come home, one day soon, and build a country far better than the one left by their fathers.

Strangers to Ethiopia may wonder what I mean. For nearly all my life, international news has made Ethiopia synonymous with poverty, famine, and civil war. But Ethiopians have a long memory and know the richness of our country's long history. While ancient Egypt fell to the Greeks and the Romans and ancient Nubia collapsed in chaos and confusion, ancient Ethiopia remained unconquered. Menelik's dynasty once governed a vast corner of the Horn of Africa and beyond into the Arabian Peninsula.

For centuries, our strength and prosperity grew through vibrant international trade, our Red Sea ports connecting the economies of South Asia and the Mediterranean. When those economies collapsed in the 500s AD, ours did too. The ancient Ethiopian kingdom of Axum in the highlands of Eritrea and Tigray (the home to stelae or obelisks built with unmatched skill in ancient Africa) soon faced isolation, economic depression, and external invasion.

And with good reason. Ethiopia's medieval splendor was unlike anything else in Africa. Our art and architecture were unparalleled. At the dawn of the twelfth century, the Emperor Lalibela oversaw the construction of the rock-cut churches still carrying his name. When Portuguese explorers first saw those churches in the 1520s, they feared no one back home would believe their story. From this height of success, history once again took Ethiopia full swing. Foreign invaders nearly destroyed our country in the 1530s and 1540s. Two centuries later, the central state in Ethiopia collapsed. We fell into a period of civil war and instability called the Era of Princes from the 1760s to the 1850s. But through all of this, we never gave up hope.

When Italy occupied Ethiopia in the 1930s, we never gave up hope. The rapacity of the fascist troops, and Mussolini's use of poison gas, nearly drove us to despair. But even then, my grandfather, who was emperor of Ethiopia at the time, understood he had to find a way out. Something from his faith in God and humanity gave him hope.

Rather than fight and die, my grandfather did something no emperor before him had ever done. He went into exile, as an act of hope.

His critics at home called it a pointless decision, but time proved them wrong. For years, his ringing appeal to the League of Nations served as the conscience of the free world. When that free world finally awakened to the fascist threat, my grandfather returned home from exile at the head of Allied armies. With this act, he secured Ethiopia's independence once and for all. He was no longer simply an Ethiopian but something more, and in the following decades he led a wave of independence movements across the continent. He became the father of free Africa.

And yet again, as with Axum and the Era of Princes, all of our progress seemed to slip away in a single moment. My family is now in partial exile for the second time in a century. Communist revolutionaries overthrew my grandfather's government in 1974, deposing Menelik's ancient dynasty. Our country sank into civil war in the 1970s and famine in the 1980s. But even then, we never gave up hope. It was an extremely difficult time. It was a time of despair that seemed to have no ending! We rallied Amnesty International and other organizations in defense of our prisoners of conscience. We mobilized local communities in our new homes around the world to raise funds for food aid to help our people eat.

But now, with this history behind us, and the communist revolutionaries long out of power, Ethiopia and Ethiopians need to reflect less on the past and more on its hope for the future. I want to talk with my fellow Ethiopians about where we find ourselves today. We are at a crossroads, a time to reflect about our common humanity, about our common challenges, about our environment, about our personal relationships, about family, about values, and about what we hold dear. People can reflect on all these things only when they have time to think and ask what we want to get from these reflections, especially in these uncertain times back home.

I see hope, a bright light at the end of the tunnel. Although we rarely learn from history, when we face challenges to our common humanity, whether pandemics or wars or crises that challenge our collective wellbeing, then we build mechanisms to overcome them. It is human nature to kick into gear to confront the problem, to challenge it, to rise to the occasion. This claim I make is not borne out of simplistic reflections, but out of what I've seen, what I myself have reflected on, and out of the lessons I have taken from my own life.

Do I have hope? Yes, I do have hope. But it's a measured hope, a hope that comes from suffering, from living life as a refugee, from watching my family tortured and killed in revolution, from watching helplessly during my country's civil war. All these moments have given me a better sense of who I am. They have given me a better sense of the values and faith that center me, that center all of us to hope always for better things, despite our human frailties.

My hopes are personal, they are national, and they are global. What I hope for personally is that I won't have to witness another decade of civil strife and famine and war, and that I can do my part in aiding the birth of a stable society that will be a productive member of the international community and will achieve as a country the greatness it has achieved in the past. That's what I would like to see, or at least begin to see on the horizon in my lifetime. And for my children, I hope they will have an even greater opportunity than I to live in Ethiopia and contribute to it.

At a national level, I know if I went to any Ethiopian on the street and asked them, "What do you hope for, for your family and your country?" I am sure, without question, they would all say "peace." Without question. *Selam*, they'll say. Because everybody has been affected by the refugee crises, by the communist Derg revolutionaries, by our current ethnic problem, by the lack of job opportunities that drives people to the Middle East, Europe, and around the world. All of this is because we don't have stability and peace at home. Even today, in 2020, after finally reaching peace with our neighbors in Eritrea, we have stumbled into another crisis in Ethiopia itself—ethnic tension between the Oromo, the Amhara, and the Tigray.

After this crisis is over, what's next? The next thing would be a reconstruction in every sense, reconstructing our attitudes, reconstructing our state of mind, our basis of security, and how we want to develop. There should be rapid development and opportunity for all. If we can achieve this, then all the war and civil conflict will not have been in vain. Our complete focus must be on reconstruction.

Job opportunities are key. When I think about the current economic environment in Ethiopia, I see a tremendous need for job creation. High-impact investment should focus on this. We have a growing population of young people. This itself gives us hope, but it is also our biggest challenge. If you don't employ those young people, if you don't educate those young people, if you don't feed those young people, then it aggravates everything else and creates the crises we've witnessed. We meet this challenge first with stability, and next with job creation.

Water is also key. Drought has been a trademark of Ethiopia since the 1970s and 1980s, but we hope this can be put behind us forever. My own work on the Water

Initiative for Africa contributes to this process by providing clean and reliable water in marginal rural communities. Water is essential to our health. We must learn how to utilize this scarce natural resource and avoid conflict in the future. But more importantly, we must learn how to make it healthy even while it is still scarce.

The Grand Ethiopian Renaissance Dam (GERD) is another great example of the progress we have made. The dam is a product of the twenty-first century, but its original conception and location date back to geological surveys conducted under my grandfather in the 1950s and 1960s. GERD is not simply a source of pride for Ethiopia. It is a source of hope for the greater Horn of Africa. Providing new power sources to Sudan, South Sudan, Eritrea, and even to Egypt can contribute to collective regional peace and prosperity. Other projects like it can fuel the larger development of the region, but this must happen in an equitable fashion, leading to mutual benefit, not conflict.

In terms of other projects, because countries like Ethiopia have started from a low base of development, we can learn a lot from other failed models of development and thereby accelerate our country's growth. With the rapid advances of the twenty-first century, we will be aided by the deployment of new technologies unimaginable to previous generations. My hope is we will learn from other people's mistakes and utilize models with technology to advance growth much quicker and more equitably than previous models in agriculture, in industry, in science, in every field.

By utilizing our water resources efficiently and by utilizing new agricultural techniques, we will have a lot of arable land we've not been able to use. We must utilize the crops that best fit the general environment, as well as move away from subsistence farming and into large-scale farming. One chief cause of the famines is a lack of incentive behind large-scale farming and the lack of equitable distribution of land. We need to maximize productive land use so everyone benefits, and we need to incentivize people to do just that.

Above and beyond these national hopes, I have hope at a global level, for Ethiopia's place in Africa and the world. Above all, I hope all Ethiopians can come back from exile. I hope Ethiopia's diaspora plays a role in building this future, that they, like all other communities in this tapestry of America and around the world, will contribute to their country of origin and their country of heritage. And I hope other people of African descent will also look to Africa as a place full of potential for their future. A key factor in our future, given Ethiopia's historic role as a pan-African model of freedom and independence, is for Ethiopia and Africa to work together as one. That's the hope, the vision, I want to set forth, not only for the diaspora to contribute to Ethiopia, but for the larger African diaspora to contribute to the continent as a whole.

Africa is the last frontier in terms of development and potential for investment. It has the youngest population with magnificent dynamism. But it must have good, measured leadership, stability, and peace for the next generation to contribute in the coming century. Africa must move away from being a victim and being marginalized to become an equal partner.

Ghana is the epitome of a country that has shown great promise. It has worked so successfully with its diaspora. It has built a solid foundation of education and built a prominent role both in African affairs and in international affairs more globally. It has gone through its own pains and changes, but it has finally stabilized. I think this makes Ghana a great example, a cause for hope for other African nations. Likewise, South Africa has been a model in its struggle for reconciliation. This struggle has not always delivered the promise many hoped for. But it has been a shining example of reconciliation and of how to avoid massive bloodshed.

Ethiopia's reconciliation would have to follow a different model. South Africa faced racial apartheid. Ethiopia has faced a gross inequality of income, of access, and of resources. This inequality has crossed ethnic, linguistic, and geographic lines for generations. We need to find a way to balance those tensions. And we need to find a way to build a society that can balance local governance with central governance.

We have not yet found the leaders for such a reconciliation process. It must be our government, our religious institutions, our grass-roots regional leadership, and our civil society. My hope is it will be everyone because it will take all of us to do it. It must have the support of the international community as well, in the same way post-apartheid reconciliation was not just driven by South Africans, but by considerable international support.

All my life I have talked about Ethiopia's resilience, and this resilience is what gives us hope. Ethiopia's history and resilience in the face of challenges prove we can survive the worst and still overcome. Our history and our resilience weave a compelling story, from Menelik's time to my grandfather's, and on to tomorrow. It is not simply a story to cherish and enjoy, but one to hear as a call to action. In the twentieth century, Ethiopia's diaspora went around the world in exile like *Nigist Saba* in search of wisdom. All of us and our children will be like Menelik, returning home to a strange and mysterious land to help build it anew.

135

Egypt

Chapter 19

Mouaz Abouzaid

Architect

Mouaz Abouaid is the founder and design principal of VERFORM design studio for architecture, urbanism, design, and research, based in Dubai, where projects focus on public interest and social impact. He is a Cairo-born architect whose primary goals has always been simple and functional buildings that also emphasize context and aesthetics. He strives to create designs to both simplify and enhance the interaction of people and the built environment. He graduated as an architect from the Fine arts Faculty at Alexandria University in 2004. His expertise encompasses multiple market sectors, including master planning, residential, commercial, cultural, hospitality and mixed-use.

Abouzaid was recognized as Young Architect of the Year twice (2014 and 201) and nominated for Architect of the Year in 2018 in the Middle East Architect (MEA) Awards. That same year he was appointed curator for the Egyptian National Pavilion at the Venice Biennale. Other recognitions include being a finalist for the MEA Mohamed Makiya prize (Personality of the Year Award), the World Architecture Festival WAFx Smart Cities Award in 2019 for his X-Space project, and the WAFx Ethics and Value Award in 2018 for his Sheltainer project, which also won MEA's Concept of the Year. For the last four years running, Abouzaid has been included in the 50 most influential architects in the Middle East.

* * * * *

About four years ago, standing at the precipice of a new direction in my professional career as an architect, I realized a fundamental truth about space design: It must be about people.

It was 2018, and for some years I had been doing research on the informal market economy in my hometown of Cairo, Egypt. There were hundreds of unauthorized markets with tent-like shops made with tin roofs and simple wooden structures, filled with piles of objects to sell. For miles on end, each shop displayed their unique take on home items like toilet seats and rugs, or more distinct objects such as vases and antiques. Its streets were made of dusty dirt, and no doors were seen on any of the shops, allowing anyone to enter at their leisure. Something about the resilience of merchants in these markets, and perhaps the unintentional recycling of objects, had somehow drawn my attention. But it was during a moment of distraction where I encountered the story that changed my view of architecture forever.

Next to one of Cairo's biggest informal markets existed a community of families and individuals who, out of necessity and lack of basic resources, were living in cemeteries known altogether as the "City of the Dead." Many of the shop owners and merchants were residents as well, but most of the cemetery community was made up of people with vastly different lives, sharing the cemetery as a home as the one thing they all had in common. Bodies of the living and dead quite literally cohabited side-by-side. Kids were growing up and playing in graveyards. May people were afraid to walk the premises at night due to the eerie and unsafe conditions. Many worked as keepers of family graves and lived no more than a couple meters to the left or right of the resting places for which they cared.

I felt great shame that people in Cairo, residents of the city I had lived in my whole life, were living in these inhumane conditions. Feeling a need to alleviate this housing crisis, I began to turn my attention away from objects in the markets and instead wondered about people behind the cemetery community. I began doing much research, asking shop owners in the markets about the cemetery residents, and gathering any records that existed. I specifically remember this lady in a documentary I stumbled upon. She was showing the reporter a stack of human bones and acknowledging with hesitancy that her family slept each night under those bones. She went on to say, "We are not living a good life here. We are not alive. We struggle to survive. We want to have a proper house." I understood then how this had been a neglected humanitarian crisis and I could no longer blind myself to it as an architect.

As much as I wanted to create meaningful change for the residents, I remember being puzzled about how to even start, and feeling incredibly hopeless regarding what kind of help I could give this community. I kept asking myself over and over, what if my family were in the bone lady's place? What if my only shelter was a patch of dirt in a cemetery? What if I had been told my whole life that I did not deserve to experience the feeling of *home*? These questions swirled in my mind for months. Even though I had no idea how, I knew I wanted to create a better kind of housing for them, one that worked harmoniously with the systems of the informal market and their already established lives, as well as the resources available to Cairo. I wanted to promise, even if only through design and true empathy, the kind of proper housing the bone lady, and anyone using the cemeteries as their home, wanted and outright deserved.

Suddenly, I began asking myself different questions: What if proper housing wasn't a far-fetched dream for this community, but a possibility? How could I recreate the feeling of "home" for this community? Waking through the informal markets with a fellow colleague one day, sharing my idea to design (or at least imagine) new housing for the cemetery community, a young student overheard us and chimed in. "We wish they'd leave us alone," Esmael said.

We turned to him in surprise and asked him what he thought were the problems, as well as what aspects were working in the City of the Dead. He was kind enough to engage us in conversation. Esmael had been a life-long resident of the cemeteries and was now a university student in Cairo. He told us how time and again the government had come to disrupt the resident's homes, kick them to the curb, or simply harass them for living there; how the government had given nothing but mistreatment and had turned a blind eye to their situation. All the residents wanted, after all, was to be allowed a peaceful livelihood and to be noticed on equal terms to other city residents.

After Esamel so kindly and honestly shared his experiences, I understood my housing design had to treat the cemetery residents as equal participants on every level, from the research down to the planning, and hopefully one day the actual building and maintaining of new housing.

To find an answer that would fuel the right design for this project, I reflected on my own journey as an architect, asking myself why I had come into this business. Funny enough, my interest in this field began in none other than the space I wanted to create now for others: home. Growing up admiring the works of my graphic designer mother and architect father, I developed a natural interest and passion for crafting spaces. When the time came to get my architecture degree, I decided to stay in Egypt with the mission of fostering a sense of place. Pretty early on, I understood how architecture could and should be a tool for social change. My job was not just about making architecture happen, but making architecture happen for and alongside people. Cairo's community of cemetery residents was now asking me to put people first at every turn.

The daily efforts of these men, women, and children to sustain their humanity and hope while living in the inhospitable conditions of a cemetery were nothing short of heroic. I felt they deserved housing that acknowledged these efforts. The project came to be named *Sheltainer*, a combination of the two key words behind it: shelter + container. Taking inspiration from the sustainability found in the recycling of objects within the informal markets, along with the need for a simple and practical solution to the lack of shelter, shipping containers became the answer. I set out to study container homes in both Copenhagen (perfect cold weather) and Dubai (perfect hot weather), where extreme temperatures seemed to be no problem at all, proving containers could work in the climate of Cairo to fulfill the need for housing.

I also wanted the containers to offer a variety of housing prototypes with the possibility for personalization and highlight a sense of home, all while maintaining the coherence of a neighborhood through similar aesthetics. The containers would be placed on empty plots of land near the market, arranged around green spaces for recreation. The idea was to foment a space that would rightfully and only belong to the people of the cemetery community.

The issue of unsafe housing in the City of the Dead spoke to a larger housing problem seen all around Egypt. My team and I wanted Sheltainer to show that by tackling a humanitarian crisis with a compassionate and proactive approach. We included the people themselves by asking them what they truly needed This allowed us to transcend

140

our judgments as architects and embrace a new professional and moral imperative we could show to designers and homebuilders all around the world.

Out of this project, and after working to fulfill other people's missions with architecture in their own companies for years, I decided it was time to start my own design and research studio, which I named *Veform*. After my deeply satisfying experience with Sheltainer, I wanted to make more out of architecture than aesthetics only some in society could afford. Architecture had to become a source for change regarding neglected physical spaces. By taking on clients who were interested in high-end projects with the promise of sustained funding, I was then able to fund the humanitarian projects I now felt were my duty to design. I began creating more of what I now call "gifts" to communities in need of architecture to enhance their lives. These projects are offered at no cost to the communities with the promise to design in collaboration *with* them based on their short and long-term needs.

When 2020 arrived and brought with it the global coronavirus pandemic, the space of home was highlighted once again. Around many parts of the Middle East and Africa, people who were living in high-cost cities found themselves obsolete in metropolitan areas and started moving out into the countryside. Many countryside communities, however, did not have the possibility of moving out, and their villages started receiving a flood of attention unlike anything they had seen before.

It was amidst these pandemic-driven migratory movements when Shereen Farouk contacted me about a community hub project in Arab Al-Sanae, a village just outside Cairo. She explained how her daughter, Doaa Morgan, who had passed away, always had the dream of helping poor communities, and Shereen was determined to make it happen. The community center had been partially built but was left undone due to poor design strategy and lack of budget, and they needed an architect to complete it. I instantly knew this would be my next project because it is what architecture was meant to do—make people's lives better and strengthen community.

During visits to the village, my colleagues worked as on-the-ground reporters of the village's atmosphere, its people, and the key architectural styles. Our mission was to capture the essence of Arab Al-Sanae through as many interviews, photographs, and visits with residents we could manage. We wanted this design to be people-centered, and for Arab Al-Sanae's residents to be just as involved in the process as we were going to be.

As a rural village housing only 24,000 residents, Arab Al-Sanae maintained itself through a strong sense of community. However, many residents expressed how their quality of life was affected when they lacked basic resources for daily survival. There were no hospitals nearby, literacy rates were low amongst residents, unemployment was high, and there was only limited financial accessibility. We were sure the placement of a community hub could truly offer new opportunities to experience life. We wanted to respect and uplift the cultural and religious traditions of the community while also offering needed services from medical to educational. Our objective in designing and building the Arab Al-Sanae Community Hub was to provide its residents with both immediate facilities and long-term opportunities to achieve true prosperity.

One of our key correspondents on the project, with whom we collaborate to this day, was Ahmed Nasr. As we elaborated on key architectural and stylistic elements for the community center, we wanted to keep up to date with the village. Ahmed became our trusted messenger and made sure to report on numbers, statistics, and countless lists of village needs. Coming from the high-tech world of Dubai and working with the most updated software, I found myself having to restructure my communication with Ahmed. He was still writing most information on paper and sending it through pictures via WhatsApp. For me, this was a small turning point that let me into the world of the village, where the design had to be integrated to work with the technology they had at hand.

Since this would be a building that stayed with the residents to use and incorporate into their daily lives, I wanted to make sure the architecture and design of the hub was socially responsive. Residents would not only be part of the building project, but the design of the community hub itself had to reflect the architectural styles displayed throughout the village. The building mustn't feel foreign, but should be welcoming, and this could only be achieved through materials.

While the hub's main material was brick, inspired by most homes in the village, other materials such as wood, palm reed, plaster, and concrete were also part of the mix. We also thought to include the triangular windows seen in house walls and fences, mostly used for storage or ventilation purposes. Placed in the community center minaret, a mosque's most sacred are, these windows had the same functionality as in homes while incorporating a cultural detail belonging to the village's identity. Additionally, the two main outer entrances to the space were designed as arches, a signature detail seen in doors throughout the village. By having all these details work towards a collaborative and integrated design of this community space, we were able to build trust amongst community members, and together create a platform to improve residents' lives.

142

Inside the community center, we kept the already built mosque and classrooms, while adding other necessary features such as an urgent care clinic, exam rooms for small medical procedures all the way to surgeries, a natal-care room, gynecology ward, a small residency for visiting doctors (since no doctors resided in the village), a pharmacy, a dining hall, a rooftop garden, and a courtyard in which residents could gather. We wanted these facilities to also highlight and host health awareness programs, availability of essential drugs, outpatient and inpatient care, natal care and children's vaccinations, skills training programs to improve employability, mental-health counseling, advocacy against child marriages, and many other social programs requested by the residents themselves.

Proudly being featured in architectural festivals and named a winner at the World Architecture Festival in 2021, the Arab Al-Sanae Community Hub has found enough funding to begin construction, and our last missing piece is government approval.

As we keep battling with the pandemic, internal migration into the countryside keeps occurring, and new projects stand on the horizon. Every year I look for new projects to create, and new gifts to give. What I started with Arab Al-Sanae, I hope to replicate each year with a new place in the world that needs something, and in 2022 it will be a new community center in Blantyre, Malawi.

The day I realized how much spaces were all about those who inhabited them, those who walked through them, and even those who built them, I knew architecture could be a powerful source of change. Through the design and planning of our built environments, we can reflect and understand ourselves. Moreover, we can reflect and understand the world's problems on a human scale. Whether it's an environmental or social issue, architecture can lead us to change what no longer works for people and what is no longer humane.

As I look forward to many other projects waiting to be discovered, I keep with me the sense of home that once led me to begin designing and re-discovering architecture. I remind myself every day that what might look like four simple walls attached to a roof can quickly turn into a profoundly powerful symbol of hope for someone in need.

Mexico

Chapter 20

Gina Diez Barroso

Educator and Philanthropist

Gina Diez Barroso is a serial entrepreneur and philanthropist committed to developing design and innovation projects. She is the founder of Diarq, one of the most important design and real estate development companies with offices in Mexico and the United States; founder and president of CENTRO, the first university in Mexico focused on design, media, and technology; founder of Diez, the leading high-end lighting company in Mexico; and is the president and founder of Dalia Empower, a global education project for professional women that includes training and mentorship to master the life skills needed to succeed in their personal and professional goals.

Gina has also started three non-profit foundations. In 1990, she started the Diarq Foundation to eradicate domestic violence. In 2004, she established the Pro-Education Centro Foundation to grant scholarships at the university level. In 2020, she created the Tati Foundation, dedicated to providing opportunities to people with disabilities.

Gina is also an independent board member of public companies and advisor for numerous organizations. The only Latin American woman member of C200.org, the Women's Executive Leadership Organization. She represents Mexico at the W20 women's initiative of the G20, and is also the leader of Empower, the new private sector initiative reporting to the G20.

* * * * *

When I turned forty-two years old, I felt happy with my achievements as a business-woman, first in publishing through *TÚ* magazine for teens, and then in construction and design through *Grupo Diarq*. However, there is a great difference between feeling happy and feeling fulfilled. I remember my grandfather, who became my role model when my father passed away, as a great visionary. He adored Mexico and its people, and he left an impressive legacy in telecommunications that endures to this day. What legacy was I going to leave?

Thinking about that question is when it dawned on me how the key to help people succeed is by giving them a good education. What frustrated me the most was to see how creative education didn't move forward at the same pace as technological developments and innovation. It also bothered me how youth remaining in Mexico were unable to study what they wanted because there were no institutions providing a high-quality education in creative careers. Such enormous talent was being wasted! After all, isn't it a nation's young people who represent hope for the future?

Complicating matters further was how many parents believed studying a creative career would be synonymous to having their kids die of hunger and poverty. These parents often prevailed upon their children to study some other career, such as accounting or law, even if their poor son or daughter had no interest in or the abilities for such careers. I also did not share the notion of teachers categorizing people's abilities according to what side of the brain they used the most (their right or left hemisphere), thereby choosing to favor and stimulate one hemisphere of the brain over the other. This was when I decided I would dedicate my time, energy, and money to creative education. I began by exploring what was available in the market and seeking an institution to potentially be the recipient of my resources. The more I sought, however, the more I realized I wasn't finding what I wanted.

One day I woke up with the deep realization I would need to be the one to create what I envisioned. I decided I would establish a new university. Although a daunting idea, I also knew whatever I set my mind to would eventually work out and come to be. One challenge, however, was how I didn't have my own outstanding academic credentials. My mother believed women should not engage in lengthy studies for a career, and certainly not a graduate degree. I studied interior design and did not go on to obtain a master's degree. Instead, I married for the first time when I was nineteen years old, divorced when I was twenty-seven with three children, remarried in my thirties, and divorced again when I was forty-one, with an additional two children.

I remember the face of my mentor, Pedro Aspe, when I told him I wanted to establish my own university. He told me I was getting into a very difficult project. He advised that since I had limited funding it would be best to invest in an extraordinary educational *model* rather than in a great building. This was a piece of advice I cherish and will always take with me.

I invited Kerstin Scheuch to work with me. Kerstin is an Austrian woman who helped me organize, plan, hire staff, and create, among other things, the curricula for the university I envisioned. I remember all the many people who told us we were wrong to attempt creating a new university and our plan would surely fail. Even the market survey we conducted concluded it would be best not to go forward with our plan. This is where the part of my character that doesn't take "no" for an answer, which annoyed my mother to no end, carried me through. We sought out people who would make my project their project. We avoided all the negative people and "haters" and decided to form a great team. Thus began the Centro University project.

We decided to travel to the top twenty universities around the world. We met with their respective presidents and asked them what they would do differently if they could. Curiously, most of them stated they would reduce or do away with bureaucracy. So, we decided our university would be created with one clear rule: *no bureaucracy*. We also came up with an innovative, whole-brain curriculum where the division of the brain between both hemispheres is not present and the whole brain is stimulated and trained to solve world challenges. We train people to stand out in a truly creative economy with innovation and an outlook for the future, not anchored in the past.

147

It took us many years of planning before we could open for business, but sixteen years after its creation, Centro is the university leader in its field. We compete with the best universities in the world. We teach seven careers, twenty-two postgraduate courses, and 200 continuing education courses. After the first ten years, we had to move the university to a different venue because we needed more space. We decided to build a new campus respectful of and committed to protecting the environment. Centro was the first campus in the world to obtain a LEED Platinum certification. We are convinced we must lead by example and be the pride of Mexico and the world.

Also dear to me are women's issues. For nineteen years I have been part of a group called the C200 Global Women's Executive Leadership Organization. I am the only Latin-American woman in this group. We have travelled to some of the best universities in the world speaking to female MBAs and PhDs. We speak to them of our experiences, inspire them, and give them confidence in balancing their lives. In short, we act as their role models.

I recall from my many visits to those universities how I had the impression that the more I spoke to these women, the more I felt there were some fundamental ingredients for success missing in their lives. I spoke to them about leadership, negotiation, finding balance in life, and about having mentors. Nonetheless, I saw how many of these women—with outstanding academic credentials—appeared fearful and didn't participate or ask many questions. I felt if they kept up in this way, they wouldn't get very far ahead, they wouldn't take risks, and they wouldn't negotiate efficiently their wages. I knew there was something more I had to do.

In 2014 I received an invitation from the Mexican Government to represent Mexican women at the W20, the women's initiative at the G20. This initiative began during the G20 summit in Turkey in which I was very honored to participate. From the outset I made it clear my participation would not be sponsored by the government or any other political body. I wanted to have the liberty to request, say, and negotiate for what I believed Mexican women needed. After the summit in Turkey, I sent on to attend the summits in China, Germany, Argentina, and Saudi Arabia.

Being exposed to so many women's needs and recalling my C200 talks at many universities and the frustration I felt seeing how many women lacked some essential abilities, I concluded that in order to succeed in life, in addition to having solid academic skills, it was also essential to have soft skills.

148

In 2017, I decided to start another educational project, this time with a global scope and dedicated to women. I founded *Dalia Empower*. It helps women entrepreneurs and business leaders or women planning to go into business gain the skills and abilities they need regardless of their nationality, culture, or background. It also assists women in public service whose voice is so important in drafting and enacting laws, setting public policy, and generating good governance. Of course, it was always clear to me we would consider men as strategic partners in this effort to achieve equality.

As with everything I undertake, I didn't want Dalia Empower to be only a place where women could take courses with no substantial impact in their lives. Therefore, we invited pedagogues, psychologists, academics, and a whole team of specialists to make sure when women take one of our courses, they change their outlook on life, their way of confronting problems, and how they negotiate or pitch projects. We understood Dalia Empower must give women tools to succeed in any of the endeavors they undertake.

In Dalia we don't empower anybody; we provide women with tools so they can find their inner power, the power that education and culture have taken away from them. This power lies inside us, and once it is awakened and embraced, nobody ever can take it away. It is the power that enables us to fulfil our goals.

We created a very potent app because we believe in both a virtual and in-person education format. We foresee growing our business by forging local partnerships with people who will establish Dalia branches in their own countries. We also created an international mentorship program for women using the app and we will increase business-to-business (B2B) relationships amongst women through our global network. Our goal is to positively impact 100 million women in the next ten years.

Today, I realize my true purpose in life is about education. I am very positive for what the future holds. The pandemic pushed us to more virtual interactions, which in turn helped us have a positive impact on women in countries around the world I never imagined reaching.

On a more personal note, I now have a real-life partner, Abraham Franklin, to whom I've been married for more than twenty years. My five wonderful children are all in creative careers. They are also independent and successful in what they do. I brought them up with the notion they should always be independent, self-sufficient, and strive to be successful in everything they do.

Life, especially in recent years, is full of doubts and questions often without answer. Still, I am certain of one thing: Someday I will no longer be in this world. No doubt my time will come long before I have accomplished everything I want to do, but I will be satisfied to have left a legacy in areas about which I am passionate: education and the development of women. After all, the young women of today are our greatest hope to achieve a better future for all.

Barbados

Chapter 21

H.E. Ambassador Dr. Andre Thomas

Global Spiritual Leader and Economic Leadership Consultant

Dr. Andre Thomas is the pioneer of the 12 Spheres of Leadership Movement, a UN Peace Ambassador, and the Ambassador at large for Vienna. He is the Co-Chair of Upturn Funds New York; Chairman, Co-Founder and CEO of Upturn Funds Caribbean; Co-Chair and Co-Founder of Upturn Funds Middle East; Co-Founder of Pleion Group Inc; and the Head and Senior Inspector of the Eastern Caribbean office of the Organization of Human Rights Defense.

Dr. Thomas founded The Greatness Channel, The Daniel and Esther Network, Greatness Publishing, Leadership Axehead

Consulting, and the Ideas and Solutions Group. He is also the founder of the Caribbean Israel Group, which includes the Caribbean Israel Leadership Coalition, Caribbean Israel Venture Services Inc, and Caribbean Israel Finance. A prolific writer, Dr. Thomas has authored 28 books on topics such as leadership, spiritual development, and the transformation of nations. He is married to H.E. Ambassador Dr. Nina Thomas and has two daughters.

* * * * *

Today more than ever there is a desperate cry for what I call *Hope to Reality Leadership*. We can't blindly deny the influx of disparities affecting mankind and gripping our world. Although these are dark realities, I believe there is a light shining brightly that will not only bring hope and change but will cause a rise in Hope to Reality Leaders, creating an awakening from the villages to the palaces of the world.

The subject of Hope to Reality Leaders is very dear to my heart. I have worked for over twenty years in the fields of spiritual leadership, business, and strategy consulting to governments, political leaders, and business organizations. Growing up in an academic, political, and entrepreneurial family, I witnessed the dynamics of national leadership and the effects it can have on a community. I am not only passionate, but I have also dedicated my life to seeing the realization of hope transpire across the globe.

Because of my commitment to this cause, I continue to champion those who have discovered their voice to help bring change and reformation. For those of you who have not reached this level of understanding, my calling and life mission is to bring people from bondage to greatness. My letter is meant to motivate and transform you to challenge yourself to create a life that serves the greater good.

You may be reading this book in anguish and pain because you are oppressed, abused, and have felt the blows of injustice in your soul. I have news for you: The injustice you have suffered, the oppression you have suffered, cannot extract your innate value. Your gifts are still within you, your ability is still within you, and your future is still within you. Do not surrender it but rather answer your pain and shame by evolving into a higher state where the pain cannot live. Responsibility is the price of greatness. It's time to take responsibility for developing the seeds of ability within us.

Hope is one of the greatest forces in humanity. As we approach the subject of hope, I must first define what hope is and then address the realities of how hopelessness can affect people. I define hope as the positive expectation created by a clear mental portrait of possibilities of the future. It is the greater future of a person or thing. Hope is an aircraft carrying a greater version of the present, seeking to land on the runways of people's adjusted mentalities and actions.

One of my favorite examples on the power of hope is a lab experiment I once read about. In the experiment, mice were placed inside a case of water and timed how long it would take for them to drown in the water. Another set of mice were put in the same water, but just before the time the previous mice had expired, these mice were taken out of the water and allowed to rest. After the rest time they were placed back into the same water. To the scientist's amazement, the second set of mice extended past the time the first set of mice had, and even lasted twice as long. Do you know why? It's because they had hope of being rescued. This speaks to how hope can inspire one to fight for survival.

Being a counselor to people from all walks of life for over thirty years, I can say without hesitation that the poorest man in the world is the man who has lost hope. People commit suicide when hope is gone. However, as powerful and relevant as hope is for an individual, it is much more impactful when the hope is translated to reality for people as a whole, and this is why Hope to Reality Leaders must emerge. When a leader discovers how to affect the hope of others, change occurs. When a leader does not understand or abuses the influence they possess to inspire hope in others, the hopes of the people are shattered.

Sadly, I have witnessed countless of leaders instill "temporary" hope for the people in which they lead. I can think of social leaders and entrepreneurs whose mission was to inspire hope in their communities to bring transformation, only to fail to deliver results year after year. I've seen political leaders inspire people to vote for them, work for them, and stand with them, yet were unable to deliver the results they promised. The world is full of hope inspirers who have been unable or unwilling to translate their visions into reality.

In my experience, I have discovered there are three types of leaders: Emperor Leaders, Hope Inspiring Leaders, and Hope to Reality Leaders. Allow me to elaborate on these.

Emperor Leaders are those who do not inspire hope and come into office whether in politics, business, or in social positions for purely a selfish reason. These leaders believe the purpose of the people is to create a platform for their personal power. I can recall negotiating an agricultural project for a developing country that would have provided a profitable opportunity for this country to have offtake agreements with a major western country for vegetable production. A project of that magnitude would have created approximately 400 jobs and brought desperately needed foreign exchange to the country. The financing for the project was prearranged and all the stakeholders were engaged. Right as we were approaching the finalization of the agreement, a particular powerful stakeholder began to ask for personal financial compensation to make sure the deal went ahead. As a result of this, a major project that would have transformed the agricultural landscape of that developing country was halted. He was an Emperor Leader who felt the resources of the country and the financing for the project must first serve him, and if he didn't eat from it before anyone else did, the project would fail. In every community Emperor Leaders abound and they certainly do not inspire hope.

Hope Inspiring Leaders are those who cause people to see the possibilities a people can achieve. They understand the power of vision. They see the future trapped in today that is awaiting the leadership to bring it into fulfillment. Without these leaders, the world would be a very dark place. I am always blessed when I meet leaders who are hope distributors because they inspire people in the classroom, particularly inspiring kids to dream beyond their status. They are in hospitals, where they inspire people to believe they will return home healed. They are in churches and faith-based institutions, where they inspire people to believe life can be better. They are in politics, where they inspire communities and nations to believe life will improve. Hope Inspired Leaders are one of the great assets to this world. They see beyond where they are, and they are difference makers.

Hope to Reality Leaders are the ones I have studied, investigated, and am now writing about. Hope to Reality Leaders understand that hope is not a fantasy. A fantasy is a picture of an outcome or desire that is not attainable because the present does not contain the ingredients or seeds for its realization. Hope is a gem from heaven. Hope to Reality Leaders are those who inspire hope and then also go on to translate hope into reality through strategy, networking, and resource acquisitions. These are the leaders who become gems on the earth.

I want you to aspire to become this type of leader. I want to inspire you to become the gems on the Earth. The ability to take great ideas and solutions from concept to reality is what makes people great leaders. In the journey of every person who has impacted their generation there have been a few life defining moments. In a person's life, they may only have an average of three to five defining moments. What are

154

defining moments? Life is lived in moments that set the trajectory of your life. The effect is either a trajectory of significance, obscurity, destruction, or somewhere in between. I had one such moment in my home in Barbados at about 1:30am when a sudden burst of unpremeditated, spontaneous, and revelatory thoughts flooded my consciousness. After my life-defining moment, I gained a wisdom and realization of the problems I was created to bring solutions to on the Earth. In other words, I discovered my gems. Here is a summary of what was revealed to me during that one moment:

- The problems of this world can be solved by the people of this world if they manifest the vision.
- The problems of a generation will never be greater than the people born into that generation, otherwise God set us up to fail.
- Ideas and solutions are within people in the form of an uncommon vision.
- If the wisdom within the visionary does not match the scope of the uncommon vision, it will become the object of the visionary's frustration.

Let's further explore the depths of the above statements.

The problems of this world can be solved by the people of this world if they manifest the vision. First, what is Vision? Vision is a clear mental portrait of the future of a thing trapped in today. It is not a wish nor a fantasy. It is the picture of the future of a thing if it submits to a process of development and actualization. If you go to a garden store and head for the aisle that has tomato seeds, when you look at the packet you will see a clear picture of what the future of each seed looks like, if it is put in the right soil conditions, watered, and nurtured. The future of the seed does not look like the present of the seed. The future of the seed is trapped in the present of the seed. To unlock its future, a specific process unique to that seed needs to be followed for its future to emerge out of its present.

Within human beings there are the seeds of ideas and solutions to the problems the world faces. These problems can be as diverse as pandemic problems, economic problems, homelessness problems, spiritual problems, educational problems, political problems, or national security problems. Their scope could be personal, family, community, local, national, or global. If you are living in a nightmare, it's hard to see past your current pain, shame, complexity, and mobile prison. Know this: You are a seed, and your current state does not have to be your permanent state. Just like a mango seed can grow and become a mango tree that produces mangoes and leaves and branches and can sustain a treehouse, you can grow and evolve into a state where

155

your current problems bow to your growth. We were not set up to fail and we do not have to surrender to our problems.

If we recognize God-given solutions and ideas are inside us and if we submit to a developmental process like the seed, we would be able to bring about great change to nations. There is, however, a big difference between seeds and human beings. Human beings have a will, and they can choose good or evil. Seeds don't. This should not cause you to surrender your God-given ideas and solutions to apathy, fear, or passivity. We can all make a big difference in this world.

The problems of a generation will never be greater than the people born into that generation otherwise God set us up to fail. For me, this is the most telling of all the statements. It says the unsolved problems of the world remain so because the agents of solutions are dead, passive, mentally imprisoned, physically imprisoned, underdeveloped, or ignorant. When you look at the history of the world, you can find great people who became agents of solutions. The Wright brothers are an example of this, as they had the solutions to flight. Lee Kuan Yew of Singapore was another, who had the solution to build his country into an economic giant out of poverty. Mother Teresa had a solution to the plight of the poor in her sphere of influence. Martin Luther King Jr. had a solution to a sphere of social injustice in his generation. Jonas Salk had a solution to his generation as he was the one who successfully tested the polio vaccine. These people were change agents because they were willing to solve a problem in their generation.

These ideas and solutions are within people in the form of an uncommon vision. Ideas and solutions lie within each of us, waiting for expression, waiting to be discovered. They are the gold that lies within people, and just like gold must go through an exploration, extraction, refinement, and placement process, people also must go through these steps to bring their ideas and solutions into reality. Allow me to break each process down to help you better understand how this works.

- *Exploration Process:* This is the process where people must explore themselves to discern the innate gifts, ideas, and solutions they contain.

- *Extraction Process:* This is the process where the identifying of the gold of innate abilities, ideas, and solutions within takes place. During this phase, one must endure a process of education, mentorship, development, apprenticeship, and work to extract a part of themselves.

156

- *Refinement Process:* This requires practice, experience, and mastery of the services and deployment of your innate abilities and skills to generate solutions.

- *Placement Process:* This is where convergence happens and your prepared and refined self meets a prepared opportunity in a prepared moment to bring out the best of you and the highest version of your solutions and ideas into reality.

All four processes are necessary to transform the uncommon vision into a vision that will impact others. This leads me to my next statement.

If the wisdom within the visionary does not match the scope of the uncommon vision, it will become the object of the visionary's frustration. Wisdom is the sequential process to take what you have in the present and create its highest potential into reality. A person who cannot cook but has in their possession all the ingredients and equipment to create a five-course meal fit for kings may complain they don't have enough, but the issue is not a lack of resources or opportunity—it is a lack of wisdom. Wisdom leverages the present to create a greater future. If a generation of visionaries increase in wisdom, you will see the greatest explosion of solutions and good ideas that will change our world for the better. This gives us all hope.

There is a global vacuum of leadership that inspires hope in the masses. However, on the verge of extinction is leadership that translates the hope of the masses into reality. Below are six attributes of Hope to Reality Leaders:

1. *They do not inspire fantasy in the masses but clearly paint a picture of the future people can have if they submit to a developmental process.*

The shape of a greater future is always found in the ingredients of today, and like a great chef, Hope to Reality Leaders will assess the ingredients of their target groups, giftings, culture, history, resources, mentality, challenges, and strengths with brutal honesty to determine what greater future can realistically be sculpted from these ingredients. A great chef does not engage in fantasy. He will not look at kidney beans, minced beef, and spices and think he can create a chocolate cake for his customers. A lying leader may do exactly that. A leader who peddles false hope can do that and keep the masses drunk and intoxicated by fantasy speeches birthed from falsehood. A Hope to Reality Leader will only inspire hope in people that can be actualized.

2. *They understand the sequential process that is required to translate hope. This entails the combining of the ingredients of a people plus wisdom into reality.*

A mango seed must submit to a process to produce a mango tree that has mangoes, and the egg of a chicken must submit to a process to produce a chicken in the egg. Many nations and people are suffering from arrested development that has prevented the intangible but real greatness within them from coming forth.

3. *They acquire the wisdom that matches the vision that they want to turn into reality.*

Wisdom can also be defined as the application of concepts and principles to create the outcomes you want from the ingredients of the present. There is diabolical wisdom that creates a worse tomorrow from the ingredients of the present, and there is greatness wisdom that creates a better tomorrow from the ingredients of the present. Hope to Reality Leaders ensure they have enough currency of greatness wisdom to see hope manifested.

4. *They count the cost of progress and inspire people to pay the price to turn hope into reality.*

Progress has a price, which sometimes is the constructive deconstruction of the present to build something greater. Progress may have to endure years of waiting for change to manifest while the process is followed.

5. *They are emotionally independent from the people they are called to serve.*

To take hope from concept to reality for a people requires an emotional and mental core that can withstand hostile, suspicious, ignorant, and passive environments. Hope to Reality Leaders must have the ability to encourage themselves and have a supportive inner circle they can count on. They are builders of the relationship network required to take hope into reality and understand how the relationship network that turns the hope of a people into reality requires a multiplicity of different relationships.

The word relationship comes from two words: relate and ship. It basically means to naturally relate with somebody because both of you are in the same ship going from one destination to another. It is not forced or manipulated. It is a discovery of a synergy in some of our goals. I must say there is no human who will naturally share the same affinity for every single goal you have. This is because we are each designed uniquely, and each have distinctive differences within us. However, there are some people with whom your goals and values will intersect and align. These are the people with whom you will build synergistic relationships. When I was younger and inexperienced, I only focused on the synergy of my goals, but life has taught me that to truly do something great and impactful, we need a synergy of both goals and values to create great partners and great teams.

6.   *Hope to Reality Leaders are committed to a life of personal growth and development.*

They are always growing and developing as they invest in themselves. They understand that unless they grow themselves, they will eventually become a ceiling hindering the development of people who follow them. It is this growth and development that makes them special. Who they are as a person today will always be greater than who they were yesterday, and who they become tomorrow will always be greater than who they are today.

As you have read through my letter, I hope you have gained a better understanding of how hope will ignite your vision and those you may influence. I also hope you have expanded your understanding of the three types of leaders. I want you to take some time to reflect on your life-defining moments and the seeds you have inside you. Many people die and take the seeds of the solutions and ideas they carried to the grave, undeveloped and with the fruit still trapped in the seed. *This must not be you.*

You may be reading this from a place of wealth and success but still feel unfulfilled. To you I say this: A tree cannot eat its own fruit, for it exists for others to eat from what it produces. Discover the solutions you were born to contribute to your generation and serve them up.

You may be reading this book working in a job just to pay your bills but feeling there must be more to life. The reason why you sense there is more is because there are seeds of solutions within you crying and yearning for expression, and when your spirit senses them, you sense the emptiness of unfulfillment because this part of you has not expressed itself. It's time for you to discover you and search out your innate giftings that are the solutions to the problems you were born to solve.

I speak to the greatness within you. The world needs more Hope to Reality Leaders. You too, can be one in the sphere of your influence.

South Africa

Chapter 22

Ivor Ichikowitz

Industrialist and Philanthropist

Ivor Ichikowitz is a South African-born industrialist, social entrepreneur, and philanthropist. He was named one of Africa's 100 most influential people in 2015 and 2020 in recognition of his role as a leading investor in the future of the continent. Ivor began his career during South Africa's political transition in the early 1990s, working to support Nelson Mandela's program of democratization, national reconciliation, economic and industrial normalization, and integration into the African Continent and the global economy.

For more than two decades he has built many successful businesses on four continents in energy, aviation, mining, retail, tourism, media and marketing, aerospace technology, and defense. Through his Ichikowitz Family Foundation he has invested in wildlife conservation, education initiatives, responsible citizenship, and youth development, including the African Youth Survey.

* * * * *

This is the African Century. It's our gift to the rest of the globe. The year 2020 was an inflection point for the world. This was the year we came face-to-face with the novel coronavirus, an unseen enemy that would be the greatest disruptor any of us have ever experienced. Stock exchanges bucked, the price of oil crashed, and the world closed its borders. No one knew what would happen.

There wasn't a playbook. Universal panic set in as a result of the collective fear of the unknown. There was only the hope of a great reset as the world realised we are in fact, in the immortal words of Bob Marley, "One love and one heart" because as long as one of us is at risk from infection, all of us are.

As I write, almost two years after the start of the great lockdowns, the question is whether we have learnt anything, and if so, what? I sit at the southern tip of the African continent. I am literally kilometres from Maropeng, the self-proclaimed cradle of humankind. Scientists will wrestle with one another (verbally, of course) about where Homo Sapiens first stood up and walked, but here in South Africa there two contenders: Taung on very edge of the great Kalahari Desert or Sterkfontein Cave in the Cradle. Then there is also Tanzania's Olduvai Gorge or Lake Turkana in Kenya. Who knows? Perhaps those first footsteps were taken in Makgadikgadi-Okavango, the great prehistoric wetland south of the majestic Zambezi River. But there's no doubt Africa is where it all began.

These are the lands from where the ancestors of modern-day America, Europe, and Asia would once have walked across our grasslands, clambered above our kopjes, and peered down the Rift Valley that threatens to cleave east from west. We truly are all one humanity, both literally and figuratively, and it started in Africa. This is the continent that gave us the library of Alexandra, the greatest university of its time at the dawn of the Common Era. It's the home of the incredible libraries of Timbuktu in Mali. It's the same landmass that birthed the medieval Kingdom of Mapungubwe with its gold smelters and traders in the south, that would in turn give rise to Great Zimbabwe, a society protected by battlements erected by stonemasons whose craft was the equal of any master crafter of Europe or of the east, though they would never have met.

162

But Africa's wealth, both mineral and human, would also be its downfall. From cradle to breadbasket, it would be several hundred years before Africans would win the right to live their own lives and choose their own leaders. From the first breath of Harold MacMillan's winds of change to our own Nelson Rolihlahla Mandela casting his vote in 1994 as Africa's last country finally took its rightful place in the constellation of Africa's states, this has not been an easy walk to freedom. Even so, it has been an incredible journey of triumph. It's been a story of overcoming incredible odds, of courage, and of humanity.

My own country, even by the outsized standards of Africa, is one of incredible paradoxes, most notable in the fact that Soweto, a sprawling, dusty dormitory township on the outskirts of the Eldorado of the twentieth century, could give the world not one but two Nobel Peace Prize laureates (both from the same street, by the way) in Archbishop Emeritus Desmond Tutu and Mandela himself. Two global saints, instantly internationally recognisable; one secular, the other of the cloth.

South Africa is a country that was a byword for oppression but also the birthplace of the world's first successful heart transplant. It is a country that could pit one group against another and then be the site of a peaceful hand-over of power through a negotiated settlement, something that's rarely been done anywhere else in the world. It's the same country where former foes could come face-to-face with the bitter fruits of their wrongdoings and heal through publicly asking for forgiveness.

The South African story is a narrative that wrong-foots the cynics and doomsayers every time. They are determined to tell you that in this country the hands on the doomsday clock perpetually hover between ten-to and five-to midnight. Sometimes those hands come perilously close to twelve. For a moment in July last year, the hands did just that. Somehow, we pulled through. Somehow, we always pull through.

There's a proverb in Africa that says until the lion learns to tell his own story, the story of the hunt will always be that of the hunter—and with that comes all the prejudices, fears, and intolerances of the hunter in his echo chamber. I have been seized by a personal mission for the last twelve years to help tell a different story to the world, and to Africans themselves, because many have had this non-African narrative hard-wired into their DNA.

Though the Ichikowitz Family Foundation, we have been able to encourage, support, and fund efforts to tell the great stories. The African Oral History Project set out to do this in the voices of the actors who were there at the time, while they are still

163

here with us. We have celebrated the hero's journey of modern South Africa through #IAMCONSTITUTION, an interactive project that infuses the next generation of leaders with the values and ethos of our world acclaimed founding document. We have also pioneered innovative anti-poaching measures blending the abilities of man, dog, and machine (even helicopters) to preserve our natural wealth which we have shared across other African stories to stop the scourge of rhino and pangolin poaching.

That is just the tiny contribution we have made. There are others who share our passion and our belief in our African homelands and the continent that birthed and continues to inspire us. This is not a continent of hopelessness, squandered opportunities, and expatriated wealth, despite what you might read or see. I tell you this not from a fervent belief but from what I have personally experienced. I have had the privilege of working in Africa for most of the last thirty-five years; I started this journey shortly after Nelson Mandela's release. I have visited and I have done business in just about every one of the fifty-four countries that make up our amazing continent.

I have seen and heard the hunter's story repeated and embellished from one Northern Hemisphere capital to the other, from boardroom to cigar-smoke-filled committee rooms, but it increasingly clashed with my own experiences. I would return from the African cities and towns of my travels to see them being written off in the media. I would break bread with presidents, politicians, and ordinary people, sharing our hopes and dreams for our continent. But then I would read these same people being publicly disparaged by analysts and experts repeating common wisdoms that were just the hoary old tropes of a misunderstood continent. Nobody seemed to be having the same experiences as I was on the continent.

It became increasingly galling as we approached the quarter century of my own country's liberation from apartheid. The more I travelled in Africa, the more I discovered an organic optimism in the young people I would meet that had little to do with their ethnicity or nationality, but everything to do with their age. I have believed for a very long time that the redemption of Africa will only be possible when those who were not born either under the yoke of apartheid or carrying the scars of colonialism's chains, are finally ready to take their rightful place as the inheritors of what is the cradle of mankind.

Now it seemed my theory was being proved in front of my eyes wherever I went, but when I tried to share this new sense of optimism with the world beyond Africa, no one wanted to listen, irrespective of whether they were presidents of countries or corporations. The only way to prove this as well as test my own sanity, which I was starting to doubt, was to have my instincts properly researched through a professional survey. It was an immense gamble, and an incredibly expensive one at that. The professional researchers said it had never been done before because the cost of testing the pulse of an entire generation would be prohibitive. We didn't care and instead broadened the scope. We didn't want something that would test political sentiment or social issues, the economy, or just their aspirations but all of it, because Africa has the youngest and the fastest growing population in the world.

These people are literally the leaders of tomorrow and no one knows what they feel, think, or even hope for, and yet it has never been more important for us to know what they think now and to chart that evolution afterwards. We wanted to find out, despite our efforts as Africans to evangelise to the rest of the world, if there was such a thing as a pan African identity, an African consciousness, an African psyche. The survey was a huge risk for me personally as it could have shown my gut instinct was totally off kilter and that the Afro-pessimists I have been battling all my life were in fact wholly justified in their long-held prejudice.

Researchers went out into fourteen countries and conducted 4,200 face-to-face interviews. They found young people in Africa imbued with optimism about the future, and they want to shape their own destiny. They found young people who refuse to shy away from the very real challenges of Africa, youth who are honest about what needs to be done and what their role has to be to achieve this. More than anything they found that the youth of Africa are overwhelmingly keen to make that difference.

There is a new generation of youth who are connected to the world, and they are out there doing incredibly innovative things with none of the resources of their peers in more developed continents. They are not just optimistic about the much-vaunted African century, they are determined to shape that century because, unlike their forebears, they have never been downtrodden by apartheid or colonialism. They do not have a hardwired mentality of being inferior in any way to anyone else. They do not know they're not destined for greatness, and because of that, they will probably succeed where their predecessors have failed.

This year, we did the survey all over again. It's part of a promise we made to ourselves that we would commit to a five-year process to ensure the survey was not a flash in the pan but a body of research that can shape how Africans see Africa, but most of all how the world sees Africa. The inaugural survey had given us more than we could have hoped for, but I was nervous because the results seemed almost too positive.

So, the researchers went out once more, in the wake of COVID-19 as biggest global public health crisis in living memory, to build on the body of knowledge AYS 19 created. This time, we added four new countries, including Angola, DRC (Democratic Republic of the Congo), Mozambique, Uganda, and Sudan.

The second edition of the African Youth Survey confirmed some of the beliefs we have, showed us emerging trends, and warned us too: Africa remains greater than the sum of its parts. The optimism we found in the first survey hasn't waned, but the level of confidence has, both in Africa as a whole and in the individual countries where the survey was conducted. The survey remains unique. So far, just under 10,000 young Africans across a total of nineteen countries have been interviewed. There is nothing else like the African Youth Survey in scope or focus.

As we promised when we started in 2019, we won't alter people's perceptions by being the ones shouting the loudest from the rooftops. We will make our point by producing properly researched and verifiable data everyone else can check for themselves. The initial objective was to change perceptions, but since then we have realised how the findings provide African countries with the tools to understand their future leaders. Through this understanding they can then unlock the door to understanding their own problems and developing their own solutions.

So many of Africa's youth today remain marginalised. The survey also became a mechanism to prove to them that they are not voiceless and nor are their aspirations just pipe dreams. It shows them how the dreams they dare to dream for themselves aren't unique because so many others across Africa share the same hopes and the same fears. Perhaps this survey will give them the confidence to continue the journeys so many have begun, to unlock their own promise.

I also hope it will help foreign investors. What Africa needs, according to the youth, is anything that will bring the greatest benefit, such as infrastructural development, water management, digital connectivity, and so on. Their greatest need is for initiatives and investments to unlock the continent's economic promise and create sustainable and enriching jobs. The youth want to preserve the natural resources that are their heritage, but at the same time they understand that a major cause of poaching is poverty and the desperation to sustain communities that don't have any other way of surviving.

There's an inherent warning too: The youth of Africa won't stand by idly. The era of one man, one vote is long gone on this continent. This has emerged in both surveys, then in full sight in Zambia in 2021. There are omens of tectonic change in other countries, particularly my own after our watershed local government elections in November. The youth of Africa aren't prepared to wait for handouts, they want to be in charge of their own destinies. They will start their own businesses and they will move to where they believe those greatest opportunities lie. They will leave their homelands for the chance of a better life.

There is much to be excited by in this survey. It dispels the narrative that took hold after the world forgot the wonders of Mapungubwe, Great Zimbabwe, and Timbuktu and instead chose to replace those with the false trope of the hopeless continent—a starving child with a begging bowl, mucus crystallising under its nose as armed militiamen rape its mother and the fat cats embezzle the foreign aid.

We still have a long way to go. Xix of the United Nations' twelve peacekeeping missions are in Africa as I write. There is conflict, there is hardship, but there is also undeniable hope. Back home in my own country there is a civil society as resilient as any other in the world, whose sheer force of will forced the peaceful recall of a sitting president, whose courts forced his subsequent imprisonment and whose people stood fast when his acolytes tried to burn the entire country down. There are many other stories like that in Africa. Slowly, the lion is winning its voice, slowly the stories are being told, and slowly the disparate pieces of the jigsaw puzzle that will ultimately show the picture of hope that is the African Century are starting to slot into place.

On the first day of January 2021, the African Continental Free Trade Agreement (AfCFTA) was signed into law. When this agreement becomes a working reality, we will have created the biggest single trading bloc in the world—a whole continent still dependent on commodity demand and massively under-industrialised. The World Bank believes the AfCFTA has the potential to increase Africa's GDP by USD \$450 billion by 2035, lift 100-million people out of poverty, and boost intra-African trade by 80%. It is a phenomenal opportunity to achieve a better life for all.

As Nelson Mandela once said, there is no easy walk to freedom. He also told us that after climbing a great hill, you find there are many more hills to climb. He was indisputably right, but he also said the task always looks impossible until it's done. Who would ever have thought it would be a young South African scientist who would spot the new coronavirus variant that terrified the world at the end of 2021? Who would have thought it would have been a brave South African epidemiologist who acted in the greatest interest of the world at large to sound the alarm, irrespective of the ensuing cost because of all the prevailing prejudice?

167

Omicron could well be the turning point in the COVID-19 global public health crisis. We don't know yet, but we can take comfort from the trajectory of the Spanish flu pandemic a century ago. Perhaps we are entering the next phase of a virus that is highly contagious but not as fatal as previous variants—a final phase before segueing from a pandemic to an epidemic the world can live with and manage if we are all vaccinated.

Almost 2,000 years ago, the Roman poet Pliny the Elder bequeathed us the immortal phrase *ex Africa semper aliquid novi* (Africa always provides us something new). The great Nigerian poet Ben Okri reminds Africans that if they are to be at the harvest among the gatherers of new fruits...

> Then you must begin today to remake
> Your mental and spiritual world,
> And join the warriors and celebrants
> Of freedom, realizers of great dreams.
> You can't remake the world
> Without remaking yourself.

If they do as he says, they will infest the world with their light, fulfil the golden prophecies, press forward the human genius, and ensure their future is greater than their past.

I believe they will, and I now have seen the research to prove it. Africa is the cradle of mankind, and in the twenty-first century there is every possibility it will be the nursery for the next evolution of our species.

Aluta continua! The struggle continues.

Malaysia

Chapter 23

Carol Lee

Former Mrs. Universe and Entrepreneur

As the first Asian and Malaysian to be crowned Mrs. Universe in 2013, Carol Lee's victory is listed in the Malaysia Book of Records as the epitome of a woman of this era, encapsulating beauty, brains, and a caring heart. Carol has amassed a diverse portfolio of work experience across the entertainment, hospitality, education, and broadcasting industries. She been a Chief Receptionist at a hotel, a model, a kindergarten teacher, a news presenter, a television host, an emcee, and started her own child enrichment center. She holds a Bachelor of Commerce in Management and Marketing from the Curtin University.

Along the way, Carol has actively dedicated much time to charity work, making a difference in the lives of the underprivileged. One of her most notable efforts was raising awareness about violence against women, spearheading the Nationwide Campaign Against Domestic Violence in Malaysia. She has also worked tirelessly to help her community as a community leader and a committee member of a resident representative council, which is an appointment by the Federal Territories Minister on a pro bono basis. Charity and community work has given her a sense of purpose in life and helped build her self-confidence.

Carol has also won numerous awards over the years, including the Parkroyal Employee of the Year (1993) and Centrac Award for Courtesy (1993), Curtin University Merit Award (2003), Most Outstanding Celebrity Award (2014), and the Asian Top Fashion Anchor of The Year (2014).

* * * * *

Has there been a time in your life where you felt debilitated by the apathetic dissonance of the world at hand, leaving you hollow and suffocated? Did it all just make you wonder, why you? I, for one, have not been spared from the hand life has dealt me. But I have also found hope in growing my own capacity to face and overcome life's challenges even while helping others and accepting help from true friends.

In traditional Chinese culture, most married couples would prefer to have sons rather than daughters. A daughter would be seen as a liability because she would eventually get married and follow her husband. This in turn would mean the parents would lose a child. Sons, on the other hand, were seen as potential breadwinners for the family, to continue the male lineage, and to take care of their parents in their golden years. Hence, the parents would usually give special attention to the sons, including further tertiary education.

Being born into a traditional Chinese family in Malaysia, I often asked why I couldn't do what a man could do, such as being financially independent enough to take care of my parents when they grow old. Instead, at a young age, I had to learn to cook, clean, and sew, whereas my brother had enjoyed the privileges of being a son. Whenever I asked or challenged my parents on this gender inequality, I would get caned for talking back to an adult as it was considered rude to do so. The common answer would always be, "Because you're a girl." Caning seemed to be a norm for Chinese families back then to discipline their children. The best part? We were given the liberty to choose which cane to buy when we went to the *pasar malam* (night market in Bahasa Malaysia) with our parents.

Though Malaysia has progressed economically and socially over the years, there are certain areas that have remained the same or have even gone backwards. Some parents still cane their kids. In their way of thinking, they believe they turned out well despite being caned when they were young, so they think they should do the same to their kids. Even when their kids did not respond well to caning, they would still do it in the hope it would work one day. I, on the other hand, would never cane a child and would rather look for other ways to discipline a child. I knew how it felt to be caned and understood the kind of psychological impact it can have on a child, even into adulthood. One of the psychological impacts included a tendency to physically hurt myself by hitting my head against the wall. I did this to distract myself from the pain in my heart whenever it was too much to bear.

I had lost my dad to stomach cancer just before I turned twenty-one. After his passing, I had to work hard to get whatever I wanted, even when it came to my education. I didn't want to follow the same footsteps of traditional Chinese women, whose sole purpose in life was to stay home after marriage and take care of the household. Instead, I obtained a scholarship to pursue my studies toward a bachelor's degree in Commerce. I did well and even received the Curtin Merit Award from my university. I had always believed in putting my best foot forward, in hopes of achieving the desired result. I also ensured I was financially independent. I had worked as a news anchor, a television host, and an emcee. I also set up my own child enrichment center. My mum had initially wanted to disown me for not wanting to follow the "traditional footsteps" of getting married and being a housewife. However, I was glad she was able to understand how times have changed and how women can play a more active and constructive role in society.

In 2013, I represented Malaysia on the international stage in the Mrs. Universe pageant competition. It was a great opportunity for delegates from around the world to exchange their knowledge on domestic violence in their respective countries, which was the theme of the pageant. I also managed to highlight my experience spearheading the Nationwide Campaign Against Domestic Violence. Beauty pageants have evolved over the years. Women were not just judged on their beauty alone, but for other qualities, including intelligence, character, and their ability to "be the change they want to see in this world" (adapting the famous quote attributed to Mahatma

171

Gandhi, even though it has been debated whether he really ever said those precise words). I was deeply honored to be the first Asian to win the Mrs. Universe title, and my accomplishment is listed in the Malaysia Book of Records.

Even after my reign was over, I continued to contribute to my community and help the underprivileged. During this time, several people I had considered my friends betrayed my trust. To add salt to the wound, I also had friends who chose to shun me, excusing themselves from unnecessary trouble. Not only did this affect me emotionally, but physically too. I was diagnosed with Temporomandibular Disorder (TMD), which included chronic and uncontrollable mouth spasms whenever I felt particularly stressed and/or emotional. Finding out there is no cure for TMD was quite devastating. However, I had to embrace the fact this condition will be with me for life. So, instead of crying over spilt milk, I concentrated on better managing my TMD to slow down the deterioration rate.

I took a step back to reflect on my life. I realized how I would often get stuck in negative emotions, constantly asking myself, why? Why was I born a girl? Why do people betray my trust? Why are these difficulties happening to me? Many things just didn't make sense. After thorough pondering, I realized how asking these questions was both draining and counterproductive. In many of the challenges, I had allowed my emotions to cloud my sound judgment and dictate my actions, which only exacerbated the situation. The crying and victimhood certainly didn't help at all. In general, as a person who is in touch with her feelings and emotions, it explained why I often reacted the way I did. I must admit I had done some stupid things before, especially by hurting myself, but I would never do it again, no matter what. I was born into this world for a reason, and I should make the best use of it. As the old saying goes, "When life gives you lemons, make lemonade."

I had to constantly remind myself to be aware of my emotions and condition my mind to be more objective in handling different situations. I know it is easier said than done, but trust me, the power of your mind lies in your hands. After much deliberation, I managed to find a way forward, which was through talking to myself (either in my head or saying it out loud, especially when I look at myself in the mirror). What I needed was a paradigm shift on how I view each challenge. I began putting more time and effort into looking at different ways to cope with a challenge instead of wasting so much time asking questions with no definitive answers. I have certainly not mastered mind conditioning. I still sometimes fall back into my old ways. However, I am now more aware of my reactions and can shift my focus much faster toward the positive. More importantly, I am confident in identifying solutions and determining which solution is the most appropriate, as well as owning the choices I make.

172

Strong will and perseverance are some of the key elements to survive challenges and to chart your own destiny. At times, the choices I made might not have had the desired effect. When that happened, I took a step back to reflect on what worked and what didn't work, and looked for other options, instead of doing the same thing repeatedly but expecting a different result. As Thomas Edison put it when he had run through many failed attempts at creating the light bulb, "I have not failed. I've just found 10,000 ways that don't work."

Throughout some of the challenging situations, I was glad I had my loved ones and a few true friends by my side. I am blessed to have a loving and caring daughter who would always offer me a shoulder to cry on. She is one of my pillars of strength. My few true friends have spent time with me and have given me advice, which turned out to be invaluable. These true friends had also given me the impetus and additional strength to do what I needed to do for the greater good. These challenges have taught me how you only need a few true friends to have an enriching and meaningful life.

I know some of you may not have anyone to rely on when you go through difficult times. Believing in yourself, however, is another pillar of strength, even while you work to surround yourself with positive people. Be true to yourself and don't give up hope. Hope and other positive emotions are the basis of improving our mental and physical health. Keep in mind how hope cannot manifest into something good if we just sit back and do nothing about it. We need to put effort into doing what it takes to achieve the desired result unless it is something beyond our control. Trying and failing is still better than not trying at all. We may make mistakes along the way but doing so and learning from them is one of the ways we grow and become wiser. Always remember these words from Friedrich Nietzsche: "What doesn't kill you makes you stronger."

United Arab Emirates

Chapter 24

His Excellency Sheikh Nahayan bin Mubarak Al Nahayan

Minister of Tolerance

His Excellency Sheikh Nahayan Mabarak Al Nahayan is the Minister of Tolerance, which was announced in October 2017. His Excellency joined the Federal Government in 1992. He held several positions in the Federal Government including the Minister of Higher Education and Scientific Research, the Minister of Education, and the Minister of Culture and Knowledge Development.

In addition to his ministerial duties, His Excellency had previously served in many positions in national universities, including Chancellor

175

of the United Arab Emirates University (1983–2013), Chancellor of the Higher Colleges of Technology from 1988–2013, and President of Zayed University from 1998–2013.

His Excellency received his education from the British Millfield School before joining the Magdalen College at Oxford University in the United Kingdom.

* * * * *

Imagine a world where people in need do not have to ask for help because they are embedded in communities that take action to care for everyone. Imagine a world where every individual, every organization, and every government are determined to ensure a safe, productive, meaningful, and fulfilling existence for every human being regardless of where they were born or what they believe. Such a world would be united in the virtues of justice, equality, tolerance, brotherhood, sisterhood, and prosperity. It would be a world based in free and open dialogue between people of various cultures, in the full knowledge that words and reason bind us together. It would be a world without extremism, violence, war, or hate—a world of peace, progress, safety, and a better future for all human beings. Our attitudes and our actions are the only things standing between us and this world I describe.

The twenty-first century gives us opportunities to create such a world. We observed, for example, a remarkable phenomenon emerge globally as a result of the COVID-19 pandemic. Individuals, organizations, and governments all demonstrated compassion for their fellow human beings and worked to make a positive difference for others in unprecedented ways. Acts of kindness, expressions of support, and practical actions taken to help others abounded. We learned how this collectively shared compassion made a profound difference. Seeing the best of human fraternity in action has given me great hope for our collective future.

For a new world of universal hope, peace, prosperity, and coexistence to take root, we must respect the bonds that unite us as members of a global community, and work tirelessly to nurture those bonds. We must work together to overcome religious and cultural misunderstandings. We must encourage reform in our societies to eradicate poverty, achieve safety and security, and open economic opportunities for everyone. We must unleash the power of education as an effective tool for building positive relationships, dispelling stereotypical attitudes, and nurturing new ways of thinking. We must strengthen our ability to help those who are in need regardless of their politics,

176

their ideology, or their religion. We must also help make peace, tolerance, and human fraternity into fields of innovation, initiative, and causes for joint action and effective participation by all for the benefit of all. We must celebrate successful models from around the world to demonstrate how peace and coexistence within diverse human societies are positive and creative forces for progress and stability.

I am delighted to send this call to champion hope, peace, and tolerance from the United Arab Emirates to the world. As Minister of Tolerance and Coexistence in the United Arab Emirates, I ask people everywhere to work together for a world of mutual understanding, a world of tolerance, empathy, and justice. I call on all of us to dedicate ourselves to thinking and working together as one human family where we celebrate the power of engagement to shape the future and to help solve the world's great global challenges. As one human family, we must think and work together as a family of equals where everyone is entitled to respect and deserving of empathy. As one human family, we can commit ourselves to becoming champions for human rights, human dignity, and a high quality of life for all.

As we reach out in a spirit of brotherhood and sisterhood to commit to living together in peace, safety, and good health, and may we always remember our greatest hope lies in recognizing our shared humanity.

Canada

Chapter 25

Dayle Haddon
Model and Author

Dayle is the founder and CEO of WomenOne, an international non-profit organization focused on creating quality education for girls. Partnering with Duke University, WomenOne created leadership workshops and award-winning film programming for Syrian refugee girls in Zaatari Camp in Jordan. Dayle has traveled extensively on behalf of girls' education in Jordan, Turkey, Sudan, Darfur, Angola, Congo, Rwanda, Kenya, Bolivia, and India, raising awareness of the importance of educating girls in the most marginalized contexts. She has written for many publications and is a sought-out speaker globally on the importance of girls' leadership and empowerment through quality education.

Dayle has been the international spokesperson and the face of L'Oréal, Revlon, Estée Lauder, and Max Factor—the only person to have four major cosmetic contracts. She has written two international bestselling books on inner and outer beauty and living in balance and has been a regular contributor for CBS television's *The Early Show* as a beauty expert.

Invited to be part of the first Gender Equality Advisory Council for the G7, Dayle helped raise $2.8 billion for girls' education globally. She was nominated to Vanity Fair's Hall of Fame for her work with refugees and was ranked one of the top 50 US philanthropists by *Town & Country Magazine* for their yearly philanthropy issue. UN Women for Peace honored Dayle's work at WomenOne with their Humanity Award, and she was also honored by the Girl Scouts of America. She is on the board of Airbel Impact Lab, an arm of the International Rescue Committee, as well as the board of Artemis Rising Foundation. Dayle is also a member of The Council on Foreign Relations, an international think tank based in New York City and Washington DC.

* * * * *

There is a moment in your life where your trajectory can change in an instant. One minute everything is going along in the normal day-to-day way and in a flash, without any warning, your life is completely changed and is never again what it was. That is what happened to me. In an instant I lost so much: my husband, my home, my livelihood, and security. An unexpected accident had changed my life forever.

As the shattered pieces lay about me, I knew even then I had to move forward. I had to put the pieces back together somehow, however slowly, and build back a life I knew would be completely different. In doing so, I hoped to be a stronger, more compassionate, wiser, and more understanding person through my own loss and challenges. The hope I had was the light I followed, even though I wasn't sure where it would take me. I trusted where I was going as I knew I couldn't go any lower.

I had been happy and successfully living and working in Europe for more than ten years. In the wake of these overwhelming events, I had to return home. It took me some time to grieve and gain an equilibrium, but I knew I had to go back to work. I had a daughter to support and focusing on other needs would help me heal. With a successful career as a model and actress behind me, I reached out to my agents in the fashion business to start again. To my surprise, the response was, "Are you kidding. You are over the hill. You will never work in this industry again!" It was a rude awakening. I was only thirty-eight years old and never considered myself over any hill, nor would I be at any time soon. In fact, I felt more like I was at the beginning of who I was as a woman, not anywhere near an end! The billion-dollar beauty industry was saying if I was close to the age of forty, then I was not viable and not worth imaging for their products. I knew if they were saying this about me, then they were saying it about all women, and I was determined to prove them wrong.

In the early 1990s, there was little imaging of a woman in her forties and above. Most of the beauty products meant for that demographic were shown on twenty-something women who obviously didn't need them. By not being represented in the media, the industry was saying women over forty didn't count, held no value, and were therefore invisible. It didn't make sense to me, and I knew I had to change this perception from the inside out. I went to the library and did a lot of research, discovering there were over 40 million women (the baby boomers) who saw themselves differently, yet the industry was not addressing them or representing them in their advertising. It was time for a change.

I came out armed with a lot of information to support the vast numbers of women over forty who still considered themselves young, vital, and engaged, yet weren't being *seen*. No one had spoken about it before. I was definitely onto something.

I knocked on a lot of industry doors. At first, I was turned down by most of them, but I had a real conviction I was right, which gave me the energy to persevere. Bit by bit the doors started to open, and the cosmetic executives began to listen. It was a new idea to show the continuity one's own beauty has over the years and the evolution of true beauty that only experience can bring. The idea that beauty never ends and is certainly not the property only of the young.

It started with a campaign for Clairol that shattered the age barrier by featuring top models of the 1970s and 1980s on a major hair color line. Because I had done so much research on this subject of aging, they chose me as the spokesperson for their extensive domestic campaign. The idea took hold and other clients became inspired to capture this vast, new audience. I was asked to shoot for campaigns reflecting beauty over forty, speak on panels about the "invisible woman," and share the message through these venues that beauty comes from within and looks different at every age.

I was convinced that if we as women are truly beautiful then of course we would be beautiful all our life. We just had to find the most authentic ways to feel beautiful, to be in balance, and recognize our value throughout all our years. Our idea of true beauty had to be defined together and come from an inner place and radiate outwards. And it had to have the wisdom we'd garnered over the years included in the definition. The message hit a cord with the media and more importantly with the thousands of women out there who were finally being acknowledged for having value, no matter what their age.

In the beauty and fashion business the "brass ring" is to get a contract with a major beauty company. There are only a few beauty contracts available and lots of competition vying for them. I was in the right place at the right time, and it was my great good fortune to not only get one beauty contract but to secure two of them back-to-back, first with Estée Lauder and then L'Oréal for more than fifteen years. It was due to a stroke of luck, perseverance, passion, knowing I was right, and lots of hard work. I was humbled by the opportunity. It was also gratifying to receive these affirmations after the way I had previously been treated by the industry. It proved my instincts were right: The power our truth of beauty holds allows us to travel throughout all our decades with grace, wisdom, and dignity. If one is truly beautiful, then one should be beautiful all their life. It has to do with who you are on the inside and how you see the world, not just what you look like on the outside.

Throughout the more than thirty years of my career, I've had the good fortune to have worked with some of the greatest photographers (Horst, Beaton, Avedon, Hiro, Lartigue, and many more) as well as the very best makeup artists, hairdressers, and stylists. I was not an immediate success. It took a long time to work with these greats, but along the way I had the time to develop myself in an industry many dismiss as superficial, finding time to develop my own ideas on the meaning of true beauty. When I first started, I was turned away so many times that when I finally did succeed, I had to adjust the meaning of what the term being beautiful was and see for myself the humor in it all. I believe my success has been more about who I am than what I look like, and we know how we feel about ourselves has a direct influence on how we look.

While working with the beauty companies, I felt I had more to say to women who had grown up with me through my photos in magazines. I received many letters saying how they related to me and felt I understood their problems. This gave me the opening to write two books on both inner and outer beauty, sharing what I had learned and what I felt was important to highlight for women through this roller coaster called life.

182

Both books became successful in countries from the US to China, Germany, Brazil, France, and more, so I knew my message resonated.

Having done many tours for my books in numerous countries and speaking on behalf of the different companies I'd worked with as well as working personally with so many women from all walks of life and all ages, I could see that there were many of the same concerns and difficulties coming up for women after a certain age. We all have our challenges to overcome. Each of us is dealt a hand of cards to play in life. Some people seem to have been dealt a better hand than others, but we have to play the hand we've been dealt. We can't always control what happens to us, but we can control our attitude towards what does happen. Our freedom comes from the choices we make as well as the attitude we have, no matter what hand we have been dealt. I my experience, the more we are challenged, the more opportunity we have for growth if we choose well. When we make good choices and learn from our stumbles, we can transform those difficulties we face into real change, both for ourselves and for those around us.

Now, why am I speaking about a philosophy of living when we have been, up to now, addressing the subject of beauty? Because it is time to develop a deeper understanding of who we are and to come to terms with the essence of what being a truly beautiful person is. Together we must go deeper and come up with truths that help sustain us through the years and free us from the fears causing us to look backwards with possible regret for "lost" time. We know our physical body changes. That's a fact. No matter how hard you work on it there will be changes. But we can decide to move with this change and come up with deeper truths instead of desperately clinging to ages that have long passed us by.

We need to define and create a more authentic way of seeing our beauty to guide us as we travel forward through our own timeline. I consider myself very logical. So, I asked myself, "If our life has a beginning, a middle, and an end, how can any of it not be important?" All of it is ours and it all must be good because we are alive! Our beauty in each of these ages we travel through changes, and we must take the time to listen to the secrets each age has to tell us. If we try to cling to what has passed us by, we will never hear the wisdom given us from each age.

This understanding is the basis of real beauty. The understanding of where our true worth lies is something we must work on and develop. We need the substance of these wisdom years to feed us and offset other more detrimental messages that often come in so loudly, such as *we are not enough*—not pretty enough, good enough, sexy enough,

183

vital enough—I say enough of the *not enoughs*! When we value who we are, and all our parts, the shadow as well as the light, we can fully embrace ourselves and love who we are, exactly as we are, which is always a work in progress. All this translates not only as inner acceptance and love but radiates outwards as balance, authenticity, truth, sovereignty, and yes, *beauty*—a complete beauty that honors you as a person and not only what you look like.

True beauty in our forties and up is about generosity, compassion, and inclusion. It's about giving back and being of service to others. When we make the choice to *be* these qualities, we light something up inside. We become greater than we were. Our vibration becomes more refined, and we just shine brighter. We become truly beautiful no matter what our age. Physical beauty is a gift, like a talent. It must be cared for, yes, and not dismissed. We have but one body. It is our vehicle. We must tend to it the best we can, so we can move around, touch and be touched, take action, create things, and more importantly (with our experiences garnered over the years) add to our developing wisdom and understanding to deliver all our promise and all our beauty.

I have been given a lot in this life and I am deeply grateful. I've had my share of challenges, more than some and less than others, but at that moment in time where I lost so much in one go, I knew I had to eventually give back to gain my own balance. It was a long road but something I had wanted to do for many years. The hope of traveling this path gave me the courage and the conviction to move forward.

I started as a UNICEF Ambassador working in the field in many countries in Africa and South America. At a certain moment after numerous trips in often heartbreaking situations I saw a need for a smaller NGO and decided to start my own charity, WomenOne, focused on quality education for girls. I felt education was important because it changed so many difficult problems. When a girl is educated, incidents of violence go down and occurrences of HIV Aids are lessened. Mothers with an education raised fewer and healthier children and would send their children to school as well. With an education a girl not only lifts herself and her family up, but also the community in which she lives.

WomenOne has now worked in countries as diverse as Haiti, Jordan, Turkey, Senegal, and The Gambia. We've created leadership workshops in Syrian refugee camps and worked alongside great partners like UNICEF, Save the Children, and UNWomen. We have focused our efforts now in Nanyuki, a small town in Kenya about three hours outside Nairobi. Working with our partner on the ground, we are supporting young girls to become leaders in their community. I am more inspired by the passion and

184

determination of these young girls who, though they have very little, want to be so much in the world. Their hope for themselves and their families, their commitment to their place in the world, their dreams and ambitions all inspire me to do better, work harder, and be more daring for them.

My journey has come full circle. I started off in a world of glamour, fashion, and beauty that at first didn't want me or value me as I grew older. Through conviction and perseverance, I managed to change their minds. Along the way I had to reinvent myself, transforming my own focus on where my value truly lay.

I had the incredibly good fortune to encounter these inspiring young girls through my work with WomenOne, girls who faced tremendous challenges, obstacles, and trauma, yet kept going in the face of it all because they saw a dream for themselves. Many of the girls are the first in their family to go to school. They have hope for their future. They have hope to be many things and it's this desire for something to happen in the future that propels them and in turn each of us forward. We hope for a better life, a better future. We hope to be more than we were and in doing so we find growth, positivity, resilience, courage, and strength.

Hope requires action to make it happen and is the secret ingredient of possibilities. We don't know who we can be unless we hope for more for ourselves and then do something about it. Hope is the grounds for believing something good may happen. This is our birthright. Hope is what picks us up when all else has failed. We have hope when we feel we have something to give, something to share that fulfills us and makes a difference. True beauty and happiness mean having a hopeful life where anything is possible and you have the courage to follow your dreams.

Italy

Chapter 26

Jennifer Missoni

Wellpreneur

Jennifer Missoni is a holistic health coach and former actress. Though the granddaughter of Rosita and Tai, founders of the prestigious and eponymous Italian fashion house, she was always more fascinated by stories and stage lights than hemlines and patterns. Jennifer's passion for the performing arts took her to New York and Los Angeles. She studied with famed acting coach Susan Batson in New York before working on several television productions, including recurring roles on *Gossip Girl*, *Damages*, *Royal Pains*, and guest-starring roles on *Fringe*, *Medium*, *Army Wives*, and *White Collar*. She made her big screen debut in the horror film *Playback*, starring opposite Christian Slater.

187

In her mid-twenties, Jennifer suffered a traumatic event so severe it wreaked havoc on her overall health. When medical care proved insufficient, she shifted her focus from the performing arts to alternative healing methods, eventually starting her own business working with private clients as a health coach. Jennifer currently resides in Varese, Italy with her husband and two children. She is currently writing a book to share all the tips and life lessons from her inspiring healing journey.

* * * * *

I write this letter to share how true love found me in the most unexpected way and how, just as unexpectedly, the solution to healing from a debilitating illness was sitting right in front of me all along.

I first met my husband when I was five years old, and Tommaso was nine. It was at a time in my life when my mother was constantly receiving calls from teachers at my kindergarten about how I was chasing boys and throwing myself at them—I'd never been shy in this respect—and I was completely infatuated with this pudgy little boy. We were at a family get-together at my grandmother's house in Crans, Switzerland. Our families knew each other both socially and professionally through the fashion industry, so it was only a matter of time before we crossed paths.

It was *settimana bianca*, the Italian winter holiday to celebrate *Carnevale*. I had smeared my mouth with some lipstick I found and was chasing a very frightened Tommaso around the house in a mad attempt to kiss him. That week, I finally convinced him to marry me. My cousin Margherita served as the officiant, and we had a small wedding ceremony in front of a vintage credenza. I was elated, but the feeling was fleeting. When it was time to don our costumes, Tommaso dressed up as The Joker, and it was my turn to be frightened. In a costume like that, I didn't want anything to do with him.

Over the years, Tommaso and I would run into each other from time to time. It was inevitable because his uncle produces high-profile fashion shows and events in Milan, and my grandparents, Rosita and Tai, founded the Italian fashion house Missoni. Our encounters were both sporadic and brief, as he lived in Milan and I lived in Varese, an hour north in the countryside. Besides, in 2004 at the tender age of nineteen and intent on pursuing acting, I moved to New York. As I would later find out, Tommaso also moved to New York in 2004.

188

I had always dreamed of becoming an actress, and my life in Manhattan revolved around a rigorous schedule of acting, dance, and voice lessons. In my personal life, despite constantly having my heart broken, I never stopped falling in love. I knew someday I would meet someone who would love me the way I loved—unconditionally. Even when my last relationship went quickly downhill, with me financially supporting an abusive boyfriend, I never gave up hope. I let myself be open to the experience of falling in love again and again.

In 2006, I found myself at a party at the National Arts Club in Gramercy. I was sitting with my friend Katia when out of nowhere a guy approached me and started speaking to me in French. Poor kid, he was clearly trying to impress me, but it wasn't working. I'm fluent in French and dove right into a conversation with him. He was taken aback and looked confused. Suddenly his eyes shone with recognition. He immediately switched to his native Italian. "Jennifer!" he said. "It's me, Tommaso!"

It took me a while to place him. He looked nothing like the boy I had chased and married so many years ago. The Tommaso in front of me was a thin, lean rocker. He wore skinny black jeans with black leather Converse sneakers and had a shaved head, which he was hiding under a colorful cap. He was a completely different person. He had moved to New York with a friend—two directors focused on fashion content, curious if they could find the same success here they had found in Europe.

Several years later, when Tommaso and I would talk about this chance encounter, he would say, "When I saw you sitting there across the room, it was love at first sight." It's still extraordinary for me to think he was able to feel that way without even knowing who I was.

Tommaso and I became fast friends. I knew right off the bat he was somebody I could trust, somebody I could completely be myself around. I'd take him along to an acting class every Tuesday and Thursday morning, as I thought it could be useful for him as a director to understand the process actors go through. We'd also go out on the town frequently, and I would help him swiftly escape women who had latched onto him for the evening.

One of my favorite places in New York was Cipriani downtown on a Sunday night for karaoke. One night, Tommaso and I went there together and left around 4:00 am. We were walking in SoHo on West Broadway when I suddenly started to feel differently about him, like maybe he was more than a friend. For a reason I can't remember, I sat down on a nearby stoop. Maybe I was tired, or my feet hurt. Tommaso sat down next to me, and before I knew what was happening, he leaned in to kiss me.

Though I had just had a shift in my feelings towards him only moments before, I was taken completely off-guard. "What are you doing?" I exclaimed, erupting in laughter.

In his heavy Italian accent, he responded: "Do you like it when I kiss you, or do you feel repulsion? Please tell me, I need to know!" To give him an answer, I kissed him back. It was April 17, 2006. Even to this day, whenever we think back to this moment together, we can't help but laugh.

After that night, we were inseparable. It didn't take me too long to realize he was the one. Even though I sensed his slight hesitation to commit, I knew it was just a matter of time before he realized we were meant to be together.

The next milestone in our relationship was a month-long trip we took on the Trans-Siberian Railway. We traveled from Moscow to Beijing with another couple and a Russian friend who served as our guide. We had agreed that if we could survive on a train together for nine days, we'd be ready to move in together. It was exhilarating to be with him on this trip because it was so different from traveling with my family in comfortable hotels with set itineraries. Tommaso has an incredibly adventurous spirit, which inspired my own sense of adventure. I had experiences I would have never been able to have on my own, experiences that were completely life changing.

As an equestrian, one of my dreams was always to ride a horse with my eyes closed. In the Mongolian desert, near the end of our trip, I did just that. I got on a horse, closed my eyes, and let it take me wherever it wanted. It didn't matter where I went. Everywhere was desert, everywhere was safe. That was what being with Tommaso felt like—complete safety and freedom. If there was one thing I learned from this trip, it's how getting out of your comfort zone can often lead you to discovering parts of yourself you didn't even know existed.

Once we returned to Manhattan, I moved into his loft in TriBeCa. It was thrilling to be in this meaningful relationship with the man of my dreams, while taking advantage of all the excitement and opportunity New York City had to offer. As our relationship and trust grew deeper for each other, our professional lives also blossomed. I accepted my first official acting job on a television show, and Tommaso found his own success as a director. But three years later, in 2009, everything changed.

190

On New Year's Eve 2009, I experienced a traumatic event which resulted in my body completely shutting down. It took me several years and many health professionals to later learn the trauma had caused my endocrine system to stop functioning. I was a twenty-four-year-old girl trapped in the body of a much older woman. I stopped getting my period and went into early menopause.

We had just come out to Los Angeles, and I was at a turning point in my career. I'd just secured a new manager and a promising agent. I was very focused on my professional goals, yet despite leading a healthy lifestyle, I rapidly started to put on weight. This wasn't exactly helpful for a young actress trying to make it in image-obsessed Hollywood. A friend recommended a local doctor who immediately diagnosed me with hypothyroidism. With my little knowledge about health back then and desperate to feel my best again, I started on thyroid medication without getting a second opinion.

The weight started coming off, and I felt a boost in energy. I still wasn't getting my period, but I was happy I had gotten some answers and was seeing immediate results. Little did I know I was heading into a terrifying state of hyperthyroidism, along with all its debilitating symptoms. I constantly felt nervous and jittery, had heart palpitations, and lost a drastic amount of weight—symptoms my doctor didn't seem too concerned about. I started having anxiety for the first time in my life and had frequent obsessive thoughts I couldn't control. It was one of the darkest times of my life, and I felt like there was no end in sight.

My illness began to affect my personal life. How could it not? It was inevitable, as I was in a constant state of anxiety and depression. Tommaso felt helpless, and that helplessness expressed itself as sadness, anger, and frustration. Conflict seeped into our relationship, and intimacy became complicated. I knew in my heart there was a way out. Just because I didn't know how to get better did not mean I would give up hope. On the recommendation of my trusted family doctor, I found a wonderful psychotherapist and began a life-changing journey of cognitive behavioral therapy.

Throughout the years together, even though I felt ready to get married, Tommaso was hesitant. He needed to know I would be physically and emotionally ready to start a family and live a happy life. When I began hormone replacement therapy with a new doctor in Manhattan, my physical symptoms seemed to disappear, so Tommaso and I decided to get married then. But it didn't take long for me to realize the root of the problem had never been solved—the hormones I was given were a Band-Aid at best.

After living a bicoastal life for four years, we fully moved to Los Angeles in 2013. The following year, as fate would have it, I was getting an IV in the doctor's office and shared my story with the patient sitting next to me. She recommended I see Mirela Lisicar Rohan, her acupuncturist extraordinaire, who was helping her through similar issues. I had already tried two highly recommended acupuncturists to help get my period back, so I was skeptical. But when Halle, who would later become a close friend, added that her menstrual cycle had returned, I wasted no time in calling to schedule my first appointment.

After five years of amenorrhea, my period came back a month after starting twice-weekly sessions with Mirela. I also took Chinese herbal formulations she prescribed. I got off my thyroid medication completely. Her opinion was I never needed it to begin with. These instant, drastic changes in my health were what sparked a fire in me to learn more about alternative healing methods. But healing my body, as it turned out, was only the start of my life-long healing journey.

In 2015, a few months shy of my thirtieth birthday, I was driving in Beverly Hills when a sudden panic attack hit. I pulled over, took out my cell phone, and called a number I never, ever thought I would call. It was a last resort.

It wasn't my first panic attack. Ever since my body became healthy and hormonally stable, panic attacks had started to occur with an alarming frequency. I often experienced several of them a day, which left me helpless and bedridden. Basically, the emotional impact of past trauma, which required a lot of healing, waited to reveal itself once my body was physically capable of handling it! How incredible. This made me realize how we are never given anything in life we are incapable of handling.

A few years prior, I met a guy at a party, and we spoke openly about the anxiety I was experiencing. He confidently stated the meditation practice he'd been doing for years had the power to get rid of it. He mentioned the David Lynch Foundation in Los Angeles, where he had learned Transcendental Meditation. I was familiar with Transcendental Meditation (commonly referred to as TM), as most members of my family had practiced it since the 1970s, including my maternal grandparents. It was never something that interested me. The simple fact my family was so enthusiastic about it made me distance myself from it even more. Besides, I didn't think meditation was an option for me. I had a natural tendency to overthink things and my brain was always going a mile a minute. I couldn't imagine sitting still with my eyes closed for even one second.

192

That day in my car on the side of the road, I called the David Lynch Foundation in Los Angeles, and asked when I could come in. Lucky for me, their next introductory lecture was only three days away. I'll never forget the Sunday afternoon I walked into the center on North Highland Avenue for the first time. I immediately felt like I belonged there and knew my life was truly about to change.

Transcendental Meditation is one of the simplest yet effective tools you can use to instantly shift your energy and mood. For only twenty minutes, twice a day, you can bring peace and serenity back into your life. I had tried other types of meditation before, but they never worked for me. It was through TM I was finally able to ground myself through the repetition of a mantra, chosen for me by my teacher, which is a unique aspect of this practice. I wish I had known how simple it was to begin with, and how there was no reason to be intimidated. Even children are capable of practicing TM. In fact, the David Lynch Foundation has done incredible work integrating this practice into the curriculums of several inner-city schools.

At first, there was too much trauma in my body that needed to be released for me to do the full twenty minutes. With my teacher Lynn Kaplan guiding me, we decided it was best for me to just stick to ten minutes. Slowly, over the course of a year, we increased the number of minutes until I reached the sweet spot of twenty minutes, twice a day. The fact I had to really take my time shows just how powerful this practice can be. Countless veterans and survivors have benefited from TM because of how it can increase gamma brainwaves and help restore the amygdala to its original setting.

Within the first few days of learning TM, I saw an immediate shift in energy and mood. I felt happy for the first time in years! I started to see everything differently and became reacquainted with my natural chemistry of joy. I could finally see the light at the end of the tunnel as excitement slowly creeped back into my life. I felt calm, and my natural state of being transitioned from hopelessness to happiness. I followed up with Lynn frequently, knowing this practice would be a part of my life forever.

It took me a long time (and years of psychotherapy) to realize what I had was PTSD from my adolescence and childhood. The trauma I had experienced on New Year's Eve in 2009 was the straw that broke the camel's back, and it sent my body into a perpetual state of shock.

The hope that meditation reinstated into my life has been far beyond anything that any doctor, medication, or alternative healing method has ever been able to offer. I know this because I spent nearly a decade trying everything that was out there. So often, both in love and in life, the solutions we're seeking are the simplest.

Today, I'm so grateful I'm able to enjoy the love I strongly believed I deserved for so long, and that my partner was able to stick with me through several dark years. We have two beautiful children and are back to living in Italy. I have been meditating now for nearly eight years. It's the first thing I do in the morning as soon as I get up.

On the surface, it was meditation that got me through the most difficult parts of my life. But what really guided me towards healing was the same thing that had originally guided me towards finding love, and that was *hope*. Despite everything, I always held onto a magical combination of patience and trust, knowing one day everything I had ever dreamed of would eventually come and find me.

Hungary

Chapter 27

Dr. Edith Eva Eger

Psychologist and Author

A native of Hungary, Edith Eva Eger was just a teenager in 1944 when she experienced one of the worst evils the world has ever known. As a Jew living in Nazi-occupied Eastern Europe, she and her family were sent to the heinous Auschwitz death camp. Her parents were sent to the gas chambers, but Edith's bravery kept her and her sister alive. Toward the end of the war, Edith and other prisoners had been moved to Austria. On May 4, 1945, a young American soldier noticed her hand moving slightly amongst several dead bodies. He quickly summoned medical help and brought her back from the brink of death.

After the war, Edith moved to Czechoslovakia, where she met the man she would marry. In 1949 they moved to the United States. In 1969 she received her degree in Psychology from the University of Texas, El Paso. She then pursued her doctoral internship at the William Beaumont Army Medical Center at Fort Bliss, Texas.

Dr. Eger is a prolific author and a member of several professional associations. She has a clinical practice in La Jolla, California and holds a faculty appointment at the University of California, San Diego. She has appeared on numerous television programs, including CNN and the Oprah Winfrey Show. She was the primary subject of a holocaust documentary that appeared on Dutch National Television and is frequently invited to speaking engagements throughout the United States and abroad.

* * * * *

Some of my favorite words are four-letter words, but I don't mean the naughty ones. I mean words like *life, love, hope, risk,* and *kind.*

Each person is born, and each person will die, but between those two events is something we call *life,* one of my favorite four-letter words. The question is how you will live it. Life can and will pass you by. You must be willing to take a *risk,* another of my favorite four-letter words. Take a risk to do what you love, to do what makes you happy. Take a risk to try connecting with another person. When I take a risk to connect with someone but don't get what I wanted, I never think the other person is rejecting me. No one rejects me but me. It's about managing your own expectations. If you do have expectations, you must ask yourself if they are realistic or unrealistic. It's better to be a realist than an idealist. This doesn't mean you shouldn't have dreams, because you should, just avoid confusing romanticism with realism.

When I was taken away to the Auschwitz death camp, I was a sixteen-year-old girl very much in love with my boyfriend at the time. He used to tell me my eyes were beautiful, and my hands were beautiful. Separated from him at the camp, everything became about the uncertainty of life. I would ask people to tell me about my eyes and about my hands because it reminded me of my boyfriend and the constant thought that if I just survived this day, then maybe tomorrow I would see him again, and show him my eyes and my hands. Wrapped up in that word, tomorrow, was *hope*—yet another four-letter word. It was only later I found out he had been shot dead the day before the camps were liberated.

The hope for tomorrow kept me going despite the uncertainty I faced every day. Even the simple act of taking a shower was full of uncertainty because I never knew for sure what would come out of the faucet—water or lethal gas. I also didn't know where I was or even if anyone knew I was there. I felt like had been discarded, thrown out, I felt I must be good for nothing, or that something must be wrong with me. It came so very close to breaking my spirit. It would have been easier to die than keep living. I lost everything in Auschwitz except for two things—my older sister Magda and my mind. The last thing my mother said to me before she was taken to the gas chambers was this: "No one can take away from you what you put here in your own mind."

This is why the battle against COVID today is so important. During the worst of the pandemic, when everyone had to go on lockdown and people were dying in great numbers, life was full of uncertainty that for me echoed what it was like at Auschwitz. I knew if COVID continued unchecked, it would eventually break the spirit of humanity. The rapid development of vaccines and treatments kept this from happening.

Suffering, you see, can make you stronger. Suffering is feeling, and you cannot heal what you don't feel. The opposite of *de*pression is *ex*pression. What comes out of your body doesn't make you ill, but what you keep inside surely can. Helping someone means guiding people to look for the light in the darkness, to look for the hope in hopelessness.

What is hope? It's something you must never give up. I expressed hope in the death camps by changing even hatred into pity. I felt sorry for the guards who had been so brainwashed they could believe the lies they'd been told and could do such horrible things to people just for being who they were. I prayed for those guards. I even saw how some of them were *kind*, yet another important four-letter word.

When people in positions of authority and leadership tell people a lie over and over again, people will begin to believe it, which is why *you* must always be willing to question authority rather than following it blindly. This is what makes people and groups susceptible to fascism. It's what fuels prejudice, which means to pre-judge. When I first came to the United States in 1949, I was shocked at how black people were treated. I went to use a public restroom that was labeled *colored*. A white woman rushed over and told me not to use that bathroom and pointed to the one for whites. I played dumb, but after that I always made a point of using the "wrong" restroom.

People need to know it's okay to not feel so good, it's okay to be disappointed, but it's not okay to be discouraged. Give up the saying of "Yes, but…" and instead always say "Yes, and…" Yes, and I'm hopeful. Yes, and I'm a one-of-a-kind unique person. Yes, and no one can do what I do quite the same way I do it. Yes, and God only made *one* of *me*. You celebrate all of what makes you different from everyone else. Yes, and differences can exist within a framework of unity that empowers everyone.

I recently spoke at a church, and I talked about a boyfriend I had for six years and how we celebrated our differences. He was from a farm in Nebraska in the United States. I'm a Hungarian girl. I knew nothing of Nebraska. Yes, we were different and we could empower each other through our differences. It's about not having an agenda and authentically meeting people where they are. You can be you, and I can be me, for we are all utterly and completely unique, and it doesn't mean I am better than you or you are better than mean. We can empower each other through our differences if we are *kind* to one another and meet people where they are.

If you want to communicate effectively with a ten-year-old child, you need to meet them where they are and adjust what words you will use. I'm not going to tell a child they are experiencing cognitive dissonance. That would be meaningless to them. This is why it's important to do your research before spending time communicating with people of a different country or culture.

Meeting someone where they are is one thing, but as a psychologist I also treat people. I do not, however, treat people where they are but treat them as if they were what they're capable of becoming. I respect everyone just by virtue of their humanity. This is not always an easy thing to do! There was a fourteen-year-old boy who had been caught up in a David Koresh type of cult. During his first session with me he leaned on my desk, looked me in the eye and said, "Hey doc, I'm going to kill all the Jews." What should I have done in this situation? I could easily have told him how I saw my own mother dragged away to the gas chambers. I had to remind myself—people don't just come to me, they are *sent* to me.

I turned to God for wisdom. I asked God what was this all about? And God told me to find the bigot in myself. Whatever you don't like in someone else, find it within yourself first because it is a reminder of what we all have in common, which is being

198

human. We are all human beings, and we are not perfect. This is why love and forgiveness go hand in hand.

Love is not what you feel, it's when you give yourself a gift, and the gift is forgiveness. Why? Because it's *for giving* away, so you don't have to carry negativity, so you can let go of whatever is hurting inside you, such as pain, anger, and bitterness. If I didn't let go of all the pain of Auschwitz, if I continued to carry this pain, then I would still be a prisoner to this day. The boy becoming a man who says to himself, "I don't want to be *anything* like my father," is a prisoner because he has not forgiven his father.

Love must begin with love of self, and it's about letting go. Self-care and self-love needn't be narcissistic. After all, if you don't love yourself, why should anyone else? For me, forgiving myself was one of the hardest parts of my personal journey. Moving past survivor's guilt was incredibly difficult. I completed university with honors but didn't even attend my own graduation ceremony because I allowed myself to think it was wrong celebrate such an achievement when so many others had died in the camps. This was my survivor's guilt. I had to forgive myself and regain self-love.

Whenever I'm about to say something to someone, I ask myself, is it necessary? Is it important? But most importantly, is it *kind*? If it's not kind, then it's not the best I can do. God gave each of us one mouth but two ears because it's more important to listen than to speak. What you say to others is so powerful it deserves to be considered and even rehearsed before you say it, as if you're acting in a play. Your role in this play called life has very real impacts on other people. Kindness is the way to ensure the impact you have on others is positive. Avoid saying, "How are you?" as well as "Why don't you…" because life is better for you and others if you refrain from asking questions and giving advice.

What you say to yourself is also important. Pay attention to your self-talk. Does your self-talk empower you or deplete you? If it's depleting you, then you must change it. Change the way you think and you can change your life. When people say they'd be so happy if they look as good as I do when they reach my age (I will be 95 in September 2022), I always give the same response: You must be happy *inside*. If you are, then it won't matter to you what you look like on the outside, but as it turns out you will naturally look better too!

My wish for you and everyone in this world today at this moment has everything to do with my favorite four-letter words:

Life ~ Celebrate yourself as the completely unique, one-of-a-kind person you are.

Love ~ First love yourself, then love others.

Kind ~ Be kind to yourself and be kind to others.

Risk ~ Be willing to take risks to truly live life to the fullest.

Hope ~ Look for it constantly and never let go of it.

Benin

Chapter 28

Djimon Hounsou

Actor and Nonprofit Organization

Djimon Hounsou is a two-time Academy Award-nominated actor for his work in Ed Zwick's *Blood Diamond* (2006) and Jim Sheridan's *In America* (2002). He most recently appeared in John Krasinski's hit *A Quiet Place 2* and Matthew Vaughn's *The King's Man*. Upcoming projects include Zack Snyder's *Rebel Moon*, Alex Parkinson's *Last Breath*, and the animated *Paws of Fury: The Legend of Hank*.

Born in Benin, West Africa, Djimon moved to Paris at the age of thirteen to pursue a Western education. As an adult, he was discovered by designer Thierry Mugler and subsequently, modeled for and appeared in several iconic music videos for Herb Ritts and

David Fincher. Small roles followed before his breakthrough performance as an African who leads an uprising to regain his freedom in Steven Spielberg's *Amistad* (1997, earning him a Golden Globe nomination and an NAACP Image Award). He later shared a SAG Award nomination with the cast of Ridley Scott's Academy Award-winning Best Picture, *Gladiator* (2020).

In 2009, Djimon opened the UN General Assembly with a speech about the impact of climate change on developing nations. He has also appeared before the US Senate on behalf of the Runaway and Homeless Youth Act and participated in a hearing and summit for the International Arms Ban Treaty. On December 2, 2019, the International Day for the Abolition of Slavery, Djimon announced the formation of the Djimon Hounsou Foundation (DHF) at the United Nations. This nonprofit organization aims to reconnect the African Diaspora with the motherland and combat modern-day slavery and human trafficking.

* * * * *

I was born in Benin, a west African nation previously known for more than three centuries as the Kingdom of Dahomey, which was the primary regional power in that part of the African continent until it was colonized by France in the late 1800s. It is rich in culture and spirituality, with both firmly rooted in a deep understanding of the forces of nature. This belief system and way of life is called Vodun in West Africa, though most know it more commonly as Voodoo. Where I find great hope in the world today is in honoring the history of the people of Africa and their ways of living, keeping the legacy of those traditions and perspectives alive in the modern world. The way I do this is through a two-fold path in my professional life in the film industry, and through projects and opportunities in my personal life.

Moving from Benin to France with my brother was a huge change, especially since I was only twelve years old at the time. During my childhood in Benin, I simply wasn't aware of things such as discrimination between blacks and whites, and to suddenly be surrounded by it at such a young age was a lot to cope with. It was a whole new culture to which I had to adapt. I excelled in school, especially at math and science, but I had dreams far beyond the academic path being imposed on me by school. You see, when I was a child in Benin, cowboy movies were occasionally shown in the village. I knew from watching those films I wanted to be an actor. School in France didn't seem like the right path to get there, so I willingly dropped out.

Granted, I also ended up having nothing and was homeless for a time. While this also didn't seem like a good path to my dreams, I kept a hope alive in me that it would somehow work out. Holding fast to my dream of being an actor gave me hope. This is a kind of hope that's visceral for me. It's like planting a seed and then carefully nurturing it until it sprouts, then continuing to care for it so it grows and eventually blossoms and bears fruit. Maintaining this kind of hope is real work! If you lose focus on the dream, the plant will begin to wither.

I also like to think of hope as a muscle that needs to be worked to build and maintain its strength. Of course, there will be times when a loss of focus means the muscle isn't getting the workout it needs. But the good news is there is muscle memory! Regaining focus on your dream and getting back into the habit of working this muscle quickly gets you back on track because of muscle memory.

Never losing site of my dream and nurturing hope even during the dark days of being homeless on the streets of Paris hoping to not get caught and deported, which is what could easily have happened to me since I dropped out of school, was difficult. Then, out of the blue, a photographer who noticed me said I should give modeling a try. It seemed like a long shot, but I did it, which is how I ended up meeting French designer Thierry Mugler. He opened the door to my modeling career and my first trip to the United States, which was the perfect place to pursue my dream of becoming an actor, which I did.

Actors don't always get to pick and choose only the most meaningful projects, especially in the early stages of one's career. It was my great fortune to play roles such as Cinqué in Stephen Spielberg's 1997 film *Amistad*, as well as the fisherman in *Blood Diamond* forced to work in the diamond mines. These were very important roles to me because they were chances to fully lean into and embrace narratives and characters reflecting the historical experience of so many Africans caught up in the slave trade of old as well as more recent experiences of slavery through forced labor. Just as important, whenever possible I choose roles that present positive and uplifting images of the African man and the integrity of the black man.

Outside my professional life, I am outspoken about the urgency of climate change, not just because of the existential threat it poses for all life on the planet, but also as a racial and social justice issue. It's why I spoke at the 2009 United Nations Summit

203

on Climate Change in New York City. You see, in my home region of West Africa in countries such as Benin and Mali, agriculture isn't just a job, it's a way of life. To see the devastating effects on this way of life because of climate change is heartbreaking. I witnessed this first-hand through my work as a global ambassador with the international humanitarian group Oxfam.

The impacts of climate change ignore the borders nation states. While West Africa's contribution to global warming is negligible compared to more developed nations, the poor farmers there will still experience its negative impacts, perhaps even disproportionately so. As I said in my speech at the UN, "The bottom line is that the world's wealthiest nations can and should help the neediest to plan ahead for the future, to avoid the humanitarian disasters that we have seen ravage these communities."

I have also been fortunate in being able to establish the Djimon Hounsou Foundation several years ago. The idea is to champion a visceral connection between the countries of the African diaspora and the motherland and to heal the wounds that slavery left behind. The mission and purpose of the foundation is two-fold: 1) Strengthen Africa's intergenerational identity and self-awareness by reconnecting the Peoples of the African Diaspora with their motherland and celebrating *Unity in Diversity*; 2) Combat modern-day slavery and human trafficking to stop exploitation, loss of freedom and identity, and educate about the causes, stakes, and consequences of slavery.

My desire for everyone, and especially my own son, is to be fearless regardless of how others may treat you. You do not have to let the reality of others, or the way others treat you, or the assumptions of others become *your* reality. Keep your dreams alive, nurture your seeds of hope, and then keep your hope muscle strong through constant use. I deeply believe humanity longs to better itself, and we each have a role to play in doing so. Honoring the history of Africa and its rich cultural legacy is what gives me hope. I am focused on doing whatever I can to reconnect the African diaspora to its roots in the motherland for the purposes of hope and healing. As the inscription on the Reconciliation Statue of Cotonou says:

Acknowledge and forgive the past
Embrace the present
Shape a future of reconciliation and justice

204

Venezuela

Chapter 29

Ramón A. Domínguez

Hall of Fame Jockey and Racing Advocate

Ramón Domínguez began riding horses at age sixteen in his native Venezuela, first in show jumping and then later in thoroughbred flat racing. In 1996, he migrated to the US and started riding on the South Florida racetracks. In 2001, he became the winningest jockey in the United States. He repeated the feat in 2003, and in 2004 he won the Isaac Murphy Award for having the highest winning percentage among all American-based jockeys.

In 2012, Ramón topped the New York Racing Association (NYRA) riding circuit for the fourth straight year with 322 victories and was also the winner of the George Woolf Memorial Jockey Award. In

2013, he was the recipient of the Mike Venezia Award. He also won the Eclipse Award for Outstanding Jockey in 2010, 2011, and 2012. On June 13, 2013, Ramón announced his retirement due to head injuries he suffered in a fall at Aqueduct Racetrack. His lifetime career wins are 4,985. On April 25, 2016, his induction into the National Museum of Racing and Hall of Fame was announced.

In 2017 Ramón was inducted into the Delaware Park Wall of Fame as well as the Saratoga Walk of Fame. Since his retirement, he has remained involved with racing through the invention of the humane riding crop 360 GT, advocating for the Permanently Disabled Jockeys Fund (PDJF) as well as thoroughbred aftercare. Ramón is the President of the New York Racetrack Chaplaincy (NYRTCA), Ambassador of Brooke USA, a member of the concussion advisory board for NYIT, and is co-owner of the Exacta Box platform.

* * * * *

I was born in Venezuela's capital city, Caracas, but when I was five years old, my family moved about an hour-and-a-half outside the city into what was at that time a more rural setting. Both my father and my grandfather had jobs related to horse racing. Back when I was a kid in the 1980s, betting on horse races was very popular, especially the Pick 6 exotic bet. There were betting machines in various locations, and everyone dreamed of picking the winner in each of six consecutive races to win big and be set for life. There were always long lines at these betting machines leading up to the weekend's races at Venezuela's largest and most popular horse racing track, the La Rinconada Hippodrome, where my father had one of his jobs.

When I was thirteen years old, I started going to the track on weekends with my father, helping him out with small tasks. Once the betting deadline was reached midday, I'd help my father take some of the machines to the restaurant at the track. I'll never forget the first time I watched a live horserace, close to the rail and near the finish line. When the pack of horses, their jockeys riding low in the saddle, raced passed me with their hooves thundering on the dirt track, it was the most thrilling thing I had ever experienced. In that moment I knew I wanted to become a jockey.

I had an uncle who lived about six hours away in the country, and he had many horses. I had saved up enough money that I could afford to buy a horse from him. I chose a filly (female) and brought her back to our home. Having my own horse is how I learned to ride so well on my own, and I almost always rode bareback.

I told this to my parents, but it was like a kid in the US telling his parents he wanted to become a professional baseball or football player when he grows up. In other words, most parents don't take those dreams too seriously. But my passion for the sport only increased, bordering on an obsession. Two years later, I was still entirely focused on horse racing and once again told my parents I wanted to become a jockey. My grandfather was there and said I should focus on getting a good education and become a doctor. I was so upset my dreams were being dismissed.

My parents must have felt bad about this because as a kind of consolation prize, they let me enroll in a nearby horse show jumping school. I was so happy to just be around horses and have a chance to ride them. Every afternoon I would take two different buses to get to the show jumping school, and my time there was truly wonderful. I learned so much about riding and jumping. One day, when returning home, my bus was full and I had to stand. Hanging onto the handrail with one hand and holding my riding crop and helmet in the other, I heard a voice call out to me from the back of the bus. The young man asked if I was a jockey and I told him I was a show jumper. He explained how he was learning to be a jockey at a nearby thoroughbred training center and encouraged me to stop by to see if there might be a spot for me.

The very next day when I was riding the second bus, I stayed on right past the show jumping school and got off as close to the training center as I could, but it was still a long walk from where the bus dropped me off. I introduced myself to one of the trainers and he told me to come back the next day. I did, and they put me on a horse with just a pad (not a saddle) to see how I handled myself and the horse. I had great balance to begin with and always rode my own horse bareback, so this was no big deal to me. The trainers liked how confident I was riding bareback, and they soon had me helping exercise the horses, including at near racing speeds.

Soon I had reached the upper limit of what I could do at this small training center, so I went to another training center that was much bigger and had more jockeys coming in and out to train on their horses. I interviewed there and once again got to be involved in exercising racehorses, but once again I felt like I quickly advanced as far as I could go there. What I wanted to do was race, but this training center did not provide a pathway to becoming a licensed jockey.

By this time, I realized there weren't any official jockey schools at that time anywhere near me in Venezuela. The only way to get licensed was to go spend time at one of the rural racetracks. My parents agreed to take me to one in the same area where my uncle lived, but he warned me it was not going to be an easy life. I would have to live in one of the tack rooms where the equipment is stored (saddles, bridles, and so on) along with four other young jockey hopefuls. They slept on horse pads on the floor. I had a hammock, so I slept on that.

There was no plumbing or bathrooms or anything like that, just barrels of water you'd ladle out and pour over yourself to take a shower and washing your clothes by hand with regular soap. And the flies! Wherever there are horses there are flies, and I mean *lots* of them. You can't escape them. Eventually you just get used to them being everywhere, including every meal you cooked and ate. It was all very primitive, and I was feeling incredibly homesick and missing the comforts of home and family.

Two weeks into this experience, my parents came to visit. When they saw how sad I was and living conditions, they said I should come back home with them, but despite how I was feeling I said no way. That's how strong my desire was to become a jockey. Then my parents also took me to visit another aunt and uncle who lived not far away from the racetrack. They worked in the oil industry (there were lots of oil wells and refineries in this rural area of Venezuela) and lived in a beautiful home. They said I would be welcome to live with them. Once again, I said thanks, but no thanks. I needed to be at the racetrack if I was going to achieve my dream of becoming a jockey, despite the hardships of the living conditions.

After seven months at this rural racetrack, I got my jockey license, which was specific to just that racetrack. I rode in more than a dozen races there, but I never won a single race. Then I finally got a break. A man who had a high-up executive position at a big racetrack was organizing a jockey promotion, an event where jockeys and apprentices from the rural racetracks compete. He talked to my father and said he might be able to get me into the event.

There was an ex-jockey at the track who oversaw jockey license approval. I approached him and said I wanted to get a license. He offered me an exercise license, but I said I wanted a jockey license. He took one look at me and laughed, saying I was too tall. When he found out I was eighteen years old, he said I would grow even taller and end up too heavy. But after he watched me doing the various apprentice tests, he was quite impressed with how well I performed and offered me the jockey license.

208

Now that I finally had a jockey license at a big racetrack, what I needed next was an agent. A good agent is key because of their extensive experience. They help choose the best horse for a jockey to ride based on their relationships with many different trainers. The apprentices who came from the rural racetracks who had tons of wins had a relatively easy time getting a good agent. But how was I going to land one? After all, I hadn't yet won a single race! One day there was an agent at the track who I knew was one of the best, and he approached me and asked if I had an agent. I said I didn't, and he offered to work with me! This was the opportunity I had been waiting for.

But it didn't quite go the way I thought it would. For months my agent was putting me on subpar horses that just weren't fast. I wasn't winning races on such slow horses. Then one day the agent finally said, "Okay, Ramón, today's your day. I've had you riding slow horses all this time because I knew you weren't yet ready for the next level. Now it's time to see if you are." He arranged for me to ride a truly spectacular horse in an upcoming race, a horse that was heavily favored to win. But I was naïve and lacked experience. The horse was overeager, and I should have calmed him down to a less furious pace out of the gate. Instead, I encouraged him to let loose way too early, and paid the price. During the last part of the race, the horse was too tired and another apprentice jockey nudged just ahead of us at the finish line. I totally blew it! I came in second and the spectators in the grandstand were all booing me. That horse should have won that race, and it was my fault it didn't. I was devastated.

In the aftermath of such a horrible performance, I felt completely hopeless. I remember thinking to myself how I would have done anything to turn back the clock on that race and not make the mistake I had made. With some time and reflection, however, I realized it was one of the most important things that has ever happened to me. I will be forever grateful for it, despite how painful it was. Why? Because of what I learned from it. I would certainly never make those mistakes again! I also began to incorporate this self-evaluation process into my riding to be brutally honest with myself after each race to say what I did well and what I could have done differently. I went on to win 53 races that year.

Once I started to become more successful, a desire grew in me to move to the United States, which is a common dream among jockeys. At that time, it was difficult for a Venezuelan city to get a passport and visa. An apprentice jockey friend of mine at the track mentioned he had a connection at the place where people go to get passports. We went and somehow his connection got me past what was possibly the longest line of people I'd ever seen. They were all waiting to get passports, and I got mine without waiting in line. Instead of the usual dark blue passport, they gave me a burgundy one with a gold embossed front. It was beautiful.

But what about a visa? I made an appointment at the embassy to get one, but it couldn't be a work visa, as those are very difficult because it requires being sponsored by a company in the US. I tried to get a tourist visa, but they wouldn't give me one at first since I didn't have any hotel reservations already made. Luckily, however, I had a secret weapon with me, which was my mother! She has a very magnetic personality. She was working with a man there at the embassy to get her visa, and they called me over because she told the guy I was with her. Thanks to her charm, I got the visa and never looked back!

I went on to achieve great success as a jockey. Out of 5,000 races, I won 4,985 of them. This isn't to say hope came easy. Every person goes through ups and downs and times of discouragement when life is difficult. I saw many jockeys come into the sport for all the wrong reasons, seeking fame and fortune. What always kept me going through the difficult times was surprisingly simple: Passion for my profession. I got to do exactly what I loved my whole life. It was all I ever wanted.

United States

Chapter 30

Evanthia "Evie" Evangelou
Activist and Nonprofit Organization

Evie Evangelou is the President and Founder of Fashion 4 Development (F4D). She first introduced F4D's global awareness campaign and the First Ladies Luncheon initiative in 2011, inspired by her career in the international arena of cultural diplomacy and international relations, specializing in entertainment, arts, fashion, beauty, travel and tourism, and trade development.

Previously, Evie served as interim Deputy Secretary General for the World Federation of the United Nations in New York City, where she worked with more than 100 UN member states, countries, and missions, as well as numerous non-governmental bodies focused on education, cultural affairs, and humanitarian causes. Kensaku Hogen, a former Under Secretary-General of the United Nations Department of Public Information (UNDPI), appointed her to be a Special Consultant for Cultural and Educational Affairs and programs within the UNDPI, one of the nine departments comprising the United Nations Secretariat.

Evie was also appointed to be a strategic consultant to the special representative of the UN Secretary-General for United Nations theme "Dialogue among Civilizations" as well as the UN theme "Diversity is Beautiful." Throughout her career she has been acknowledged by the US Senate and honored by several international governments as well as being a Goodwill Ambassador for foreign countries. In 2013, Fashion Group International presented Evie with its Humanitarian Award for her work to create positive social change for humanity.

* * * * *

My parents came from Athens, Greece and settled in a Greek-Italian neighborhood in New York City, where I was born. I was an only child, and my parents were wonderful. They were very protective and wanted to give me everything. Although I was born here in the US, at home we only spoke Greek. When I went outside to play with other children I spoke Greek to them, and they would never answer back. This often sent me home in tears because I couldn't figure out why no one would talk to me. When it was time for me to begin school, I still didn't speak English. Luckily, I was sent to St. Demetrios, a prominent Greek American day school in Queens, where I could learn English at school. And I was the best student in Greek class.

Everyone in my home was inspiring to me. My mother was a strong woman who worked hard and ran her own beauty salon, even while making sure everything was taken care of at home in terms of cleaning and cooking amazing Greek meals. My father was a quiet, patient man. He used to tell me to "fly straight," by which he meant always being transparent and clear with people, treating them in caring ways so you'd never have to be looking nervously over your shoulder.

One evening when I was maybe six years old, he and I had walked to a Greek deli not far from where we lived to pick up a few things we needed. I remember this because it was in the middle of a big snowstorm. Later, as everyone was getting ready for bed, he discovered the cashier at the deli had given him way more change than he was owed. He immediately got suited up to go back out in the storm. I asked him why it was so urgent for him to go back out in a blizzard. He explained to me that when the cashier went to close out the register for the night and it was short, he'd have to make up for the shortage out his own pocket. My father said he wouldn't be able to go to sleep knowing that. He was a big believer in the Golden Rule of treating others as you want to be treated and was always a man of integrity and fairness.

My grandmother also became a very big part of my life after her husband (my grandfather) died. She moved in with us and because our house was not so large, she and I had to share my bedroom. My grandmother was a wonderful person, always full of light and laughter. We laughed together all the time, and our laughter was very healing. She also let me do things my parents would not have approved. My grandmother was my best friend and we spent most of our time together. Even after I married, she came to live with me and helped care for my children. She was such a good role model for how to be warm, open, and welcoming to people, and to refrain from judging them. She was all about acceptance and tolerance. I also admired her because she was always so happy and content.

Fast-forward to a very different time in my life. My aging mother had recently fallen and required surgery, so she was staying with me during her recuperation so I could help take care of her. It was a very busy time for me at work and traveling a lot to speak at different events around the world. I began noticing I wasn't feeling well a lot of the time. Sometimes I even had trouble breathing. I was always a healthy person physically, so I figured it must be due to stress and anxiety.

Over time these problems worsened until at one point, as I was returning from a trip to Milan, I knew I had to find out what was going on. My feet were incredibly swollen, and I had to be in a wheelchair because I couldn't take more than a few steps without losing my breath. I couldn't even wear shoes my feet were so swollen. I called a doctor to come to the house. She checked my vitals, but nothing there seemed to be amiss. Then she checked my oxygen levels, and they were extremely low. She said in no uncertain terms I needed to go to the hospital emergency room right away for a thorough examination to determine what was going on with me.

A trip to the hospital is exactly what I had been avoiding, probably for too long. Whenever I'm sitting in my kitchen, I can see an image of the sacred heart of Jesus hung above the doorway. After the doctor left, I remained sitting in the kitchen, looking at that image, and then I heard a voice. This voice was not in my head, it was in my ear. It said, "Go to the hospital and let them do what they must do. I will carry you."

I immediately called my son to come get me and take me to the hospital. Just getting ready to go out was an incredibly difficult task. At the hospital, they began running all kinds of tests to see what could be ruled out. When they ran a series of blood tests and were looking at the results, I could see their demeanors had changed. They were gravely concerned but wouldn't tell me anything definitive. It was the middle of the night, and I was on a bed in a hallway of the emergency room because no regular beds were available. The next morning, I was visited by another team of doctors. The lead doctor did not have good bedside manners. He just came right out and said I had cancer, it was advanced, and it was bad. He couldn't say yet what kind of cancer it was, but it was clear it had spread to my lymph nodes and my blood.

They finally found a bed for me, but I was in for quite an ordeal. I was sharing the room with an elderly woman who had constant fits of screaming and shrieking for no apparent reason. I was having a lot of trouble breathing. People kept coming to draw more blood for additional tests. Unfortunately, I'm a phlebotomist's nightmare thanks to my tiny veins. They were constantly pricking me with needles, and I felt like a pincushion.

I must have blacked out because the next thing I remember was waking up in the intensive care unit (ICU). I had been intubated with a breathing tube. I had a feeding tube as well. Now I couldn't even speak and had no idea what was going on. I was incredibly tired. The thought did briefly occur to me that this might be my time, and if it was then I was okay with it. But it was only a fleeting thought because I knew it was my not yet time. I still had a lot of work to do on this Earth.

It was my faith in Jesus and the voice I heard that gave me not just hope, but the *assurance* it was not yet my time to depart this realm. I was in surprisingly good spirits because I was determined to fight and get through this. I summoned my father's patience, my mother's strength, and my grandmother's joy. They were all inside me and would see me through. I had a purpose in life, and I wasn't about to give up on it. My daughter came to visit, and I wrote down a lot of notes for her about a big event I was working on so she could call people and keep things on track.

For my whole life I've been devoted to working through the arts. My first campaign was about healing the world through the spirt of the arts. My calling is to bring peace, unity, love, healing, and hope to people all around the globe, and it has always felt

214

to me like the best way to do this is through the beauty of different cultures and the arts—music, singing, dance, art, fashion, and so on.

Back in the ICU at the hospital, the doctors finally arrived at a firm diagnosis. I had Hodgkin's lymphoma, which is a rare cancer of the immune system, but it's also treatable and even curable. It didn't feel like it at the time, though, as I was in the hospital for six weeks that first time. Luckily, I had an angel helping me. His name was Fernando. When he first saw me in the ICU and I was writing notes down for my daughter, he couldn't believe it. He'd never seen that before. Fernando was a good soul and the kind of person who was always trying to be as helpful as possible. If it weren't for him, that first hospital stay would have been significantly longer. He would come in my room and talk to me and help me exercise my lungs, which was important because that's what helped me get off the machines sooner than later. Thanks to his help, in week five of my stay they removed all the tubes. It took four years of treatments and a stem cell transplant, but I was eventually cured.

There are things I learned from this time of suffering. First, coming to terms with your own mortality makes everything else in life more urgent because you realize how quickly your life can end. I also believe the saying, *what doesn't kill you makes you stronger*, but there's more to it than this simple phrase conveys.

Suffering is what allows you to have greater empathy and compassion for others who are suffering because you've been there and know what it's like. If you haven't experienced it, it's hard to relate to others who are suffering. This means you can be helpful to people going through something similar. For a long time, it was hard for me to even talk about my journey through cancer. But now I talk about it freely because I know how important it is for others who are going through it. When I share my story with someone who has cancer and they hear about how I made it through, it gives them hope, and few things in life are better than giving hope to others.

We are all here on this planet together, we are all connected, and we are all the same. We all cry, we all laugh, we all suffer to one degree or another. Love is what lifts us out of the darkness. If we can all think of each other as ourselves, then there's hope for humanity and a better, more beautiful world for everyone, like heaven on Earth.

Ecuador

Chapter 31

Eduardo and Sebastian López

Father (Former Minister of Energy and Mines) and
Son (Businessman)

Eduardo is an international speaker on sustainability issues in the energy and business sector. He is a visionary citizen and passionate about the development of the energy industry, and a faithful believer that countries can become true powers if they are supported by state policies with vision and agendas to 2050 where the priorities are education, productivity, and self-sufficiency. In both the public and private sectors, he has dedicated himself to demonstrating commitment to excellence, ethics, support for laws, respect for cultures, and good practices that constitute a fundamental pillar of the generation of long-term, mutually beneficial global relationships and the engine to build a better world.

Sebastian is a businessman from Houston. He is currently the Director of International Research and Business Development for SERTECPET (an oil and gas multinational corporation dedicated to sustainable upstream, patent creation, oil services, integral solutions manufacturing, technology development, and R&D). Sebastian's passion within this company is R&D, where he commercializes patents and new technology developments. Sebastian opened SERTECPET in the USA, from where he spearheads new technology developments in the Middle East. Sebastian is also an entrepreneur focused on mental and physical health, for which he is creating his new company, ALMA.

* * * * *

Ecuador is a tough environment for many of its citizens. I had a good quality of life, but it was always frustrating to see how much unrealized potential there was for so many, especially given Ecuador's wealth of natural resources. What I saw even from a young age was how corruption and competitive in-fighting could get in the way of sound development that would benefit everyone. This was a constant topic of discussion in my family, and it helped me see how devoted my father, Eduardo López, was in trying to make things better. It was about being able to see what *could* be despite the constraints of the prevalent mindset of society and government. Trying to get others to see what *could* be was a constant challenge, but it was one my family was willing to accept to improve society.

I grew up in Ecuador's capital city, Quito, but my parents were both originally from Ambato, which is a couple hours south of Quito, so we traveled there frequently to see family. I loved traveling around Ecuador with my parents because I got see so much nature and the beauty of Ecuador. I developed a very strong attachment to my country as a place of natural wonders and gorgeous landscapes. Forging a deep connection with nature is powerful because it helps put into perspective your own place in this world apart from your career and social networks. Feeling connected to nature elevates a feeling of commitment to the planet, to yourself, and to your society because you realize everyone is also part of this beautiful natural world. It is my connection to nature that has helped me be very aware of my actions and the impact my actions have on the world around me. Connecting to nature or a higher power is how people can discover their purpose in life.

My father was an incredible role model who gave me hope. He was in the oil industry, which many labeled as corrupt. There was a lot of corruption in the government as well. Despite these hostile conditions, my father fought the oversimplified label of corruption by always being a man of honesty and integrity. He instilled those values throughout his company, and eventually went on to bring those values to the whole country and its government.

When he became Minister of Energy and Mines, my father's work was exemplary, eliminating immoral practices and creating an atmosphere of hope with clean practices and dignity for the people working in the ministerial office. Everything under his oversight was performed with the utmost transparency, which helped save and maintain many of the country's natural resources. Even when he stood in the way of illicit economic interests, and even when his actions were questioned, his integrity, honest words, and most importantly the truth, were his greatest allies in showing everyone how the country's interests were unquestionably put first. In a country rife with corruption in both industry and government, his honesty and integrity inspired real hope in many that things really could get better.

My father also stood out as an example in how to run an oil company in a way that respects both people and the planet. He always emphasized how important it was for the company to pursue and achieve different corporate responsibility and ethical certifications. This was a rare occurrence in Ecuador's energy and mining industries, and my father helped raise the bar and pave the way for other companies to follow his lead. The impact he has had is appreciated by many to this day, and those impacts extended into other government departments, and even to other governments in nearby countries such as Colombia. My father accomplished all this without ever compromising his core values of honesty and integrity.

The hope I have for my own path in life, as well as for the oil industry, is to continue my father's commitment to honesty and integrity while constantly seeking new ways of doing things and holding ourselves to ever-higher standards to make the world better and safer for everyone now as well as future generations. My hope for *you* and everyone is that you will connect to a higher power to discover your purpose in life, that you will always look beyond your present circumstances to see what *could* be, and to believe in your own potential to improve your life and the lives of others.

* * * * *

Growing up in Ecuador, I often felt like an outsider. Everywhere I looked there were limitations. Ecuador felt like a very constrained, even marginal country. It lacked access to technology, the schools and universities weren't very good, and it seemed like everyone had a very limited mindset. Luckily, however, I was a dreamer. All those constraints and poor conditions didn't stop me from dreaming about something better. I felt like an outsider because everyone else was just going about their day-to-day lives. They all thought it was silly of me to dream about things being better or accomplishing great things. Their mindset was one of just accepting things the way they were, but that never made sense to me. Why not change things? And I was always willing to work very hard at making my dreams come true.

I was a dreamer thanks to my maternal grandfather and my father. They always said if you aim for the sun, then you'll at least reach the moon, which was their way of saying dream big and you'll go far. My father was a big motivating influence on me because he told me I could do anything, build anything, and be anything I dreamed of if I put my mind to it. If there were obstacles, just find a way to work around them, over them, or through them. He said to always look at life through the lens of hope, opportunities, and happiness. My grandfather was a very gentle, kind, and loving person. He also believed in me and said I could do and have everything I wanted in this life. This unconditional love and support from these two men in my life meant everything to me and set me on my path toward my dreams.

For people who don't have those kinds of role models in their lives, one pathway to unlocking your potential is by connecting with the universe or a higher power that helps you become more self-aware. Your dreams must come from within yourself. Connecting with a higher power helps you become more deeply self-aware of how you are part of a much greater whole, which is how you discover what makes you happy and what resonates with your soul. When you do this, there will be no limitations to what you can accomplish because you have something of value to bring to the table, something you can share with the world to make it a better place for others.

When I graduated from high school at age eighteen, my big dream was I wanted to become a pilot. Unfortunately, at that time aviation school was simply too expensive for my family to afford. The door to that dream was closed. This felt like a huge setback to me. But I told myself everything happens for a reason. There were so many doors of opportunity that I realized although this one had closed, surely some other door would open. Of course, that is exactly what happened. And in hindsight, I have

220

helped many more people improve their lives and the lives of their families through my oil company than I ever could have done as a pilot. I have even been able to elevate the whole country through the work I did within the national government. Being a pilot wasn't a big enough dream!

As I see my son, Sebastian, making his way in the world, my hope for him is to always remember the love and lessons I've shared with him over the years. I hope he can hold on to his noble heart and his core values. I hope he will always remember, just as my father and grandfather told me, that he can do, build, and be anything if he puts his mind to it. Whatever dreams and goals he pursues, I hope he will always think about how it can benefit the world around him, and to always be ethical in all he does. Even when his path becomes difficult, I hope he will remember he already has everything he needs inside to see himself through.

For the world, my hope for everyone, and especially leaders and corporations, is to focus on actions that will make the world better for everyone. Every person, every company, every government, has a role to play in modeling behaviors that respect this planet we all share while also respecting each other as human beings. We are all connected to each other and to this beautiful Earth we call home. Our greatest hope lies not in just wishing for a better world but taking concrete actions to make the wish come true.

Bhutan

Chapter 32

Dr. Lotay Tshering
Prime Minister

Dr. Lotay Tshering is the serving Prime Minister of Bhutan. He is also a practicing surgeon and has been in the profession for over two decades. The head of the third democratically elected government also has his name prefixed with numerous philanthropic activities that have touched many lives.

From the start, it was his passion to help people and save lives that motivated him to become a doctor. Today, the country's medical fraternity would attest to the fact that he spared no weekends or public holidays to offer his medical services to the people.

With the burning desire to improve his country's healthcare system, he made a political debut in 2013. He fell short of votes, which led him to spearhead His Majesty's Kidu Mobile Medical Unit. It was an opportunity to practice his surgical art through charitable platforms while accompanying His Majesty in different parts of the country.

Dr. Tshering made another attempt at politics in 2018 that took him from the berth of party president to the helm of the Cabinet. His spirited phrase of "building the health of the nation with the stroke of a pen than treating one patient with his surgical scalpel" rang true with both local and international audiences.

Living up to his words, Dr. Tshering strives to make every day of his five-year term count, dedicating weekends for his hospital visits. In addition to being a urologist, he holds an MBA from the University of Canberra. He is also a recipient of prestigious *Lungmar* scarf and the *Druk Thuksey* medal from His Majesty The King.

* * * * *

Memories of curiosity and nervousness during the initial news of an emerging novel coronavirus from Wuhan in 2019 are still vivid to me today. Emotions welled up due to reasons ranging from the virus being new and the dearth of knowledge about its severity at the time to its possible impact on a small society like ours. For a medical person like myself, I knew it was only a matter of time before the contagious gusts from our close neighbours would reach us. The impending risks to the global population, especially the physically weak, was apparent. Moreover, we are a country with limited health infrastructure and human resources. The poor health behaviours of our people are mostly symptom-driven, which was no consolation.

Then again, there was a tinge of hope it might turn out to be like the earlier outbreaks of Severe Acute Respiratory Distress Syndrome (SARS), Middle East Respiratory Syndrome (MERS), and Ebola back in the day. Despite the intrusion into some countries in the region, Bhutan dodged outbreaks of those. However, that was not going to be the case this time around.

Without leaving much to chance, surveillance measures were installed at the airport and other entry points as early as January 2020. The daily news of the virus in the papers and on television were anything but reassuring. Many Bhutanese quarters insisted on closing the gates altogether to tourists and other travellers. Other countries had, by then, started imposing travel restrictions. By March, countries around the world had already recorded more than 3,000 deaths. These were countries we normally looked up to for reference. How grave was the situation? Will nations be wiped out? Will humanity be able to withstand the devastation?

Like waking up to a nightmare, our safe haven saw its first case of COVID-19 on March 5, 2020, prompting panic and fear among people. We were now part of the pandemic. What would it mean for this nation of about 700,000 people? Above all, how will our King, for whom the lives, safety, and wellbeing of his people are non-negotiables, react to it? This is why I choose to delve into what transpired on the night of March 5. Looking back, that night was the unfolding of a new chapter for Bhutan, and the beginning of a story of hope I share now with the world.

Soon after the Ministry of Health confirmed the case of the tourist who had travelled to the western part of the country, we gathered at the health ministry around 5pm. I am not sure whether it was the system we had in place or the denial of the fact COVID-19 had entered the country, but we ran the RT-PCR test three times on the first case. It was a grim scenario, but amid the frenzy for further action, I remember a gleaming sliver of optimism that night.

His Majesty the King joined us at the ministry and immediately put together a team to bolster the efforts of our health officials. The chiefs of army and police were commanded to spring into action. Overnight, the extent of the disease spread was scanned and necessary actions to trace and isolate contacts were completed. We took a war footing. This set the tone and standard of our battle against the pandemic. As commanded, I shared with and through the media to provide a national update to everyone on the situation.

For the first time in our country's history, all locations the first infected person visited were placed into "lockdown." This was a foreign word I always had a strong aversion to using, hoping it would never come to apply for us. Much to our dismay, such a call had to be made, not once but several times, to declare what we called *dodruel kakdam*, an equivalent local term for lockdown.

Bhutan began its unique battle with the pandemic. His Majesty was in the lead, and the guiding command was clear: Bhutan must strive for zero deaths from COVID-19. He did not stop for a single day after that. His Majesty travelled across the country to lead, inspire, guide, and monitor. It made me realise the extent to which leadership is truly put to the test during times of crises. In expression of humble gratitude to His Majesty for his selfless leadership in times of adversity, people from all walks of life came forward to offer services and make both cash and in-kind contributions to help.

Of the many inspiring anecdotes, I especially remember a man from a remote village who was waiting at my office on an April morning. He had some spare money wrapped in a worn-out envelope, insisting he wanted to support in his own small way. Later I learnt he had lost his harvest to wild animals, yet he was not deterred. There were also other farmers who walked in with their annual yield of rice and vegetables. Later, when the untimely monsoon destroyed vast areas of paddy fields, His Majesty offered relief, but all farmers across the affected areas graciously declined the assistance. They didn't want to put any more of a dent in the nation's coffers, even if it meant reducing their standard three meals a day to just two.

Hotel owners offered their properties for quarantine, schools closed but teachers came together to devise ways of staying connected with students, political parties united to support the government, and monks sent prayers and spiritual reinforcements reverberating into the air. With just a brief appearance on national television of His Majesty encouraging young people to partake in safeguarding and building the nation in such unprecedented times, the spirit of volunteerism soared.

Thousands of Bhutanese youth of the DeSuung (literally meaning Guardians of Peace) program, who became the main frontline workforce, engaged in skill-building programs and many developmental projects. It was not just a superficial display of allegiance but genuine gestures of courage and hope for Bhutan. Such is the power of adversity.

Quarantine, isolation, and lockdowns became part of daily language and conversations. Over the last two years, every wave that came after an interval of four to five months led to another lockdown. Subsequent action to prevent the spread and eliminate the disease from the community followed. This helped us get through the ominous Delta wave, which originated from neighbouring India with whom we share porous borders spanning almost 700 kilometres.

We maintained zero-COVID deaths throughout 2020 while across the world hospitals turned into morgues, and both cemeteries and crematoriums were inundated with bodies. But the immediate and frequent lockdowns also meant immense suffering for people. Offering respite to thousands of people, Bhutan created a National Resilience Fund and introduced interventions to support people's livelihoods. It even included interest waivers on all personal loans of the Bhutanese.

226

As if combating the disease for the nation wasn't enough, major transformation initiatives were launched during this time of upheaval. Massive skill-building among youth through innovative programs on a scale never considered before was rolled out across the country. Now both civil service and education are being overhauled. Massive infrastructure development is being carried out to kickstart a national service program called Gyalsung. It seeks to redefine the purpose and spirit of nation-building among our young people, which will impact generations of Bhutanese. It is clear we are seeking to not just come out of the pandemic but use it to reset and relaunch ourselves with and for higher standards.

If this is not a message of hope, I can't imagine what is.

If Bhutan has earned international renown for successfully handling the pandemic, it is because of the leadership of His Majesty. We don't have the technological advancement, economic might, or even expertise in size or number to deal with crises of such magnitude, but we have a leader with the heart and ability to translate vision to reality, empathy, and the capability to inspire and rally. Today, I have come to understand that if Bhutan can sustain these special characteristics, then we can triumph over any kind of national crises hereafter.

As I write this, Bhutan is entering into the second phase of our COVID-19 management plan. It is a calculated step built on the successes so far. From maintaining zero-cases in the community, when the virus was unknown and aggressive, we can now shift our focus. Omicron is less virulent. More than 90 percent of Bhutanese have been vaccinated, including children over five years old. This accomplishment is allowing Bhutan to ease restrictions and revive the economy. But we remain persistently resolute on our policy to save lives at all costs.

Then again, this comes naturally to Bhutan because we are synonymous with our development philosophy of Gross National Happiness (GNH). We are occasionally asked how we practice GNH. Just as GNH is primarily about going beyond self and embracing collective wellbeing and happiness, the pandemic is a reminder of just how dependent we all are on one another. In the grand global panorama of things, everyone is connected.

The pandemic showcased how there is room, will, and disposition for unity. Our unique system is beyond conventional definitions. It revolves around the integral values of human bonding and respect. In this reawakening message from Bhutan during this pandemic, unity is our true hope and our future.

Georgia

Chapter 33

Prince Juan de Bagration-Mukhrani
Businessman and Philanthropist

His Royal Highness Prince Juan Bagration-Mukhrani of Georgia is descended from one of the world's oldest royal dynasties as well as from the Spanish Royal Family, the British Hanoverian monarchy, the Imperial House of Hapsburg, and the German-Bavarian Wittlesbach Royal Family. Born and raised in Madrid, he returned to his homeland in 2014 to serve his country. Together with the support of leading families from around the world, he adds to the development of Georgia by attracting foreign investment and promoting Georgian culture.

Their Royal Highnesses Prince Juan and his wife Princess Kristine are founders of The Georgian Foundation, which was conceived out of a desire to contribute to the development of Georgia by supporting education, cultural, and various social projects. While managing his foundation, Prince Juan also oversees and advises on other prominent investments. He also works in the traditional Georgian winemaking industry with his labels Prince Ioane Bagrationi and Prince of Georgia.

* * * * *

In life, hope and faith lead to miracles.

I was born on August 18, 1977, on a hot summer day in the city of Madrid. Spain was home to my father and mother where they were also born. My mother belongs to a Spanish aristocratic family, while my father was the direct descendant of one of the world's oldest royal families and related to several other European royal families. Soon after my birth, I was brought to my mother's family country estate, which was located close to Madrid, in El Escorial. It was a place that gifted me with the most wonderful childhood memories. When I was baptized in Madrid, my godfather was HRH Infante Don Luis de Baviera y Borbón and my godmother was Olga, a Russian émigré who was the widow of a wealthy Spanish count. On that day I was given the name Juan (Spanish for John).

Miss Patricia, the nanny who had brought up my mother and her five siblings, was from Ireland. She dedicated her life to our family. Considered a second mother by most members of our family, she was very kind, intelligent, and well spoken. Many of our concerns were often shared with her. One day after playing soccer with other children in the nearby village, I returned home with a few new words in my vocabulary. They were bad words, and I thought it would be fun to share them with my cousins. Miss Patricia overheard our conversation and without saying a word took me by the arm straight to one of the bathrooms of the beautiful residence. She let the cold water run and then took the hand soap and washed my tongue with it. I quickly learnt to choose my words better.

"Words have an extraordinary power, both positive and negative. Words have the force to create, they are givers of life and may also be equivalent of death. At the same time, none of our words will disappear and will be our revealer before God."

~ His Holiness and Beatitude Ilia II Catholicos-Patriarch of All Georgia ~

It was at Mater Gracie, a kindergarten in Madrid, where I met my very first friend whose name is Ignacio, but who I used to call Gogi. We were three years old and became unconditional friends. I spent the following years with my family, going to school in Madrid, and improving my swimming and horse-riding skills in Menorca. I also developed a passion for motorbikes thanks to my father and the possibility of riding them at my mother's country estate twenty minutes from Madrid.

I attended elementary school at Colegio Retamar in Madrid, and it was there at the age of seven I received my First Communion. Having been brought up in the Catholic faith, it was the most special day in my life. My father asked me what I would prefer for a gift, a motorbike or a party for me and my friends, to which I replied, "A motorbike, *and* a party to show the bike to my friends, dad." My father gave me both.

When I was eleven years old, my father said to me, "Son, your godmother has proposed to send you to study at a boarding school in Switzerland. It will be very difficult for your mother, your sister, and me to be far from you, but it is a great opportunity for you. Your uncle, King Juan Carlos of Spain, went to study there. You will have friends from all around the world and learn foreign languages. It is your decision, so take your time to reflect on the offer."

One hour later, I was on the phone calling Olga to thank her for her gift and to promise her I would make good use of it. The school was Collège Alpin Beau-Soleil. After three days with my family in Villars-sur-Ollon, I was dropped off at the school and given my room, which was to be shared with two other students. The first one to arrive was a boy from Japan who was accompanied by his mother—a very elegant, beautiful lady. After a brief introduction, she took out a pack of cigarettes and smoked one by the window. I was very impressed by the Japanese family and quickly became friends with Mitsuhiro.

On the first day of class, I met all my classmates. It was a very international group, and our teacher asked everyone to introduce themselves and name our nationalities. There were students from India, Spain, Germany, Turkey, Japan, South Korea, France, and the United States. When it was my turn, my classmates were surprised to learn about the country of Georgia, which at the time was part of the Soviet Union, and how my family had been forced to leave it and live in exile since the 1920s. I always carried the hope in my heart that one day I would return to my homeland. In 1991 the Soviet Union collapsed while I was still in boarding school.

"I am a relative of Jesus Christ. He made me King of Georgia by His grace
and wish. No one should try to replace the Bagration King,
not any of the nobles or any foreign rulers."

~ King Ashot Bagrationi, 809 AD, First King of Georgia ~

The Bagration dynasty of Georgia is Europe's oldest royal family and the second
oldest royal dynasty in the world, after the Japanese Imperial family. The Bagrations
have been ruling since the sixth century as "Kings of the Kartvels" (Georgians) and
as Kings of the Kingdom of Georgia since the ninth century. As members of the
branch of the Parnavazians, their history began in the fourth century BC. According
to history, Bagrations are descendants of King David of Israel. The holy robe of Jesus
Christ, which was brought to Georgia after His crucifixion, is buried in Svetitskhoveli
Cathedral in Mtskheta. It is represented in the center of their Coat of Arms, as is
King David's harp and the sling he used to defeat Goliath as it is written in the Bible,
along with Saint George, patron Saint of Georgia. The Bagration royal family ruled
Georgia from the ninth century until the beginning of the nineteenth century, an
uninterrupted reign of more than ten centuries.

Spending five years in boarding school in Switzerland gave me many riches, but the
most valuable one of all was to experience sharing life with friends from so many different cultures and religions, and I loved them all.

A few years later in the early 1990s I was on my first visit to Georgia and felt a very
strong and welcoming energy. It was something I had never felt before, and it made
me instantly feel at home. The country had recently been through very difficult times,
yet people were still kind and generous. During one of the many dinners I attended,
I asked my friend David, my host during the visit, not to reveal my identity to the
family we were meant to visit three days later. "Please just tell them my name is Juan,
and I am visiting from Spain." The day arrived, and I was greeted by many at the
house of Mr. Zurab and Mrs. Natia. A *supra*, a traditional Georgian feast, was organized in honor of my visit. You could barely see the tablecloth because of all the
Georgian dishes laid out, along with vegetables, bread, and wine. The evening went
late into the night with numerous toasts by the *Tamada* and accompanied by Georgian
polyphonic singing, which is recognized by UNESCO on its List of the Intangible
Cultural Heritage of Humanity. A Tamada is a Georgian toastmaster at a Georgian
supra or at a wedding. A Tamada should be wise, good with words, and charismatic.
With each ritual toast he sets the mood and guides the conversation. The first toast is
in the name of God. Georgia is one of the earliest Christian nations, a country where
all religions and ethnic minorities have lived together in harmony for many centuries.

The other fundamental toasts are to Georgia, to peace, to our Holiness and Church, to the people who have passed away, to children and future generations, to our parents, to our ancestors, to women, and to our guests.

It was possibly the best supra I have ever attended. Everyone was especially welcoming and joyful, and the music and singing were of extraordinary beauty. The many different wines were also exceptional, and all made from grapes only to be found in Georgia. The experience of the supra tradition forever impressed me. On the way back to my hotel, I asked David why in Mr. Zurab's home the television was placed on top of a chair instead of a table. After some time, David confessed the hosts had sold their TV table to host me the best way they could. You see, Georgians believe guests are a gift from God, whether they are part of a royal family or not.

Life continued in Madrid, where I lived with my family and went to university. However, since my first visit to Georgia, I always had the wish of returning to my homeland to serve my country and establish my home. During the next decade I lived in southern Spain but would regularly visit Georgia whenever possible. During one of my visits, a Georgian priest named Father Levan who was a good friend suggested I convert to the Christian Orthodox faith.

"I am ready now, if you wish it, Father," I replied. He noted I would need a godfather and godmother. I said David, who was with us, could be my godfather, but I didn't have anyone in mind for a godmother.

"God will decide," said Father Levan. After a few minutes we arrived at a small church behind the Patriarchate of Georgia. While Father Levan opened the gate of the church's courtyard, one of the parishioners passed by. Her name was Tamar. She kindly accepted our request to be my godmother. During the ceremony I was baptized as Ioane, the Georgian name for John. To the right of the altar there was the Icon of King David the Builder of Georgia, and to the left the Icon of Queen Tamar, referred to by Georgians as King Tamar for her greatness. The date was the January 19, the celebration of Epiphany, which commemorates the baptism of our Lord Jesus Christ in the river Jordan.

A few years later, I brought a foreign business delegation to Georgia. During my stay I met a Georgian nun at the Patriarchate who told me I should get to know more Georgian people my age. "There is a wonderful young lady named Kristine living in Paris who you should meet." I asked Mother Anastasia to call Kristine on her phone. We had a short conversation, which I found very special. I didn't speak to her again until a few months later. In the meantime, I was planning to fly to Georgia to spend three days in Zarzma, a monastery near the Georgian border with Turkey. My stay in the monastery played a very important role in my life.

On the day of my departure, I texted Kristine, who told me she was arriving to Georgia that same night to visit her mother. We agreed to meet on the following day to go for dinner. The next day I said I'd pick her up at her house, but she told me it was a very small street I would have trouble finding. After I finally convinced her to share her address with me, it turned out the house was next to the flat where I was staying on Silver Street in Tbilisi. Three months later we were married. A few years later after our religious wedding in Svetitskhoveli Cathedral, our first child was born in Georgia. He was named Bagrat after my best friend, my late father. Bagrat was born on January 19, 2022, the Day of Epiphany, and the same day I had converted to the Christian Orthodox faith. The meaning of the name Bagrat is "Gift of God."

During the first months after moving to Georgia, I had the great blessing of spending time with His Holiness and Beatitude Ilia II Catholicos-Patriarch of All Georgia. It was in the beautiful valleys near his birthplace. I was feeling a great joy and peacefulness. When I shared my feelings to His Holiness, he said to me, "Fish need to live in the water."

When I study the history of Georgia, it seems nearly impossible our country managed to survive the invasions and hardships it went through in its history. Today, Georgia is one of the safest countries in the world, with all the qualities to become one of the most popular and prosperous nations. The breathtaking nature of Georgia, its rich history and culture, together with the famous hospitality of Georgian people are all great reasons to visit a country with its own alphabet, the birthplace of the first Europeans, as well as the origin of winemaking, which Georgia proudly traces back to 8,000 years ago.

I wish peace, health, and prosperity to you and your families, to all cultures, religions, and beliefs. I would like to invite you to visit Georgia and experience its many wonders. May we all have the faith to spread hope across the world.

United States

Chapter 34

Sylvia Alice Earle

Marine Biologist

Sylvia A. Earle is Explorer in Residence at the National Geographic Society, Founder of Mission Blue/Sylvia Earle Alliance, Founder of Deep Ocean Exploration and Research, Chair of the Advisory Council for the Harte Research Institute, and former Chief Scientist of NOAA. Author of more than 230 publications, leader of more than 100 expeditions with thousands of hours underwater, she is a graduate of Florida State University with MA and PhD degrees from Duke University and 34 honorary doctorates.

Her research concerns the ecology and conservation of marine ecosystems and development of technology for access to the deep sea with special reference to securing protection of intact wilderness from the depths of the high seas to mountaintops globally, as well as nature-based solutions to climate change and loss of biodiversity.

She is the recipient of more than 150 national and international honors and awards, including being named *Time* magazine's first Hero for the Planet, a Living Legend by the Library of Congress, Netherlands Order of the Golden Ark, winner of the 2009 TED Prize, the Princess of Asturias Award, the Explorers Club Medal, Royal Geographic Society Patrons Medal, and the National Geographic Hubbard Medal.

* * * * *

"What's on your mind?" I wondered as I kneeled near Wisdom, the Laysan albatross calmly warming her recently laid egg. She was serene as a stone, with only a flick of her dark eyes briefly noting my presence. She blended in as just one of thousands of other birds, some nesting, some flying, a few noisily walking in grassy areas among the US Army barracks on Midway Island that housed soldiers during World War II. But Wisdom is a special bird. Marked by a band in 1956, she is the oldest known wild bird. Meeting her was a pilgrimage of sorts for me.

Wisdom was learning to fly across the ocean around the same time I was learning how to dive under its surface. Watching her now, I wondered if *she* might wonder about changes in the ocean she has experienced that threaten the future of her species, and of all birds, all humans, and all we hold dear.

The ocean she knew as a fledging is now significantly warmer and more acidic. Millions of tons of plastic trash and millions of miles of fishing lines and nets now clog Earth's vast ocean spaces, and they are poisoned by an on-going flow of unnatural, synthetic chemicals. These strange additions have been matched by alarming subtractions: loss of about half of the tropical coral reefs, mangroves, and seagrass meadows and 90 percent of the sharks, tunas, swordfish, and numerous other large sea animals. Squid, krill, and small, silvery fish that have fed seabirds for thousands of millennia have disappeared by the ton into the insatiable maws of industrial-scale fishing vessels, with disastrous declines in both birds and the animals that link them to the give-and-take energy flow of ocean food webs—the vital carbon cycle in action.

236

Wisdom has witnessed and somehow survived an era of human-induced planetary change that geologists mark as the beginning of the Anthropocene. The ocean, home for most of life on Earth, source of most of the oxygen in the atmosphere, driver of climate and weather, stabilizer of global temperature, and governor of Earth's basic chemistry, is in trouble, and therefore so is Wisdom. And so are we. Like other terrestrial creatures, with every breath we take, every dop of water we drink, we are inextricably linked to the existence of the living sea.

As a fledgling scientist, I was led to believe no one could really predict let alone change the weather or chemistry of the planet. The ocean was thought to be a realm apart from life on the land, a mysterious space so vast that nothing humans do could alter its nature. Waves of migrating birds swept overhead while underwater I swam beneath shimmering masses of small fish so numerous they blocked the sun, turning mid-day brilliance to deep twilight. Rarely, I glimpsed sea turtles, champion long-distance swimmers that stay ever at sea except when, twenty years or so after hatching, mother turtles come ashore to place enough eggs in sandy nests to give their species a chance to survive a formidable gauntlet of mouths ready to engulf a tasty turtle. I saw many more crowded in pens in Key West, Florida, struggling to escape their destiny as featured delicacies in local restaurants.

Biologist E. O. Wilson observed that depletion of wildlife on the land tended to first focus on the large, the slow, and the tasty. The same is true of ocean wildlife but includes vast numbers of the small (shrimp, clams, crabs, lobsters, herring), the fast (tunas, swordfish, dolphins, whales) and many not considered edible (krill, menhaden, lanternfish) but are ground for oil and food for domestic animals, which would be comparable to grinding songbirds to feed chickens. From miniscule microbes to the most massive mammals, the fabric of life woven around rocks and water make our home planet habitable. Earth, a four-and-a-half-billion-year-old biogeochemical miracle, in the blink of a geologist's eye, has become less hospitable to life owing to the actions of one species that appears to be highly successful but for one potentially fatal flaw: By comprehensively consuming nature to foster our prosperity, we have unwittingly destabilized the systems that keep us alive.

As a young scientist scuba diving, I was mesmerized by the number and size of sharks, grouper, barracuda, and tarpon that seemed as curious about me—a strange creature in their midst—as I was about them. Coral reefs sheltered a dazzling cross section of more than half of the major divisions of animal life that exist. Sightings of marine mammals in Florida were rare in the 1950s except for dolphins that seemed to enjoy the ocean as much as I, playfully leaping at the bow of the small boats I used to access offshore reefs. Inquisitive, plump, and gentle—large, slow and tasty—manatees in the region had declined so much by mid-century that extinction seemed imminent. Another notoriously playful animal, the slow and tasty Caribbean monk seal, once ranged south to Brazil, adorned beaches in Miami, and existed in the Gulf as far north as Galveston but last seen in 1952, but was declared extinct in 2008.

Wisdom, my albatross friend, flourished through the early years of the Anthropocene, watched during nesting seasons by park personnel who recorded the time of her arrival and subsequent departure for months in the open sea. She and her lifetime mate flew many thousands of miles, typically staying aloft for days, riding the wind and dining on the ocean's moveable feast. Meanwhile, I logged thousands of miles on research vessels at sea and thousands of hours under the sea, sometimes staying submerged for weeks at a time in undersea laboratories, sometimes gliding to great depths in small submarines to witness and record the nature of rapidly-changing ocean systems.

From above and below, now in the twenty-first century, stark changes are obvious and are clearly cause for concern. If present trends continue, some predict there will be more plastic in the ocean than fish by the middle of this century, global temperature will be too hot for most corals and kelps, and other critical planetary boundaries will be transgressed, breaking through Earth's "safety net" of conditions suitable for civilization. If we did not *know* this, we would continue to do what we have always done and, according to present models, within ten years or so we will reach cataclysmic, irreversible "tipping points" that put at risk everything we care about: health, prosperity, security, and even our existence. But we *do* know. The living ocean keeps us alive, and we now have a chance—maybe the last best chance we will ever have—to return the favor. By protecting life in the sea, we safeguard our own. Our fate and the ocean's fate are one.

Whether above or below, what reasons are there for hope? In the twentieth century, people acted to protect cherished places and wildlife that would now be gone but for changed behaviors and changed laws. By 2000, about twelve percent of the land and a fraction of one percent of the ocean were proactively protected with a global network of parks and policies aimed at saving and restoring planetary health. In the sea as on the land, as caring replaced killing, the abundance and diversity of life showed signs of recovery. Now, about fifteen percent of the land and three percent of the ocean have high levels of protection. There are more turtles, whales, and manatees in the twenty-first century than existed when I was a child. Protection works!

238

More than 70 nations are now committed to high or full protection of at least 30 percent of the land and ocean under their jurisdiction by 2030, and some are championing 50 percent by 2050. Actions are underway to spare large areas of the High Seas from industrial fishing and deep-sea mining. Within ten years, scientists aim to accurately map the entire sea floor and explore the physical and biological nature of the vast living space between the surface and the great depths below. There are many pathways to making the world a better place for our children, but nothing else matters if we fail to respect the systems underpinning our existence. With knowing comes caring, and with caring there is hope we will protect the ocean as if our lives depend on it, because they do.

In February 2022 on Midway Island, among the thousands of albatrosses observed, one young mother banded in 2011 as hatchling N333 was seen feeding a hatchling of her own not far from where her mother, Wisdom, nests. The resilience of nature is surely cause for hope.

Hong Kong

Chapter 35

Didi Wong

Keynote Speaker and Film Producer

From being an award-winning international keynote speaker, angel investor, a Hollywood film and TV producer to a best-selling author, speaking coach, and philanthropist, Lady Didi Wong is breaking the doors wide open for those who want their dreams to come true. She has been honored by the Women Economic Forum with the Woman of the Decade for Entrepreneurship and Venture Capital award and was named a Woman Who Means Business in *O, The Oprah Magazine*. She has spoken at the United Nations and was knighted by the Royal Order of Constantine the Great and Saint Helen, just to name a few of her accomplishments.

Behind the screen, she has executive produced alongside Larry King, Al Pacino, Johnny Depp, Robert Kiyosaki, Dick Vitale, and many others. She also starred in *Impact*, an internationally awarded documentary on her path to becoming a speaker. Her philanthropy includes helping Pope Francis expand his foundation into the US; being the President of the Women Economic Forum Los Angeles; serving on multiple boards; contributing to the legacy of Martin Luther King Jr.'s statue in Atlanta's Peace Park; and being an ambassador for the Reef Life Foundation.

Lady Didi discovered her joy in teaching clients how to increase confidence, connection, and cashflow. Her company, The Yes Academy, offers courses in speaking, pitching, marketing, and investing. Her superpowers shine when she is balancing her four children, her projects, and travels—all with a smile on her face.

* * * * *

"You will never make it in America as a foreigner."

These were the exact words my father wrote to me when I was twenty-three years old. After reading his letter, my world turned upside down. Up until then, I had always been the perfect daughter. Never had I gotten into trouble, not with cigarettes, alcohol, boys, tattoos, school grades, or general behavior. You see, my sisters Coco, Kiki, and I (the middle child) were all raised to be very proper and well-mannered. All three of us were educated at Benenden School, a Royal all-girls boarding school in the beautiful, quiet countryside town of Cranbrook in the county of Kent, about an hour's train ride from London, where you can find lots of manicured greenery, horses, sheep, and goats. It was the school Princess Anne attended before us, and we learnt to speak English like the Queen.

It was not my style to be disobedient.

As a Chinese daughter, what you may think of as the stereotypical upbringing you see in films such as *The Joy Luck Club* or *Crazy Rich Asians* or even the recent Marvel hit *Shang-Chi* all possess true elements of how a son or a daughter of a typical Chinese family must behave. Their actions were already dictated and expected to go a certain way. We are taught to accept the teachings and words of the generations above, even

242

if they are wrong and hurtful. The idea is if they are older than you, you must respect them, no matter what.

When I read my father's letter, I didn't know what to do because my soul was telling me I had found my home in America, and the one person I looked up to the most in the world was objecting to it. At this point, there was no hope for me because pretty much everything I needed to operate my life financially, my parents paid for. I was living a great life in the expensive neighborhood of Soho in Manhattan, next to boutiques like Dolce & Gabbana, Prada, and Hugo Boss. Rent at the time in the late 1990s was already $2,500 per month. I was in a beautiful loft with big open space, beautiful hardwood floors, exposed brick, a little outdoor garden space next to a French bakery, and credit cards to use whenever I pleased, though I had never taken advantage of that privilege.

My parents told me they would only pay my rent. It was a threat or, if you see it positively, an enticement to tempt me to go back to Hong Kong. All other expenses I would need to take care of myself. This meant no more credit cards and no more privileges. I was (partially) cut off, and this became the beginning of my own journey in staying true to who I am and going for what *I* feel is best for *me*.

I remember the exact moment when I decided I wanted to live in America.

I was fifteen years old. My parents took us to the famous backlot Studio Tour at Universal Studios Hollywood where I saw the most awe-inspiring flashflood scene from the movie *Big Fat Liar*. Thousands of gallons of water came rushing through, nearly drenching all the passengers, but it just missed us. It created so much excitement in the trolley. Fake thunder and lightning crashed all around us and the loud rain was piped in from above. It felt like we were in a huge thunderstorm, and it was as real as it could be. Those fantastic effects, happening in just seconds, left a huge and lasting impression on me. I am still stunned at how Hollywood creates magic with all manner of special effects. This experience changed me. I fell in love with America and the entertainment capital of the world. I knew I wanted to move to Los Angeles. It is a big part of why I love being a television and movie producer and financier today.

This burning desire of mine to live in the United States was not easy to accomplish as there are no strings one can pull to become a US resident or citizen. It is a matter of following the system. My parents had no idea my H1 work visa was about to expire. I was blessed to be working for Vera Wang in her public relations department for my first job after graduating from Boston University. Vera was so kind to refer me to work at the New York City Ballet because she knew she wouldn't be able to sponsor me, but she knew her friends there would have more "pull" because they are a much bigger company. She asked them to hire me and help sponsor me to stay in the United States.

Unfortunately, my application was denied twice with the New York City Ballet, and I knew I had a long and hard road ahead just to stay in the country, let alone find another good job or company to believe in me so much they would try again to sponsor me, not to mention making enough money to keep up the lifestyle I previously enjoyed since my parents were no longer paying for all my expenses. Being the consummate public relations girl I am, I was telling all my friends about my visa being denied and how I might have to leave the country if I didn't find another company to sponsor me. That's when I connected with Pier 59 Studios owner Prince Federico Pignatelli della Leonessa, who was generous enough to help sponsor me. My application under Pier 59 Studios was accepted for two full years. Hooray!

But the journey continues. It was not all sweet and dandy despite that piece of good news, because my heart was not in alignment with what I was doing. I came to America to pursue the dream of being on Broadway, not working at an organization where I wouldn't be able to go out on auditions and had to kowtow to celebrity assistants. What did I do? I quit my glamorous job where I got to wear beautiful Tracy Feith and Diane Von Fürstenberg dresses and stylish heels every day. I quit the title of Director of Public Relations and Special Events. I quit having the benefit of working with such celebrities like Madonna, Mariah Carey, Jennifer Lopez, and Puff Daddy (at the time) or top photographers like Patrick Demarchelier, Annie Leibowitz, Steven Meisel, and Mario Testino. If I only had two years, I decided I better go do what I came to do.

The next week after I left Pier 59 Studios, I found myself in a Chinese restaurant making table reservations for people, along with the unkindest supervisor rudely telling me I could not book the 7:30pm tables because we had to keep them for VIPs. I picked this job just so I could have the freedom to go out on auditions and work on my craft, taking dance, singing, and acting classes. To this day, I still think the freedom of time is the best freedom there is. If you make a lot of money but don't have the time to spend it or are so tied to work you never take a vacation or spend time with your loved ones, then what are you working so hard for?

As my time in America expanded, my relationship with my parents started to deteriorate. On top of not liking the idea of me choosing to stay in America, they also didn't like how I was dating black men, or any color of men besides yellow for that matter.

244

Another letter came in, and this time it read, "Your mother and I will disown you if you marry a non-Chinese man" because they knew I had been dating men of all races. In the same letter, they also threatened they would no longer pay for a roof over my head. Now I was fully cut off.

What a blessing in disguise this was! Why? Because I truly had to fend for myself now and do everything I could to survive in this country. This taught me to be resilient, to have courage and perseverance. As fate would have it, quite soon after I received that letter, I did meet a man named Michael whom I have called my husband for almost twenty years. We fought through thick and thin to be together. He *is* the "non-Chinese" man I ended up marrying, but we had to hide our marriage for six long years. Let me rewind a little to tell you the story of how we met.

I was walking up Broadway to my acting class at BlackNexxus on a beautiful January day. This school was recommended to me by a friend because it was home base for acting coach Susan Batson. She has worked with many of the top actors ing the world, including Nicole Kidman, Tom Cruise, and Jamie Foxx just to name a few. As I walked into the building, there was a very handsome man who held the door open for me. When we got into the elevator, we realized we were both going to the same floor. As I checked in with the receptionist to sign up for class, I then realized he was going to be my teacher. I thought nothing of it, except it was a small class with four other men and I was the only female. We had to work on a prison scene, which was very challenging for me as I am a proper Chinese girl with a proper British accent who finds swearing uncomfortable. The script had lots of profanities. As Michael was teaching the class, he was swearing so much it really turned me off. I did not enjoy the class whatsoever and was pretty sure I would never go back, at least not to his class!

A couple months later, I received an email from him telling me he no longer taught at BlackNexxus but was on Broadway in a show called *Take Me Out*. He invited me to have coffee and see the play. I accepted his invitation. We had our first date at a hole-in-the-wall type restaurant called Rice 'n' Beans, which served delicious Brazilian food. It was an intimate and unpretentious atmosphere, which I loved. The bonus at the show was him getting completely naked on stage in his play, so I got to see the goods! I knew after our first date I was going to marry him.

We only dated for six months before we got married. In fact, his way of asking me to marry him was, "Honey, do you want to get legal?" To this day, it destroys me I never got to experience every woman's fantasy of a romantic on-one-knee, engagement-ring-in-hand kind of proposal. And no fairy tale wedding either—no

245

white dress, no walking down the aisle with my dearest father, and no gathering of friends to celebrate. We were married at City Hall in New York City where the officiant called out, "Next!" right after we said our "I dos."

Every time I see a proposal in a movie or a television show, I become sad and teary-eyed. Though I missed out on all that, I gained a whole life of having the privilege to finally live in America for good. No more leaving the country every three to six months. No more answering the dreaded question "Why are you back in the US so soon? What are you doing here?" at airport immigration where they check my passport. I guess this is one the biggest gifts Michael gave me—my green card.

The lesson here is that sometimes fairy tales are not like Disney movies. The pure and deep love we had outweighed the traditions and expectations of society. It is okay to marry the one you love in a courthouse because a life with the right person often holds more magic than any stagecoach, white dress, or castle can bring.

The first time I brought Michael back to Hong Kong, we were already secretly married. My mother was so uncomfortable with him as my "boyfriend" because he is black (and white, but the white doesn't count) and has curly hair that she continued to set me up on dates with rich men. I do intentionally write "curly hair" because this was a main topic of conversation with my mother. She would often comment on how it would not be good for me to have children with curly hair. I appeased her by going on these blind dates while I was a married woman.

These were dreadful times because my parents' social gatherings, of which there were many as my father is one of the most prominent criminal barristers in Hong Kong and served as a judge on the Supreme Court. I remember one evening when the whole family was invited to a dinner at one of the top seafood restaurants in Hong Kong with "Auntie Lam," a very wealthy woman married to the late Lim Por Yen, who founded the Lai Sun Group and was the biggest shareholder of Asia Television. Together they had Peter Lam, who is a very well-known billionaire in Hong Kong. My parents hang out with many tycoons and leaders, and he is usually the one to whom they go for help when they get in trouble. It was important for us, the next generation, to act properly.

When we were about to walk into the private room at the seafood restaurant as a family, my mother told me to keep Michael walking behind all of us. She introduced him as "Didi's friend" from America who is just visiting Hong Kong for the first time. Her body language was pretty much casting him off as an outsider and while words such as "never mind him" were not spoken, they were clearly gestured. It was eating me up inside how he was being treated. But I couldn't say a word to "save face." He was referred to in Cantonese as *Hack Guai*, a slang term for black people. It was better he didn't know what was being said.

As I mentioned before, disobedience was not in my blood up until I graduated from college, but it was necessary for me to break through the barriers to live my truth and my purpose. And I know this is not just associated with a Chinese family—it happens all over the world with Jewish families, Middle Eastern families, Indian families, and all other races. I would have forever been known as my father's daughter Didi rather than being respected as a woman in my own right.

My rollercoaster relationship with my parents is one I continue to live. And the love and gratitude I have for them far exceeds the trials and tribulations. All children have dreams and sometimes these dreams do not match their parents' wishes, but just like baby birds, sooner or later they must leave their nests and fly out into the big world alone. They have big hopes and dreams for their futures. Having these dreams is what has given me hope and driven all of my happiness and success over the years. The Roman poet Virgil said, "Love conquers all." Even though my parents and I don't agree on some issues, I still love them unconditionally. I understand they are only doing their best from what they know, and the intention is just for me to live a good life. My love for my parents, my sisters, my husband, my children, my friends, and even some strangers I meet all end up being just *one love*. It is all one and the same. So, pour out as much love as you can in this lifetime, to as many people as you can.

I know I am one of a small number of Asian daughters who was blessed enough to enjoy a life I have the freedom to create. I know too many who are trapped and have the guilt of doing what her parents expected of her, becoming a lawyer, a doctor, or an accountant, having respectable jobs or being housewives and staying home to have babies. I know I am not living the life of the normal Chinese daughter because I have chosen to be a public speaker. We were not taught to speak up. We are supposed to be subdued, and for sure we are not meant to air our dirty laundry for the world to see. I am going against the norm. I am stepping out to speak up so I can be a female figure for young ladies to have someone to look up to.

I have often been asked who I admired growing up and I cannot really think of many Asian women who have gained international success or recognition. I cannot think of many Asian women who are walking the life I want to walk. I want to be a woman who can inspire other Asian and non-Asian women to break out and find their own truth. This is why I love being a keynote speaker. It's why I love making documentaries and films. It's why I do so much philanthropy. I want to give hope to all the women of younger generations. I want to inspire them to lead the way and make a good life for themselves rather than losing their dreams once they have become a mother. I want to inspire them to break away from the stereotypes. They can be great mothers, great businesswomen, and great leaders, all at the same time. I am doing my best to lead the way.

Hope is a four-letter word that upon hearing or reading it gives you a glimpse of joy and a sense of goodness. Joy and goodness are what I want to find and maintain every day of my life and are also what I seek to give to everyone I encounter. I call it "spreading good dust" wherever I go. It is befitting to have this beautiful opportunity to write a letter to the world, to express and share my personal take on this little four-letter word. I hope my experiences as a 100% Chinese woman from Hong Kong, raised in England and now living in America, may encourage your own feelings of inspiration, insight, and hope as well.

Palestine

Chapter 36

Reem Khouri

Technology Founder and Activist

Reem Khouri is passionate about impact. She is the co-founder and executive chairwoman of Whyise, an impact analytics software solution selected in 2019 by the World Economic Form as one of 100 startups contributing to the fourth industrial revolution. She is also the founding partner of Kaamen, an impact design company that has worked in the Middle East, Asia, and Africa with governments, companies, and non-governmental organizations (NGOs) to design models for exponential economic and social returns.

Reem is a board member of Ruwwad for Development, a non-profit community development organization working with disenfranchised communities through education, youth volunteerism, and grassroots organizing. She is also a member of the board of trustees of the Taawon Welfare Association, a non-profit civil society organization supporting vulnerable Palestinians to live in dignity through sustainable development initiatives. From 2020–2022, she has served as a member of the World Economic Forum Global Future Council on Human Rights. She previously worked with Aramex, one of the leading global logistics and transportation solution providers, serving on its sustainability council.

Recognized as one of the World's 100 Most Influential Arabs Under 40 by *Arabian Business Magazine* in 2015 and 2016, Reem was also named a Young Global Leader by the World Economic Forum in 2018.

* * * * *

I am writing this letter…

As a Palestinian
As a refugee
As a woman
As a global citizen (as a result of being a refugee)
As a social entrepreneur

This combination might not seem like a recipe for hope, but as it turns out it is, and today more than ever. I struggled immensely with this letter because it came at a time when there were many things to be angry about, too many injustices and aggressions being committed against every aspect of my identity.

I even wondered if I should write this letter at all. I was outraged. I was angry. Then again, who said hopeful people can't be outraged and angry? They do get outraged, and they get angry, but then they do things differently:

They do not give up.
They do not let anger win.
They believe in humanity and therefore fight with hope and determination to create change.

And so, I picked myself up to write this letter despite what is going on in the world and in my country because of a simple truth: Injustice and inequality are not and cannot be sustainable.

Our lives are interconnected and so are our traumas. Martin Luther King famously said, "Injustice anywhere is a threat to justice everywhere." The world and globalization keep showing us again and again how interconnected we are. COVID-19 has been a recent big example of this, but history has shown us how a recession, a war, and sometimes even a letter from one country can affect nations. Perhaps the biggest epiphany I had was realizing that while our traumas are intertwined, so is our healing, yet we rarely talk about the need to collectively heal to ensure we stop our generational abuse towards each other and our planet.

Many people experience or have experienced generational trauma. Some of us were and continue to be systematically oppressed and exploited, enduring racism while others have witnessed or continue to live through decades of injustice, wars, and atrocities. Some have lived or continue to live through natural disasters such as tsunamis and earthquakes. And then there are the less visible traumas of economic and political systems widening the gaps and making billions of people more vulnerable or poorer with little to no access to shelter, food, water, healthcare, or education.

Some of us are still enduring trauma and some are still processing trauma from earlier years or our parents' and grandparents' trauma. But we are not healing—yet. Instead, we are committing atrocities against each other because they were committed against us or against our parents and grandparents.

Accountability matters, and so does the belief we can be liberated from the traumas of the past. Then the focus becomes how we can collectively heal so we can stop this cycle of abuse and have a world where…

- We are equal across borders, genders, race, and ethnicity.
- We celebrate our diversity.
- We honor our cultures and history.
- We restore and celebrate the rights and heritage of indigenous populations across the globe.
- We encourage our curiosity and inquisitive minds.
- We ensure everyone's access to knowledge, food, healthcare, shelter, and most of all, opportunities.
- We regenerate rather than exploit our resources.
- We value humans over capital.

251

- We value the environment over profit.
- We prioritize people and their rights over systems and borders.
- We travel freely.
- We value collective prosperity over individual prosperity.

We cannot address these issues in silos. We cannot think human rights are separate from climate change. Or that racism is separate from women's rights or poverty. These are all interconnected.

Our economic and political systems are built on the foundation of exploiting resources, which only further aggravates the injustices both within countries and between countries. Our checks and balances are faulty at best as they are held hostage by the very systems they should be holding accountable. The United Nations is a prime example of good intentions held captive by a merciless economic system that cuts off funding when an outcome is deemed undesirable.

While these realities seem to have made us reach an impasse, these challenges also make the world ripe for change, ripe for innovation and creativity, ripe for alternative models for how we govern, how we operate, and how we thrive.

Let us design the models of the future where...

- Universal human rights are practiced and safeguarded by all.
- Universal basic income is the starting point.
- Universal healthcare is accessible and available to all.
- Education and knowledge are free.
- Every enterprise is by default a social and environmental enterprise.
- Social justice is everyone's agenda.

And we can even throw in a universal blockchain-enabled passport/ID to disrupt the concept of nation states and the manmade borders imposed on us!

Healing starts with acknowledging the injustices we created. It entails more than an apology. Facing a rigged system, some have tried to amend the rules, and yet the reality remained unjust for many of us. We need a restoration and acknowledgment of rights, civilizations, and heritage. And most importantly, a system that can enable the preservation of everyone's rights rather than only a few.

Collective healing requires collective action and a new social contract between all of us. Let us design a new system so we can all thrive and hope.

252

United States

Chapter 37

Dr. David Fajgenbaum

Physician, Scientist, and Author

David Fajgenbaum, MD, MBA, MSc, is a groundbreaking physician-scientist at the University of Pennsylvania where he is one of the youngest individuals ever appointed to the faculty; co-Founder and President of the Castleman Disease Collaborative Network; and national bestselling author of *Chasing My Cure: A Doctor's Race to Turn Hope into Action*. He is also a patient battling a deadly disease which he discovered a treatment for that is saving his life and others. He recently co-founded Every Cure, a non-profit organization to scale his approach to discovering his life-saving treatment to more diseases and joined the Board of Directors for the Reagan-Udall Foundation for the FDA.

253

David has published scientific papers in high-impact journals such as the *New England Journal of Medicine* and *Lancet*, has been recognized with awards such as the 2016 Atlas Award, which he received along with then Vice President Joe Biden, and was profiled in a *New York Times* cover story as well as by Good Morning America, CNN, Forbes 30 Under 30, and the Today Show. He earned a BS from Georgetown University, an MSc from the University of Oxford, an MD from the University of Pennsylvania, and an MBA from The Wharton School.

*****

Between watching my mom die from cancer, nearly dying five times myself, and eventually discovering a treatment that is saving my life, I've learned a lot about hope. I've come to understand how hope cannot be a passive concept—it's a choice and a force. Hoping for something takes more than tossing out a wish to the universe and waiting to see if it will occur. Hope should inspire action. And when it does inspire action in medicine and science, that hope can become a reality beyond your wildest dreams.

Growing up I was always hopeful, maybe even too hopeful. I basically believed in something I now describe as the Santa Claus theory of civilization: For every problem in the world, there are people working diligently—in workshops near and far, with powers both practical and magical—to solve it. Or maybe they've already solved it. This kind of faith can have unfortunate effects, especially in medicine. Believing nearly all medical questions are already answered means all you need to do is find the person who knows the answers. And if Santa-doctors are working on those diseases for which there are not yet answers, there is no incentive to try to push forward on these diseases when they affect us or our loved ones.

I know better now. My mother's death opened my eyes to the fact good things don't always happen to good people and we don't have solutions for all diseases. In fact, I learned we don't even have treatments for most diseases! Only around 2,500 of 12,000 diseases have an FDA-approved therapy. That said, I still believe in the power of science and medicine, I still believe in the importance of hard work, and I am still hopeful. But my adventures as a doctor and a patient have taught me so much about the often unfair disconnect between the best science can offer and our fragile longevity, between thoughts and prayers and health and well-being. I wrote a book about my journey called *Chasing My Cure: A Doctor's Race to Turn Hope into Action* and I'll share highlights and lessons from my story here.

In August 2010, I went from being a third-year medical student at the University of Pennsylvania training to become an oncologist in memory of my mom to being admitted to the intensive care unit with all my organs shutting down. A retinal hemorrhage made me blind in my left eye. I gained seventy pounds of fluid because my liver and kidneys were failing, and I needed daily transfusions to keep me alive. After many weeks, my doctors explained to my family I wasn't going to survive. A priest came into my room to read me my *last rites*. Beyond the devastation of the moment, I remember wanting to give up as I struggled to take each breath and knew I only had hours left to live.

This moment when I was receiving my last rites and wanted to give up was the start of my *overtime*. Overtime is time you didn't think you'd have where every second counts. It's time I've tried to make the most of. But the truth is all of us are in overtime. During times like these with COVID seeming to take people we love right out from within our grasp, fear is an understandable feeling—fear for ourselves and our loved ones. But let's use this sense of overtime to focus on the most important things in life and to liberate us to be our best selves.

At the last possible moment, eleven weeks into my illness, I received my diagnosis: idiopathic multicentric Castleman disease (iMCD). It's a rare disease where the immune system attacks and shuts down the vital organs for an unknown cause. It sits at the intersection of autoimmunity and oncology. About 5,000 new cases are diagnosed each year in the US among individuals of all ages. For my subtype, one-third of us die within five years of diagnosis and another one-third die within ten years.

I was immediately given a combination of seven cytotoxic chemotherapies in a last-ditch effort to save my life. It worked! Amazingly, I was so sick before the chemotherapy I felt better with every dose of it. My dad never left my side for the months I spent hospitalized. One of my favorite moments together came shortly after I started the chemo. It was New Year's Eve and I had lost my hair and had a huge belly due to the liver and kidney failure, but I was so thankful to be alive. We decided to go for a walk around the hospital. As we passed the lobby, we noticed a gentleman who was clearly drunk on New Year's Eve. He was swaying in his chair. On our next lap, we saw he had fallen to the ground. My dad helped him into his chair and then the gentleman said to us, "Thanks so much, good luck to you and your wife." I looked around confused and then realized he thought *I* was my dad's pregnant wife, which was a low point emotionally. But we laughed so hard.

I learned how facing my horrible moments with laughter was such an important way for me and my family to reject Castleman's dominion over me. It cleared my mind and stiffened my resolve. It was entirely up to me to determine what was and what wasn't funny. Perhaps most important, humor is social. For me and my family, there was never a better way to reset our collective resolve than laughing together.

I was also feeling more hopeful being under the care of the world's expert for my disease and getting the chance to see another patient who had been as sick as I was and who was now doing well on the same experimental drug I would go on. This patient put a face on my future, and it made me more hopeful than I had been in months.

After nearly six months hospitalized, I was finally discharged. Two things kept me going. The first was the love of my life Caitlin who I had dated for three years and dreamed of one day having a family with. We had taken a break shortly before I became ill, and I was so glad we both wanted to start dating again. The second thing keeping me going was an experimental drug being infused into my body every three weeks. Though siltuximab didn't work for me initially, we hoped it could keep me in remission and prevent a relapse. It was the first drug to ever undergo a large clinical trial for Castleman disease. Like any good patient, I followed the advice of my doctors who believed this drug would work and I hoped with everything I had it would keep me in remission.

Then, about one year later, I relapsed and nearly died for the fourth time. Perhaps the most devastating aspect of this relapse was how it happened to me while I was on the experimental drug we hoped would keep me in remission. Chemo saved my life again, but my doctor explained to me I was approaching the lifetime maximum dosing for my chemotherapy and there were no more drugs in development. There weren't even any promising leads.

Despite my immune system consuming all my energy as it attacked my organs, despite the accumulated toxins and chemotherapy making my thinking cloudy, I had the most clear and important thought of my life: I could no longer just hope my treatment would work. I could no longer hope someone else, somewhere would perform research to save my life. If I were to survive, I had to get off the sidelines and act. If I didn't start fighting back to cure this disease, no one else would and I would soon die. I was finally done with the passive kind of hope, the hope that waits for Santa Claus and gets in the way of action. Of course, passive hope had helped me through multiple relapses. I don't think I would have survived the third one had I not met the patient who looked so healthy.

But, at last, I understood how hope on its own is often not enough. In my case, hoping my treatment would work and hoping some researchers somewhere would unravel iMCD was keeping me from taking action. I could see the road to what I was hoping for may be long, and I knew it was likely I would never get to the hoped-for end. But I needed to start trekking. I promised Caitlin, my dad, and my sisters I would dedicate the rest of my life—however long it may be—to finding a treatment for me and patients like me.

I found a researcher at the University of Pennsylvania who provided me with some space in her lab to work on my own samples and I started an organization called the Castleman Disease Collaborative Network. I learned how little progress had been made for CD in the previous fifty years. We needed to understand what was going on in my disease so we could try to figure out a new treatment. But we clearly needed to take a very different approach. And we did.

We wouldn't just raise funds and hope the right researcher with the right skill set and the right biospecimens would apply for funding to conduct the right project at the right time. We would connect the entire community of physicians and patients, crowdsource the most high-impact research ideas from them, and recruit the top experts to perform those specific studies. And if we could figure out what was going wrong in my disease, I knew we wouldn't have the time or resources to develop a new drug from scratch. Our only viable option would be to identify already FDA-approved drugs to target the problem we would identify. We just had to hope a drug already existed that could be repurposed.

I soon began to feel the power of a closed circuit of hope and action. I assembled a volunteer team, connected patients and physicians from around the world, and began to advance an ambitious research agenda. I also graduated from medical school and was engaged to Caitlin. The more I imagined a family with Caitlin, the more the effects of fear and doubt dissipated.

As action led to meaningful progress, it inspired further hope for my future. The more I thought about the thousands of other patients with my disease, the more I was inspired to act. Hope was the essential condition and fuel for my taking action. Fear disintegrates. Doubt disorganizes. Hope clears the way, pushes out the boundaries, and gives us space to build and grow. My hope was inaugurated by the strength my family and Caitlin gave me. Hope wasn't something precious I had to preserve; it was something strong, stronger than I was, and I clung to it for dear life.

But then I relapsed and nearly died for the fifth time during a month-long hospitalization. Thanks to chemo, I survived, though barely. I knew I wouldn't make it to our wedding day on May 24, 2014, unless I found a treatment for myself.

The first thing I did when I got out of the hospital was perform a series of tests on my blood and lymph node samples which indicated a particular communication line in the immune system called mTOR was highly active and a possible culprit.

Fortunately, an inhibitor of this communication line existed. It was discovered in the soil on the island of Rapa Nui in 1965. Researchers had figured out it worked well for preventing kidney transplantation but had never imagined it would be used for my disease. Now, fifty years later, I had data suggesting it could be effective for my disease. This was all I needed because I didn't have any other options. I was the first patient with my disease to start taking sirolimus.

As of my writing this, today marks 101.94 months I've been in remission on this drug. I say 101.94 months because I know I can't allow myself the luxury of rounding up. I don't know how long this will work for. But I also refuse to round down because I'm so thankful for every moment of remission I've had. *The New York Times* called this "Doctor, Cure Thyself," which is a bit of an overstatement. It should have said "Doctor helping himself a little bit right now and hopefully a lot longer," but I don't think it would have fit. Importantly, this remission enabled me and Caitlin to get married. We had our first child four years ago and a second child nine months ago. I joined the faculty at Penn Med seven years ago to dedicate my life to repeating this work to find treatments for other patients and other diseases. As I think about the moment when I wanted to give up because I felt there was so little hope, I am so thankful I kept fighting and turned my hope into action.

We've also now administered this treatment and other treatments we've identified to save many more lives. But despite our best efforts, we can't help everyone. The patients we can't currently help motivate us to continue to push with everything we've got.

One of the concepts that gives me the greatest hope in medicine is knowing there are around 2,500 drugs approved to treat about 2,500 diseases, but many diseases share common mechanisms. Thus, many of the 2,500 FDA-approved drugs could be effective for many of the 9,000 diseases lacking treatments. Unfortunately, several barriers prevent drugs from being repurposed for use in every disease they might help. We're now launching the MATRIX Drug Repurposing Initiative to create a world where every drug is utilized for every disease it can help so no patients suffer while there is a drug within reach at their neighborhood pharmacy.

We are hoping for a world like this, and now we're taking action. My life fundamentally changed when I stopped just hoping for a treatment and started hoping and acting. Action doesn't guarantee achieving what you're hoping for, but I've learned both hope and action have been essential in saving my life.

In fact, a lot had to occur for this to happen. Broadly speaking, I had to turn my hope for a future family with Caitlin into actions enabling me to survive. I had to let Santa Claus go after I realized what I needed wouldn't appear under the tree unless I put it there. By the time this book comes out, I hope it will be way more than 101.94 months since I'll have last been sick. While I can't be certain this will be the case, I'm doing everything in my power to make sure my hope turns into reality. I can't help but feel like this is a new overtime for me and my family, and I hope the lessons from my journey are helpful to you and yours.

Uzbekistan

Chapter 38

Lola Tillyaeva

Wellbeing Activist and Entrepreneur

Lola Tillyaeva (Till) is a wellbeing activist, entrepreneur, author, humanitarian, and former UNESCO Ambassador of Uzbekistan. She is an inspiring voice within the wellness space, empowering people through her ideas, vision, and experience, helping them to discover greater wellbeing and self-knowledge. In September 2020, Lola published her widely acclaimed self-care guide *Be Your Own Harmonist: Awakening Your Inner Wisdom for Physical, Mental and Emotional Well-being*.

A devoted humanitarian, Lola is the Founder of the You Are Not Alone Foundation, a charity established in 2002 that provides homes, education, and critical medical assistance to severely underprivileged children in Uzbekistan. She is also the visionary behind The Harmonist, a maison de parfums inspired by the ancient Chinese philosophy of Feng Shui, where she spearheads the Harmonist's advanced sustainability initiatives. Showcasing its ongoing commitment to the environment, in 2021 The Harmonist became the first brand within the luxury perfume industry to eliminate all plastic from packaging, making it 100% recyclable.

For her significant contributions to humanitarian and charitable initiatives, Lola received the Global Gift Humanitarian Award at Cannes and the Grand Prix of the Charter of Paris Against Cancer. Lola holds both bachelor's and master's degrees in international law and a doctorate degree in psychology, all from leading universities in Uzbekistan. She is also a graduate of Gaia School in Malibu, California, where she studied Herbal Medicine and Earth Education.

* * * * *

Since I was a child, I've been searching for answers to core questions about myself, particularly those involving the indelible connection between body and soul. Some of the answers I've found are based in science, others in spirituality. But the greatest hope for the future of human progress lies in the merging of science and spirituality because one cannot be separated from the other.

Since ancient times, many wise thinkers have pondered the meaning of human existence, happiness, freedom, and destiny. Countless works have been written on these subjects and millions of opinions expressed, all of them essentially derivative of, and secondary to, the central question: Who am I? This question has been clearly resonating deep within me since childhood and has propelled me along a path of exploration in search of inner freedom, peace, an understanding of the world around me, and the healing needed for some of my serious health problems.

I'm a little over forty years old now. I've taken in and processed a huge amount of information, checked it against my personal experiences and the experiences of close friends and acquaintances, and learned how this awareness has the power to change habits as well as thought processes.

Who am I? It's a question as timeless as humankind itself and one I imagine you've asked yourself often. For me, one way to answer it is...

You are the Consciousness embodied. You are a pure being, without limits, without age, without death. You are the being who experiences the entire universe while simultaneously containing the whole universe within yourself. Because you are aware, you can hear with your ears and see with your eyes; you can feel with your skin and smell with your nose.

You are eternally free, and your true nature never changes. Changes occur merely in the things you experience: your body, your thoughts, and your emotions. Remember, for instance, when you were a child and contrast this image with yourself as an adult now. Your body is no longer the same, yet it's the same you. You constantly experience a kaleidoscope of emotions and values. Yesterday you might have been angry, but now you're happy. Once, you had a certain point of view, but now you think differently. You operate simultaneously on physical, mental, and emotional levels, yet it's still the same you.

However, we can lose sight of our true selves if we get caught in the web of our daily lives, and this in turn interferes with our natural balance. We mistake our emotions and experiences for our true essence, and we associate ourselves with our moods so closely that in difficult moments, we forget our sense of the present moment. We're so absorbed by our problems and thoughts we no longer see the space, the difference, between these and our true selves. Our thoughts often lead to stress and a sense of dissatisfaction. The physical or mental pain we experience prevents us from finding harmony in ourselves, from feeling the Being of our authentic nature. We lose ourselves, and the vital connection to our Source. Yet it's within our power to restore balance between body, mind, and soul, and lead us back to rediscover our natural eternal beingness.

After receiving my master's degree in International Law from the University of World Economy and Diplomacy in Tashkent, Uzbekistan, I realized being a lawyer was not my calling Instead, I went on to study for a doctorate degree in psychology at Tashkent State University. Just after I left school, I began volunteering at an Uzbekistan orphanage. I was so moved by the pain in those children's eyes, by the suffering and many complications they had to bear at such a young age, that I vowed to set up a charitable organization to help them. A few years later, when I was twenty-four, I founded the You Are Not Alone Foundation, a philanthropy dedicated to improving the lives of orphaned and abandoned children in Uzbekistan.

We began our work by setting up a legal department to help children who'd been wrongly ejected from orphanages, and help others reclaim housing that was rightfully theirs. Without parents or tutors, many of these children didn't have the chance to continue their schooling, so we also set up a learning center where we worked alongside teachers to prepare the children for higher education. We went on to expand the foundation's work to help children with special needs, focusing on diagnoses, therapy, and education.

From 2008 to 2018, I lived between Geneva and Paris, serving as Uzbekistan's ambassador to the United Nations Educational, Scientific, and Cultural Organization (UNESCO). I've since stepped down from that position to devote more time to researching a better understanding of human nature, behavior, and overall well-being, including studying the energy structure of food and traditional herbal healing.

I was born in a country that no longer exists. I was just a girl when Uzbekistan declared its independence from the Soviet Union. I still remember that time very well, especially how the fantasy of the promised communist utopia shattered after the music, films, and all kinds of other Western influences came bursting in. I will also always remember my first trip to the United States at age fourteen when I learned the valuable lesson of our own experience being far more credible than what's imposed on us by others.

After the collapse of the Iron Curtain, the Uzbek city in which I grew up became the capital of a new state. Bright and architecturally fascinating, it reflected its history as a landmark on the Silk Road, a trade route taken by Marco Polo and other merchants who brought fine spices and silks from China to many European and Middle Eastern destinations. Because of my country's rich history, both ancient and modern, I was raised in a multinational, multicultural environment that had a profound impact on me, which still resonates today.

Each of us has our own personal history that makes us who we are. What happened to us since our birth is reflected in our thoughts, habits, and actions. It's essential for our physical and mental health to view our own lives with emotional distance and realize everything that has happened and is happening to us are merely components of our creation as whole beings. Realizing this, and fully accepting your past, can bring peace to your soul so your personal history is no longer important to you. By letting it go, you release a huge amount of energy to be available for the present moment, the here and now, the most important moment in your life, the moment when you are exactly who you are. I encourage you to let go of preconceptions and mental constructs about yourself and about other people so nothing will affect your clarity.

Our minds are fertile soil for overthinking and making destructive judgments toward ourselves and others. They conspire to keep us constantly busy with problems and worries so we won't seize the opportunities we're given to transcend our self-imposed limits. The negativity, judgments, and prejudices that divide us into separate nations, religions, political parties, social strata, and so forth are like filters covering the light emanating from ourselves and from each other. Only by removing those filters and seeing the same nature in each one of us, can we start understanding more and stop going to war against each other. If we are to reconnect, then we must seal out external noise, steel our minds, and focus our attention on the present moment.

Only by thinking of ourselves as infinite immortal beings and erasing our limits and prejudices about ourselves and others can we completely change our perceptions and consequently change the world. If we want to change something, we must first change our own attitude toward it. Only then can we positively influence our lives and the society we live in, based on a global understanding of unity that translates into an understanding that whatever we do to anyone else and to this exquisite earth we call home, we also do to ourselves. There is hope in this essential unity, and I remain hopeful our planet and all who inhabit it will be kind, compassionate, and loving.

Canada

Chapter 39

Richard Marvin Hansen

Athlete and Nonprofit Organization

Rick Hansen, C.C., O.B.C., is a Canadian icon who has dedicated his life to awakening the world to the potential of people with disabilities. He is best known as the "Man In Motion" for undertaking an epic 26-month, 40,000 km journey around the world in his wheelchair. Rick is also a three-time world champion, nine-time Pan Am gold medalist, and six-time Paralympic medalist. As a young athlete in a wheelchair, Rick had a vision to show the world that anything is possible. He is the Founder of the Rick Hansen Foundation (RHF), an organization committed to creating an inclusive world where people with disabilities are living to their full potential.

For more than three decades, Rick and his team have been focused on the removal of barriers. Now as Founder of RHF, Rick and the Foundation are rethinking how people of all ages and abilities access the spaces where we live, work, learn, and play. The Rick Hansen Foundation Accessibility Certification™ (RHFAC) is the only program that rates, certifies, and showcases accessible buildings based on their level of meaningful access for persons with mobility, vision, and hearing disabilities. To date, more than 1,350 sites across Canada have been rated through the program.

* * * * *

At the age of fifteen, my hopes and dreams were shattered along with my spine in a truck accident. I felt not being able to walk again was the greatest injustice that could have been done to me. I would have sold my soul to have the use of my legs again.

I'm writing this story nearly fifty years later. I've been married for thirty-five years to my beautiful wife, Amanda, and we have three daughters and three grandsons. I have good health, good friends, and I've led a wonderful life while relying on a wheelchair. I feel like the luckiest man on the planet, and today I wouldn't trade anything for the use of my legs.

For decades, I've shared my story widely to instill a sense of hope and resilience in others. During this time of unprecedented health, financial, and social challenges brought on by the COVID-19 pandemic, hope and resilience are what we need to see the tremendous opportunities for positive change.

My shift in perspective came by way of lessons learned during my life's journey. I'm sharing some of those lessons here in hopes of inspiring you to be part of the creation of a better, healthier world where we can live with respect and dignity and where everyone can reach their full potential.

You need to have hope.

I went through a very dark, turbulent time after my accident. I had always been an adventurous, athletic young man and I could not even begin to imagine how life could ever be "normal" in a wheelchair. I clung to the only thing I knew for sure—that I had survived. I faced one day at a time in those early days. As my healing and recovery progressed, so did my mindset. I became mindful of the things my body *could* do rather than what it could not. I celebrated those strengths, and I used them as motivation to move forward.

One of the things I could do was move my arms. I attached rubber bands to the sides of my hospital bed to exercise and keep them strong. My next goal was to sit up in the hospital bed for my sixteenth birthday just a few months after the accident. Once I accomplished that, I could visualize myself getting out of the bed and into a wheelchair. From there, I learned to wheel with my right arm to move toward the left, and with my left arm to go right. I was in motion again. The baby steps of progress gave me momentum.

As my physical recovery progressed from the hospital to rehabilitation and then home, I began to accept the obvious reality that living what I had previously thought was a normal life was not an option. Even though I was entering a scary and uncertain time as it may feel to you in today's world, I could see that possibilities did exist for me to live a full life. That's what hope is.

The greatest barriers we must overcome are in our own minds.

At the time of my accident in 1973, people with disabilities in the United States and Canada were still fighting to secure their civil rights. Inaccurate and damaging stereotypes about disabilities were commonplace. I believed many of them myself. These mental and attitudinal barriers in my own mind were some of the greatest I would have to face.

This realization came one summer day when I went to a lake to swim with my friends. To get to the water, there was a path down a hill. It was unnavigable by my chair or crutches. My friends offered to carry me, but instead of accepting their help, I sat alone in the car feeling sorry for myself while they went off to have fun. After pouting for a while, I realized the freedom to live my life as I wanted meant I would have to lean on others from time to time. I had to put my ego aside and ask for help.

My dad and my brother have piggybacked me to fishing holes and I've used adaptive technology to camp, boat, fish, and travel. I've even bungee jumped into a gorge in my wheelchair. I've had these experiences because I accepted that the key to enjoying life is not independence but a healthy *inter*dependence.

I reframed my thinking in many ways over time. I don't see my wheelchair as a limitation, rather it's freedom to be mobile. The anger and blame directed towards the driver of the truck I was riding in have become forgiveness. Fear has become resilience. I now know we can choose to remain captive by our own limiting beliefs, or we can free our minds of those barriers to live a full and joyful life.

Find role models and mentors who are examples of what you can be.

I've been fortunate to be surrounded by family, friends, coaches, and other wonderful people who encouraged me throughout my life. This was critical during the early years of my recovery and continues to be key to my achievements today.

While in rehabilitation after the accident, I had an incredible mentor and role model in a man named Stan Stronge. Stan had sustained a spinal cord injury during a time when just surviving such an injury was nearly impossible. Despite his situation, Stan chose to see love and beauty in his life, which helped shape my own grateful attitude. He taught me that while we can't control what happens to us, we can choose what we take away from what life deals us.

I learned from my friend, Terry Fox, how you can achieve big things by putting aside fear and taking a first scary step toward your dream. Terry and his Marathon of Hope taught me how my life and legacy would not be defined by my disability but by the purpose I found in it.

Athletics and sports have always been important to me. I had even dreamed about one day representing Canada at the Olympics. My high school physical education teacher and coach, Bob Redford, encouraged me not to let go of that dream. Bob told me that nowhere in the definition of "athlete" was there a requirement to use my legs. These people, among so many others, shaped my life personally and as an athlete. The result of these influencing forces meant there were no limits to my dreams.

A decade later, I was at the 1984 Summer Olympic Games in Los Angeles participating in a historic exhibition event of the men's 1500-meter wheelchair race, and then on the podium accepting a gold medal for the wheelchair marathon at the Summer Paralympics in England. I can still remember the incredible feeling of joy and pride in representing Canada, but most of all I felt gratitude. Because people believed in me, I moved from a place of devastation and darkness to a realization I didn't need to be cured to feel whole again. Having these powerful positive forces in my life made me let go of any limits I had placed on my dreams, and it affirmed in my mind that I must pay it forward.

Build a team that will support you.

While travelling internationally to compete in wheelchair races, I witnessed people with disabilities all over the globe being unfairly marginalized. I wanted the world to know how people with disabilities have great potential. That's when my idea of wheeling around the globe started to take shape. I wanted to show the potential of people with disabilities, and how they can contribute to society. The more athletic successes I had, the more I believed I could really do it.

The *Man In Motion World Tour* began on March 21, 1985 with a home team stationed in Vancouver, British Columbia and a small road crew. These teams were made up of incredible people who believed in me and the tour's goals, which were to raise awareness about the potential of people with disabilities and to raise funds for removing barriers. My team challenged, encouraged, and supported me while asking for nothing in return. I feel incredibly privileged to have had them with me. Without them, the dream would have been impossible.

For twenty-six months I wheeled the average distance of a marathon each day for a total of 40,075 km and an estimated 17 million wheel-strokes. We battled extreme weather, difficult terrain, packs of wild dogs, illness, carbon monoxide poisoning, fires, robberies, and financial hardships. During these challenges, I experienced moments of self-doubt, skepticism, and fear of failing.

The last leg of the tour saw us return from overseas to the US eastern seaboard and north to Canada. We were behind schedule. I was tired and dejected because it meant a frigid, snowy, cross-Canada winter trek. Every day was a grind. I wanted to quit. Amanda, part of the road crew, motivated me with her faith that there would always be a well-spring of support around the next corner or in the next town. Sure enough, Canadians got behind the journey even in the cold of winter and it was their enthusiastic support that propelled me through the last leg.

When you reach your limit, and your strength is depleted, it's okay to turn to others to replenish your faith that something better may be just around the corner.

The end is just the beginning.

We returned home on May 22, 1987. I wheeled into the heart of Vancouver through crowds of people, breaking through a ribbon marking the completion of the *Man In Motion World Tour*.

271

A stage had been set up and a banner was hung that read "Welcome home, Rick. The end is just the beginning." I couldn't even begin to think about what was next, though. I was exhausted.

The tour had sparked global awareness of and public dialogue about the experiences of people with disabilities and raised $26 million. Without ongoing effort, however, the progress would fade. There was still much work to do, and so the Rick Hansen Foundation was created in 1988 to springboard off the momentum of the tour. We have since helped make an impact on policies and legislation aimed at making communities accessible for all; we've supported research for spinal cord injury cares and cures; and we've educated people of all ages on the need to create a healthy, inclusive world for all. There have been *many in motion* to achieve all of this.

There is still so much work to do, though. Today, about one in five people in Canada live with a disability. Globally, that number totals more than 1.3 billion. As the population ages and the long-term effects of COVID-19 become apparent, this number will grow. At some point, we will all likely experience disability and face barriers in the places where we live, work, play, and learn. Those barriers keep people with disabilities from opportunities where they could contribute their resiliency, perspectives, skills, and values to improve the world. People with disabilities are creative problem solvers because they live in a world that is not built for them. And it's more important than ever to demonstrate how a healthy society can only be attained through genuine diversity, equity, inclusion, and accessibility.

Over the past couple years, our collective struggles and losses have revealed opportunities for real change in the world. If we all take on the roles of leaders, visionaries, and difference-makers, we can create a better world for all. When I look back on how far we've come, I am mindful of where we still need to be and know that together we can get there faster. Now is the time to re-energize and push forward. I believe my most important work still lies ahead of me—and ahead of you.

Have faith and keep going, one stroke at a time.

Ireland

Chapter 40

Norah Casey

Broadcaster and Investor

Broadcaster, entrepreneur, and human rights campaigner Norah Casey was formerly a Dragon in the popular television series *Dragons' Den* and is a well-known radio and television personality. The second edition of her book *Spark!* was recently published by Penguin, and her TEDx talks include "The Cure for Grief" and "The Courage to Leave" (her own testimony of domestic violence). Her digital learning platform Planet Woman seeks to empower women, and much of her pro-bono work is devoted to mentoring female founders around the globe. She serves on the European Board for Voices, established in 1997 by Hillary Rodham Clinton and former US Secretary of State Madeleine Albright. Norah is a founder of the London-based Women's Irish Network and is a member of The International Women's Forum. She is also currently serving on the Irish government Forum on a Family Friendly and Inclusive Parliament.

A journalist and former nurse, her awards include Woman of the Decade from the Women Economic Forum in Delhi; Ireland's Philanthropist of the Year award; Publisher of the Year five times; and Veuve Clicquot Business Woman of the Year. Her work to highlight domestic violence was recognized with a Safe Ireland SÍLA Leadership Award and she also received the 2019 Lord Mayor of Dublin Award. She is an Honorary Fellow of the Royal College of Surgeons and received the Honorary Graduate Award for 2018 from Blackrock Further Education Institute.

In addition to owning Harmonia Publishing Ltd, Norah is an experienced broadcaster and producer. She was the Ambassador for Dublin Honours Magdalenes and executive producer of the 2022 television documentaries *Ireland's Dirty Laundry*.

* * * * *

I am often asked what I would write to my younger self. In my mind there are always just three words: *Get out now*. Because it's what I wish I had done.

I have only in recent years talked to other women who were abused and I can see myself reflected in all their stories. But for a long time I didn't want to be one of them. I couldn't accept that I would stay with someone who did those things to me.

So often the victims of domestic abuse have to remain silent and their stories are misunderstood. There can be a complex paradox of loving and living with someone where the balance of power and control tilts. The uniquely human need to be loved and feel loved can be intertwined tightly with jealousy, anger, control, and abuse. It is so hard for those who have never experienced it to understand why someone would choose to remain in an abusive and often violent situation. It's why bystanders continue to ask what to them is the obvious question: Why did you stay?

As a survivor of domestic violence I know more now than I did then about why I stayed. And I have come to detest this question and how it makes me feel. The real question for me is: How did I leave? I want to answer both of those questions—why I stayed and how I left—because in doing so I am offering hope to others who walk in my shoes.

You may look at me as a Dragon, businesswoman, and broadcaster, and think I am different from the typical domestic violence survivor, but I am not. There is nothing special or different about me. Domestic abuse knows no boundaries and it can happen to anyone. I do, however, fit the profile. I was in my early twenties, living away from home, and it was my first real relationship. I was a nurse at the time so I had an inherent need to help people. It turns out all of these things are typical.

When I spoke for the first time about living with domestic violence for all those years, my memories were hazy. I remember the first time—the shock, the denial, the numbness. I remember the time when I knew I would leave him. And I remember the last time—a final jolt that pushed me over the edge. The middle was a bit of a blur. Bruises, humiliation, and tears all melded together in nine years of my life buried so deep I could convince myself those terrible things happened to someone else in another world far away from mine.

I know things now about the anatomy of a survivor of domestic violence, things that help explain why they stay and how they leave. I have divided them into four phases, some or all of which I share with my fellow survivors.

Phase 1: The seduction

I was seduced by a charming man who flattered me with compliments and gifts and claimed to love me very early in the relationship. I felt very special and very loved. I ignored the unease I felt deep in my gut in the early stages, believing it was all part of learning to be with someone. I began to change my behavior so as not to incite his irritation and anger.

I was geographically isolated from my family and my friends were being replaced by his circle of friends. But then I believed no one understood me better than he did. And if everything wasn't rosy, well that just comes with the territory. I told anyone who would listen he was my best friend, my one and only. There was no one close enough to me to tell me differently and no one I could share my unease with because it would be the ultimate betrayal of the whole ideal of my wonderful marriage. That was the Seduction Phase.

Phase 2: The Delusion

The second phase is complex and hard for people to understand, and some never escape. Here's how it went for me:

It was the evening before a planned holiday, a trip of a lifetime, and I was excited. Everything was packed, he managed all of the flight and accommodation details, so I had nothing more to do. We were semi-living together at this point. We went to dinner that evening and everything seemed normal. When we pulled in to the driveway, I said something. I still don't remember what it was but it irritated him. I saw him tense as he slammed on the brakes. We both got out of the car and he came round to my side as I closed the door. I thought he was just going to give me a hug to make up for the bad atmosphere in the car but he grabbed my head and slammed it against the side of the car. As he did it he said he knew it would take some time "to put manners on me."

I was in shock, completely numb. The physical pain was one thing but my head was jumbled up with confused thoughts. I sat downstairs for hours after he went to bed, just staring into space trying to deal with the fact of what he had so casually done to me. Yet I was still sitting in his house about to go on a big, no-turning-back trip where he held all the power. My passport, flight tickets, visas, and bookings were all in his control. The side of my face, my right eye, and right ear were swollen and red, and some deep bruising was beginning to appear.

I must skip the next few hours because I can't explain or understand how I woke the next morning, showered, camouflaged the bruising, and allowed him to put my bags in the car.

We didn't speak until an hour or so after the plane had taken off. He touched the side of my face with tears in his eyes. He begged my forgiveness and said he would never do anything like that ever again. He blamed stress at work and said he didn't know what came over him. I believed him. I believed he loved me and cared for me more than anyone I had ever met. A man who would take me around the world just to show me the places he loved was someone who could never really harm me.

I tell myself over and over I would never have stayed if I had known the first time he hit me would not be the last. That was the Delusion Phase.

It's like an addiction. I began to crave the nice moments, the tenderness and love, so I would work hard to earn them even if it meant accepting things that were

276

unacceptable. When he first slammed my head against the car I was shocked and numb but I was already conditioned into thinking I did something wrong, said the wrong thing, triggered a reaction I deserved. He fed me those lines even while expressing remorse. I saw it as a one-off, a total aberration. When he said it would never happen again and he loved me, I believed him.

When things were tense and he clenched his fist or slammed the door, I knew I should do everything to avoid any escalation. The threat of violence was enough to make me back down and behave. My tolerance level was rising, and I hardly noticed it happening. I see all this in the stories of other survivors.

I was in a never-ending cycle of emotions that could happen over the course of a week, a day, or an hour. Tenderness, tension, and threat followed by remorse, which led to tenderness and so the cycle began again. I only see it now through a lens of life experience and shared stories with other survivors. I went on to marry him and within six months his behaviour got worse.

Phase 3: The Reawakening

This is the phase when reality dawns but there are new obstacles to face. It began for me after a very violent incident.

I was constantly on edge. Apart from the ever-present anxiety and fear I lived with daily, serious physical harm was mostly a threat rather than a reality at least for a while for a while. Then one day we were at a lunch with friends. He had drunk too much and insisted on driving home. I didn't want to get into the car with him. A couple of hours later I walked home. It was early summer and getting dark. I didn't have keys, so I rang the doorbell over and over and knocked on the windows to try to rouse him. I figured he had fallen asleep somewhere and I needed to wake him. I started to knock on the door loudly. About thirty minutes had passed and he wouldn't answer the phone or he couldn't hear it.

When he finally came to the door in a rage, he grabbed me by the hair, pulled me into the hallway, and started beating me. He pounded my stomach, my face, he kicked me, there was blood in my eyes and I could hardly breathe. He ran into the kitchen and picked up a carving knife. I could see him from the floor in the hall. I got up and ran for the sitting room. I locked it and barricaded it, pushing everything I could move against it—the sofa, armchairs, everything. He was pounding outside, screaming at me, blaming me for making him punch me. I was really dizzy and sick and when he calmed and I couldn't hear him any more I went to sleep on the sofa. I woke up in the early hours and he was standing over me, with the knife. I went to jump up but he held me down and started begging me to forgive him. That he would never do it again.

I told work I had a bad fall. I told friends I had inadvertently got a punch from two drunk men who were fighting in a pub. I told so many lies I don't know who I told what to. Three of my ribs were broken and my cheekbone was fractured on the left side of my face.

His affection and remorse continued for a few more days. As always, I was showered in flowers and gifts and treats and promises. But less than a week after it happened when I was struggling to get into the car after a follow-up doctor's appointment he flew into a rage and started shouting and slamming his hands on the steering wheel. I can't remember the exact words, but he accused me of being a drama queen and milking the incident for all it was worth. He repeatedly asked if I was going to make him suffer for the rest of his life for one mistake.

Leaving him was not a moment, it was a gradual resurfacing from deep delusion. I didn't see myself as being abused even in the aftermath of extreme violence. I saw myself as failing in helping someone I loved, who loved me. But then a flash of reality broke through.

The final time he hit me was when my mum and dad visited. We took them to lunch, and he was drinking. I said something out of place, though I don't remember what. I was sitting opposite my mum and my dad was at the bar. He placed himself in front of my mum and leaned into me and slapped me hard across the face. I was stunned. My father returned and asked what on earth has happened to my face (one side was bright red). My mum jumped up to touch my skin and talked about a bad reaction to the fish we had just eaten. He walked away to talk to some friends. I promised myself in that moment I would leave him and never let him do that to me again.

It was partly the audacity of the slap—so casual, fearless, and brazen. It was like he was saying, "I can do that to you, and I know you won't tell a soul, not even your parents." For the first time I saw him from a different perspective—what my dad might have seen if I had told him he hit me. It wasn't quite an out-of-body experience, but it was the first time I saw him as others might see him, and he didn't look good. I promised myself I would never let him do that to me again.

278

As I was resurfacing and slowly facing up to the reality of my situation, the barriers to life without him began to take centre stage, such as the belief I couldn't get free even if I wanted to. I didn't have any money and he owned the house, but I was paying the mortgage. He used his money to fund our lifestyle while I was strapped with the bills. I had no savings. I had few friends. I couldn't even imagine a life where I had no home, alone and struggling financially. When other women told me similar things, I kept interrupting them and saying, "That happened to me." I was astonished at the similarities.

The last phase of leaving began. I would constantly weigh up the pros and cons of my position. On the plus side, I lived in a nice house, we enjoyed holidays, meals out, and there was a stability of sorts. On the downside the violence had escalated, there was little remorse from him, and I no longer craved the tender moments. I no longer loved him, and I was scared of him. I avoided him by working longer and longer hours and hoped I could survive until I had the courage to leave. I had reawakened.

Phase 4: The Act of Leaving

This is the most dangerous phase of all. There is never a perfect storm moment when you leave. Other women tell me it was the same for them. It's a gradual emergence back to reality where you see things as they are. Not a eureka moment, it was more like a slow realization nothing would change. The violence is going to get worse, and you may not survive. The illusion of love is no compensation for all the bad parts. Then there were all the barriers you hadn't considered—financial, emotional, physical—they are overwhelming when you are drained of self-belief. Overwhelmingly, women who don't survive domestic abuse are killed by their abuser when they try to leave. As the shackles binding you in a toxic relationship come undone, the threat of violence escalates.

Every Friday I promised I would tell him I was leaving and every Monday I drove to work despondent I didn't have the courage to do it. One time I told him I was thinking of leaving him. He was in a rage and I knew where it would lead, so I left the house. When I returned a few hours later he had thrown all my clothes out the window. He was slumped on the floor crying saying he would kill himself if I left him. The remorse lasted only so long.

Six months later after many failed attempts I woke very early, around 4am. I showered and packed a small overnight bag. I woke him up and told him I was leaving him. He laughed and thought I was joking. He went to go back asleep. I drove away that morning feeling like I was jumping off a cliff. I was terrified but I was also free—not fully free, but I had taken the first step. I called my sister to tell her. I had told my mum the week before. I had never spoken to them about what he was doing to me before then.

I had nowhere to live and very little money. I had to go to work that day and tell no one. I booked into the cheapest hotel I could find in London. I sat on the floor crying that night. I didn't know what I would do or where I would go. I stayed at another hotel the following night and on floors, sofas, and anywhere I could.

In the weeks that followed I lived in fear I would go back, that I wouldn't have the courage to stay away. I was ashamed and afraid. I thought leaving him would exorcise the demons but in fact I remained terrified of any chance encounter. I saw him in all sorts of places for the first year. It was enough to set my stomach into knots and the familiar butterflies to start up.

There is only one upside to talking openly about this traumatic period of my life. I felt powerless and weak during those years but then I began to understand it also gave me a hidden superpower—something I didn't realize I had until a few years ago. I have the ability to help someone who is going through what I went through. That is hope.

Being a survivor of abuse changed me but it didn't destroy me. Like many other survivors I have gone on to lead a full and successful life. I married a wonderful man and have an amazing son. I threw myself into hard work and studying. I believe some of those traits of entrepreneurship which I have relied on since were born out of this dark period of my young life. I learned failure, resilience, tenacity, determination, and risk taking all before I was thirty. The self-belief and confidence came later and took longer.

I know the lasting legacy from those nine years is an overwhelming need to be self-sufficient, to stand on my own two feet, to be financially stable, to keep my friends and family close, and to help others in need. It also left me with a strong internal radar around people who bully, control, and belittle others. I have been in hot water on more than one occasion in my personal and professional life for standing up to those who abuse their position of power.

Bystanders see that as the Dragon in me—I know it is the survivor in me. If I could not only survive but thrive after my experience of domestic abuse, then there is hope for anyone else caught in its trap.

280

United Kingdom

Chapter 41

Laura Hearn

Storyteller and Journalist

Laura is the Founder and CEO of Meraki Creative Content, a creative content consultancy that uses storytelling as a vehicle to increase visibility, credibility, and evoke meaningful conversation. An astute communicator, she has more than fifteen years of experience working as a BBC journalist and producer across multiple platforms, including radio, television, digital, and online. She has covered major news events, interviewed numerous high-profile figures, and worked with some of the BBC's leading talent to produce sensitive and highly detailed content.

A passionate believer in the power of storytelling to connect communities, Laura's work focuses on giving a voice to the underserved and inspiring fresh perspectives. She uses an editorial approach combined with a journalist's mindset to help individuals and organizations emotionally connect with their audience with clarity and consistency. Laura translates the complex into simple, relatable, and compelling content to increase engagement, productivity, trust, and loyalty.

Laura is also a dedicated mental health advocate and was a key member of the BBC's internal mental health campaign. Drawing on her own personal experience of mental ill health, she uses the tools she learnt whilst in treatment in the US alongside her skills as a storyteller to train leaders in mental health awareness. She advises organizations on how to curate a mental health strategy that encourages leaders to realize the financial and moral benefits of putting wellbeing at the heart of everything they do.

* * * * *

As a writer and journalist, I share an intimate relationship with words. From a young age I had an innate curiosity with how words could be arranged, disseminated, and interpreted in multiple ways. In any given moment we are engaging in language with ourselves and each other. We hear it, read it, write it, and speak it from the minute we wake up to the minute we fall asleep. The way we use words with ourselves and each other can literally change lives.

Throughout my professional career, I never underestimated the power of words. I have always used them to educate, inform, and give a voice to those who don't always have a platform. This sense of personal responsibility I hold is perhaps why I found writing this letter so much harder than I expected. The words written in these pages will be printed and shared across the world and have the ability to influence and shape people's thoughts and behaviours. Words are not passive; they are profoundly active in everything we do and can be used to heal or hinder.

Your greatest source of pain can in time become your greatest source of healing...

I am fortunate to have been given the gift of hope many times in many ways, and as I as write I have more hope than ever—but it wasn't always this way.

282

As a young girl I had this innate feeling of loneliness and abandonment. I felt like an intruder in my own skin and with others. I branded myself many things—a misfit, the black sheep, the ugly duckling. These feelings of being "less than" have been a dominant narrative throughout my story.

My parents divorced when I was seven, and although I have very few memories of this time, the consequences of not having my father around followed me into adulthood. Bullied throughout my school years, I moulded myself into the shy, quiet, good girl who did as she was told. I craved my dad's love and acceptance, and although we saw each other regularly, I always dreaded the moment we had to say goodbye. As the years went on, I retreated further and further into my imagination where I could be anyone to anything. The fairy-tale stories I created in my head gave me some peace and respite from the outside world, that is until they turned into a living nightmare.

I will never forget that night, the moment when my stepbrother unexpectedly turned up to collect me from a friend's house. The flashing neon lights that lit up the entire driveway as we arrived home, and the wailing that echoed from one end of the house to the other.

I was seventeen when my life and everyone else's around me changed forever. My stepfather who had so generously and unconditionally welcomed me, my mum, and sister lovingly into his home was killed in a car crash. In one flicker of a moment, the world I had just begun to feel safe in was gone. The days and nights that followed blurred into one big fog, but somewhere amid all the chaos, I decided to cram a backpack full and fly off to the other side of the world with a friend.

I have often wondered how I could be so blasé, and I wouldn't blame you for thinking the same, but just as so much of my life hasn't followed a traditional trajectory, neither did my reaction to Michael's death. Little did I know at the time how his death would not only become the catalyst for my greatest pain, but also my greatest healing.

We were almost seven months into our gap year, when the grief I had unconsciously buried began to materialise. We were flat broke, travelling on a shoestring, and opted for an "All You Can Eat" Chinese buffet. It came from nowhere, the intense rush and need to get rid of what I had just eaten. I had never done it before, but the relief from knowing I had got rid of what I had just consumed was immense. I continued my travels awash with lies and deceit until my increasingly erratic behaviour became too difficult to hide from my travelling buddy. Soon enough I was trapped in a cycle of severe restriction.

Hell-bent on a journey of self-punishment, I tortured my body and my mind for more than two decades. I controlled it, manipulated it, and denied it to the extreme. Anorexia is an ugly beast that transforms the kindest, most selfless person into a ball of anger, rage, and self-hate. It pushes and tests your loved ones to their limit, day in and day out.

I spent years searching for the one person, place, or thing that would "cure" me, all to no avail. Appointment after appointment, assessment after assessment, therapist after therapist, and hospital after hospital, I still couldn't get well. I was completely and utterly hopeless. I spent many nights wondering if I would even wake up, and often danced with the idea of ending the pain for myself and everyone around me.

Find someone who speaks your language and has walked the path before you...

I can clearly remember the time when I first felt a glimmer of hope. I was sitting on my bed in my shared flat in London, clutching a book my therapist at the time sent me. I had read more self-help books than I care to remember, always wishing for the same thing—that one of them would finally provide me with the answer to relinquish my torture. Yet, despondent as I was, something told me to open it.

I hadn't turned the third page before the tears began to roll. In that very moment, I learnt what it meant to have hope. The words I read on those few pages were so powerful they made me feel it could be possible for me to live a different way. Why, how? The words on those pages were the voice of someone who spoke my language. The author, Carolyn Costin, had been to the same depths of despair I was in and found a way out. In just a few pages, Carolyn's words made me feel less alone, understood, and hopeful. Whilst society at large still regards an eating disorder as a "diet gone wrong," it is far more complicated than that. For me, it was a complete inability to process my thoughts and feelings. I didn't know how to use my voice, words, or accept myself or others. Years of feeling abandoned, guilty, angry, and frightened evolved into the only way my mind and body knew how to cope.

And so, after many months of anxious waiting and some huge family sacrifices, I was on a plane to California and to Monte Nido, the treatment centre Carolyn founded. The relief I felt to be finally going to the source of my hope was shattered almost as soon as I arrived. The reality of travelling to the other side of the world, only to be stripped of all your belongings and have someone watch over you every time you go to the toilet, was something I hadn't prepared myself for. The seconds, minutes, hours, days, and months that followed were beyond tough. The monster that had taken over

284

my entire being pushed not only myself, but also the staff to the very limit and beyond. Despite all the tears and tantrums, and with the unwavering commitment of the staff, I kept going. Every time the monster tried to lure me back into its clutches, they shone the torch of hope as they lovingly nursed my body, mind, and spirit back to health.

Hope requires motivation and, in my case, horses…

I have often wondered what it is that keeps the human spirit alive in times of darkness. How does a hostage endure years of solitary confinement, or an athlete push through pure exhaustion? Somewhere inside us all there is an inbuilt instinct for survival and a belief that brighter days are coming.

Throughout my life, horses have always managed to brighten even the darkest of my days and have given more hope than I can ever fully express through words. Horses have taught me courage, acceptance, determination, and have helped me to grow in ways I never knew could be possible. My eating disorder had robbed me of many things over the years—my career, my friends, and almost my life, but all those paled into insignificance the day I was too weak to pull myself up into the saddle. Horses made me feel like I belonged, and it was only the fear of losing that feeling that ultimately became my biggest motivator and driver to get well.

I will be forever grateful for the privilege of knowing many horses over the years, and whilst each one has left their mark (or hoof) on my soul, it feels only right to mention Bodhi and Oria, two beautiful American quarter horses stabled opposite Monte Nido. Each morning before breakfast we would go for a fifteen-minute walk, and as I passed their stalls their non-judgemental presence reminded me of both what I had to gain and what I had to lose. Their smell and innate beauty became the highlight of my day and reignited the spark in me that wanted to live.

My definition of hope…

There is no doubt hope has been a positive character in my life, and has dug me out of some dark holes, but over the years I have had to navigate the meaning of the word in a completely different way. I was someone who spent much of my time with one foot in the past and another in the future, which seemed safer and less painful than the reality of the here and now. Consequently, much of my personal healing has been to accept and embrace the present moment, which has at times challenged my own relationship with hope.

When I began this letter, it was as a journalist naturally curious as to how the dictionary defined hope. Whilst it felt true in essence, it also didn't quite fully fit me and how I have come to know it today. So, I wrote my own:

> Hope is when you can accept the past, embrace the present, and create the future you imagine for yourself.

Where hope fits into your own story is when it motivates you to show up and take the action needed for change. This is how and where this one word evolves into its most powerful form.

Your story is your own masterpiece...

Suffering is an unavoidable part of living and I spent many of my early years avoiding it through the prism and brutality of my eating disorder. Yet whilst it almost broke my mind, body, and soul, it has also healed me in ways I could never have imagined. To go from being someone who spent more than twenty years feeling utterly hopeless to being someone who can simultaneously feel an abundance of hope whilst embracing the present is nothing short of a miracle. Through the courageous and compassionate caring of others who helped me turn the page of my own story when I couldn't, I have finally found my own voice. Each one of these people has been an unexpected gift.

We are each a collection of chapters and stories, some already told and some yet to be discovered. So, whilst the words here are just fragments of my story, you too have a story inside of you just waiting to be written, heard, read, and shared.

I do hope you find some comfort in the words I have penned here, but if nothing else my message is this: Don't shy away from your own words, voice, and story. They are your most powerful tools, and when you fully embrace them as yours and yours alone, you create a masterpiece that can inspire, educate, inform, and even entertain.

United States

Chapter 42

Matthew Stinchcomb

Technology Founder and Nonprofit Organization

Matthew Stinchcomb is a director and co-founder of Partners for Climate Action Hudson Valley, a nonprofit organization working to cultivate and connect ecological leaders in communities throughout the Hudson Valley and support them with programs and grants to bolster their efforts to address the climate crisis, repair our natural systems, and foster local resilience.

Previously, Matt founded and led the Good Work Institute, a local organization supporting a network of people and initiatives working towards Just Transition in the Hudson Valley. Additionally, he is a co-founder of Place Corps, an educational program dedicated to cultivating a call to know, love, and serve our places. Before working in the non-profit sector, Matt was part of the founding team and the VP of Values and Impact at Etsy.com.

Matt serves on the board of directors for the Schumacher Center for New Economics (Chair) and the Hawthorne Valley Association (co-chair). He is also a member of the Columbia County Climate Smart Taskforce and the Gallatin Conservation Advisory Council. He lives in Gallatin, New York with his wife and three children.

* * * * *

The weltschmerz of this moment is weighing heavily on us all. Every day there is an endless parade of dizzyingly bad news about the planet, our politics, and our culture bombarding us through apps, advertisements, billboards, newspapers, televisions, websites, emails, and conversations. It feels euphemistic and obvious to say it, but these are certainly troubling times. Some days it is even hard to know which of these interconnected heartbreaks about which to feel most hopeless.

So, it might surprise you to read I am quite hopeful about the future. I'll get to that, but first a bit of backstory.

In April 2015, I was feeling clear and confident about how to do good in the world. This was specifically because I knew business had the ability, like nothing else, to change things in positive ways. It was, I believed, only a matter of time before the whole professional world would begin to busy themselves with this important pursuit.

You see, I had spent the prior twenty years or so with a strong desire to do good through a variety of creative and entrepreneurial pursuits. Most of these things were small and met with varying degrees of success. However, as fate would have it, one of these efforts was Etsy.com, the online marketplace for handmade goods conceived of by my flatmate at the time, Rob Kalin. It was an endeavor I had joined in its early days ten years before it finally took off. So, there I was in 2015, a leader at the company, watching with pride as our values-led enterprise became the first certified B Corp to go public. We *can* change the system from within, I believed. All businesses can do well by doing good! Soon after that, I left Etsy.com to run Etsy.org, the new non-profit organization we developed there and funded with proceeds from our IPO. Our goal was to build a new kind of business school.

288

I believed then, and still do now, that "business as usual" was for the most part a destructive force in the world. If we were going to have a shot at a livable future, we needed to practice what I liked to call, "business as unusual." We had set out, somewhat successfully, to practice what I liked to call "weird business" with Etsy, so we figured why not develop an educational program that could help other people do the same?

I recruited a small team, and together we developed a curriculum, selected our first cohort of business leaders, and set to work teaching what we called *regenerative entrepreneurship*. Coming from a venture-backed tech company, we figured the way to change the world was for these social enterprises to be big, and to help folks build global brands and platforms that could have the reach and scale to change the world in bold and impactful ways. However, halfway through the first program, a sneaking set of suspicions started to overtake me:

- Was being big the same as being great?
- Were our business students really transforming the system, or were we just teaching them to sell more stuff but in less bad ways?
- Was it enough to reduce carbon emissions from shipping or use less plastic in production if no one really needed what you were making?

My inquiry continued and deepened. Were we as entrepreneurs asking the real questions? Questions like the following:

- What does it truly mean to be successful?
- How much is enough?
- Is this what makes me happy?
- Is the world better because of our work? Would our neighbors, the forests, the oceans, or the animals say the same?

These questions stuck with me, and the more I tried to answer them, the more I realized perhaps I had it wrong. The impacts businesses have in the world are not an issue of companies being "more good" or "less bad" or "downright awful." Instead, as it became clear to me, it was more a matter of ignorance than morality. It is an ignorance born from disconnection and not unique to business owners. Most of us are also unaware of the harm we are causing ourselves, our loved ones, our employees, our neighbors, and our planet because we are disconnected from the people, places, and processes behind the goods and services we offer and buy.

Let me be clear, this disconnection is not just about buying and selling things. The way we do business is just a side effect of something far deeper. This is about disconnection at the root level.

We are disconnected from ourselves, our neighbors (human and non-human), and from the Earth. It is this disconnection that enables we humans to commit atrocities, whether small or large. It is this disconnection that clouds the fundamental truth of the interconnection and interdependence of all things. I imagine there was a time when we were more aware and dependent upon the rhythms and web of life, but our technologies, our ideologies, and our systems championed a world view where we see ourselves as separate from the whole. And unless we reconnect and remember we are intrinsically bound to it all—our failures, our successes, and our futures are shared—we will not be able to make the changes needed to meet this moment.

Reconnection is the work of our time, and frankly, I'm hopeful.

I'm hopeful about the future because I believe there is a simple and clear path forward. I see it in the communities around me. I see it in the millions of small acts neighbors around the world undertake every day, and I see it myself in my own work.

What brings me hope is what I am going to call *The Work*, with a capital W.

The Work is work that recognizes and honors the interdependence of all things. It knows, loves, and serves all the beings and places touched by it. To know something means you are connected to it and aware of the impact you are having upon it. To love something means to care about its wellbeing. To serve something means to act or work in its best interest.

The Work knows, loves, and serves us and those coworking with us by engaging our full mental, physical, and spiritual faculties, and conferring joy and nourishment to all. It knows, loves, and serves the Earth by seeing how she is suffering and aims not just to sustain her, but to regenerate the systems supporting all life.

The Work is also best done locally, and at an appropriate scale. If our work is too big, there is no way we can be truly aware of all the impacts we are having on others. While we must continue to urge the world's leaders to pull the levers of change on a global level, we cannot wait for them to do so. We urgently need to take control of our own futures and accelerate and deepen efforts to address these interrelated crises in our own backyards, and do so with approaches and solutions that best honor the uniqueness of our places. We do not need the next big thing. We need a whole bunch of small things. That, I believe, is how we will build a livable future. This is the conclusion I came to with my own work as well as the work of our little business school, which we renamed the Good Work Institute.

In his wonderful essay, "It All Turns on Affection," Wendell Berry makes this same point more eloquently than I ever could:

> ...imagination thrives on contact, on tangible connection. For humans to have a responsible relationship to the world, they must imagine their places in it. To have a place, to live and belong in a place, to live from a place without destroying it, we must imagine it. By imagination we see it illuminated by its own unique character and by our love for it. By imagination we recognize with sympathy the fellow members, human and nonhuman, with whom we share our place. By that local experience we see the need to grant a sort of preemptive sympathy to all the fellow members, the neighbors, with whom we share the world. As imagination enables sympathy, sympathy enables affection. And it is in affection that we find the possibility of a neighborly, kind, and conserving economy.

The Work is about dirtying our hands in our local soils and getting, once again, to know our places and all life, human or otherwise, with whom we share them. By knowing our places, we can love our places. By loving our places, we can serve them. By serving our places, we will know ourselves, love ourselves, and serve ourselves; we will know our neighbors, love our neighbors, and serve our neighbors; and we will know the Earth, love the Earth, and serve the Earth.

I have experienced this first-hand. I live in the Hudson Valley of New York, on the ancestral lands of the Mahican (Muh-he-con-ne-ok: The People of the Waters that are Never Still). I was not born here, and only arrived about seven years ago. Nevertheless, I decided to put down roots here, and I am so glad I did. By focusing my time, energy, and work locally, I have met so many wonderful people and seen so many beautiful things.

I am beginning to know and love the nature and the communities that exist here. My love for them inspires me to be of service in whatever ways I can. I am also floored by all that people are doing here. I can see things are happening. Water is being cleaned. Soil is being built. Lives are being changed. Their work inspires me and those around me. *The Work* begets *The Work*.

Doing *The Work* in your community means learning to know and love the particular soul of that place, and then using the resources that exist locally to support the emergence of local solutions from and with local communities. It is about taking actions that honor all the history, wisdom, and both human and non-human communities that are there.

Furthermore, working together in our communities brings us together. I have witnessed how the divisions between those who think or look different from one another can break down when they work together in the service of the places they share. I truly believe our common ground is our common ground.

My neighbor, a lifelong resident of our town, and I could not be further apart on the political spectrum. Everything I read in the news or see online suggests we should agree on nothing. It tells me he does not believe in climate change and that to him I am probably just some lefty eco-terrorist. However, we recently spent a day together cleaning garbage from the trails at the local conservation area. We both spoke of our love of the woods and our appreciation of the rural nature of the place where we both live. I asked him about growing up there, and how the forest has changed.

He may not attribute those changes to the climate crisis, and he certainly wouldn't call it that, but we both agreed on the importance of conserving and protecting these woods. For both of us, it is the nature of our place that makes it most special. Our work together, in this case cleaning and clearing a trail, brought us closer. I will probably never agree with his choices at the ballot box, but I care for him, and will be there as his neighbor should he need my help. I also know he will be there for me.

It was so simple, our shared task of picking up trash in the woods. It did not require billions of dollars, global platforms, or major corporations. We did not need to start a social enterprise, a non-profit organization, or have a background in corporate social responsibility. Instead, all that is needed is a willingness, as Gary Snyder enjoined us, "to find your place on the Earth, dig in, and take responsibility from there."

Anyone can do it, and there are millions of opportunities to do so. We all work. We work as business owners, community volunteers, and employees in companies small and large. We work as politicians, religious leaders, consultants, teachers, and at not-for-profits. We work as parents, siblings, first responders, caregivers, and artists. Our work is not just about producing goods or offering services to earn money. It shapes who we are and is a vehicle for how we express ourselves in the world. Our work is *whatever it is we do*. And *whatever it is we do* will decide whether we perish, survive, or thrive. It is our choice, and I believe if there is to be any hope for us on this planet, we must choose to do *The Work* in our daily actions.

Perhaps most importantly, doing *The Work* is the process through which we will reconnect on all levels and shift the way we see ourselves in relation to the world. It is about connection. The work itself, the actual *doing*, is what reunites us with our bodies, our minds, our fellow humans, and our shared planet. It is our work, our doing, that forms and strengthens the connective mycelium between all things.

Yes, I know this idea is idealistic and even a bit simplistic, but nonetheless I believe in it. Meeting the challenges of the world seems so impossible and hopeless. The problems are too big, and the solutions too small. However, seeing and later joining the people who are doing *The Work* in your community will make you realize it is not impossible. There are things you can do about the world's problems—lots of things. And maybe it is believing it is not impossible that is just what will make it possible. So yes, I am hopeful a more just, beautiful, and connected world can be achieved, action by action, place by place, but only if we think of hope as David Orr described it, "as a verb with its shirtsleeves rolled up," and get to work doing it.

Jamaica

Chapter 43

Dawn Simpson

International Business Consultant

Dawn Simpson is an accomplished international business executive with more than twenty years of experience in international financial services with a focus on developing countries. She is a consultant to international investors, non-profits, governments, and major corporations. Her fascination and drive come from her humanitarian missions in the United States, Latin America, Africa, and the Caribbean. She is an economic justice freedom fighter with a mission to engage with international decision makers and thought leaders on international public policy.

Her background in international relations, investment banking, marketing, human resources, film, and music has forged Dawn a place with a diversified group of influencers. She was also instrumental in formulating the automated download of foreign exchange block trades at Citigroup/Salomon Smith Barney. Prior to working in the international consultancy industry, she was a Client Account Manager and Compliance Officer at Credit Suisse Investment Bank. At present, Dawn is the International Business Advisor for the Office of the Vice President of Suriname and the Director of Investments and Trade at Grassalco, a state-owned entity representing Suriname's natural resources.

Dawn is a member of the Dean's List and a graduate of New York University where her focus was Global Economics, International Human Rights, and Law. A strong advocate for a clean environment, she received the US Presidential Volunteer Service Award and is also a United Nations Peace Ambassador. She is also a film and music producer and executive producer. One her music production projects was nominated for the 2011 Grammy Awards. Dawn comes from a bloodline of influential people that includes former Secretary of State Colin Powell, Former Prime Minister of Jamaica H.E. Portia Simpson-Miller, and the current Prime Minister of Jamaica H.E. Andrew Holness.

* * * * *

Seeing the world was all I wanted when I was a little girl growing up in the suburbs of St. Andrew, Jamaica. The air was fresh, the breeze was cool, and island life was "no problem." My vacation during the summertime was at an ocean front villa in Montego Bay or with family at Treasure Beach in St. Elizabeth. My memory of the area was the scent of sweet fruit trees and Uncle Lenny taking us out on his fishing boat. When manatees would appear, my father would always excitedly shout, "Look Dawn, Sea Cows!"

My father was my hero. He used to take me to the areas where my ancestors came from in St. Elizabeth. We stopped in Rose Hall, an area he called Simpson Town. All the people there were called "red" because they were of Scottish and Irish descent. Most of the folks there had a strange accent very much different from city folks. Jamaica is a diverse country with different people, and I always wondered about our significant culture.

296

In Jamaica there are uptown and downtown people. It was a way of defining class. The elite kind of stuck together, having uptown parties and gatherings. There is also a huge disparity between the rich and poor on the island, which triggers violence. There is the beautiful side where the tourists go, and the ugly side where it's brutal and many children go to school hungry. My dad showed me the good and bad because he wanted me to be grounded. I believe he is the reason why I am empathetic and can adjust to any environment and people.

Dad was very protective and believed in education. The standard of education in Jamaica is extremely high and a lot of pressure for even young kids. To get into high school, sixth graders would have to take the Common Entrance Exam. It was good and bad exposure for a child as your name would be listed in the newspaper if you passed. My first time taking it I failed. He sent me to extra lessons, and then I passed with my name posted for scholarship to attend the all-girls Catholic school, Holy Childhood High School.

My dad supported me in every aspiration I had. I did swimming classes and at nine years old ended up on the swim team at the YMCA where I won all the swim meets. I won medals for track and field in prep school. I also joined the track team in high school, but it was extremely competitive and I couldn't devote enough time to training. It was important to me to be very active, so I played badminton, netball, and tennis. My thought was to excel at something in hopes of getting a scholarship to enter a university in the US, Canada, or England.

At high school graduation, I gave the Vote of Thanks in the presence of the First Lady and the Governor General. This was my first big exposure giving a speech in front of a large crowd. During my speech I heard the echoes of the crowd when my message seemed to touch them. I could hear my mom and dad shouting, "That's my daughter!"

One of my greatest passions is poetry. I had journals with poems I wrote at the tender age of seven years old. While in high school, I entered a poetry competition and won. A senior schoolmate of mine asked me to go with her to Tuff Gong (Bob Marley's studio) to become a Ghetto Youths songwriter. Bob Marley's children started this label to support the less fortunate youth on the island. The poetry and song writing took me on a journey of creating music, and I found myself recording in the presence of Jamaican legends like Tyrone Downie (former Wailer), Maxi Priest, Aswad, The Melody Makers, Patra, Steelie and Clevie, Steven Stanley, Mikal Rose, and Junior Reed, just to name a few.

I began to realize I was a creator, and I loved to create positive impact on people. My father's family were close, and I remember every Friday my cousins and I would entertain them. I even started a kids' club and organized a concert on my father's empty lot. I enjoyed seeing people happy and I liked being the reason behind their happiness.

After my High School Graduation, my mom went to the United States to prepare a "better life" for me and my other siblings. It was sad because I had to grow up very fast. A year after she left, my father had a major stroke after Hurricane Gilbert destroyed the island. I ended up taking care of my father and it was quite challenging for an eighteen-year-old. I had a stepmother who mistreated him, so I had to check on him very often. She felt threatened by my presence due to inheritance, so she banned me from being with my dad. I was homeless for a period around this time. I went to stay in Montego Bay with my aunt until her husband forced me to leave. I remember one morning he told my aunt he wanted me drive to Kingston with him, but I said no. He left with his sister, and they ended up in an accident and she died. I could have been the one in her seat.

Despite everything, I had nothing but hope. I had an interview at Grace Kennedy & Company and was immediately hired to do part-time sales promotion. I was a record-breaking sales promotion representative, selling unprecedented numbers of cases of product. The company saw my value and hired me full time in the Human Resource Department processing applicants and new employees. Within a short time, I was offered an executive assistant to the Director of Industrial Relations. My boss and I would travel to different parts of the island for Union Negotiations. I recorded the minutes for the meeting, and most of the time in those days I would be the only female in the room.

A year later I was offered a senior position at Versair Inflight Services to work with the General Manager. As a pre-introduction to the company, I was invited to their Christmas party. There was a raffle to win a trip for two to Disney World in Florida. The winning ticket had my name on it!

I decided to go to the United States because my mother wasn't well, and my grandmother was diagnosed with lung cancer. I took care of my dying grandmother during this time and decided to leave everything behind, including my sick father in Jamaica. Tragically, my maternal grandmother passed within two months and two months after that my father passed away. Then my paternal grandmother passed not long after as well.

298

But with death there is life.

I gave birth to my son Brandon Chris-Wayne in 1992, Gabriel Scott in 1997, Danielle Jordanne in 1998, and Alexia Egypt in 2011. With the birth of Gabriel, Danielle, and Brandon, I became a stay-at-home mother for a time. Being a mother is the greatest gift. It is important to keep children active. I placed them in sports, helping them excel at school and encouraging them to be the best versions of themselves.

When Gabriel was 11, he ran to me and said, "Mommy, Mommy, I want to run for President of my school and the election is near!" Gabriel was the type of child who completed whatever he put his mind to. Failure was never an option, and he would get upset if he got something wrong. He felt it was his responsibility to make everyone around him feel happy and cared for. He was the one who would hug grandma and ask if she was okay. Whether he knew it or not, he helped to make the hard decision of separating from his father. Gabriel was like an old wise man.

When Gabriel was four years old, he witnessed his father's anger when he threatened to kill me. We went to court, and my husband promised the judge it would never happen again. The case was dropped, but his abuse continued. I was living in constant fear of him.

I finally filed for a divorce after infidelity. I wanted to provide a better life for my children. I thought, "Would I want them to be with someone like their father?" I kicked him out of the house, telling him to never come back. I was left with three children at the time to raise on my own (Alexia was born later).

I worked various jobs through the years, often with long hours in industries such as big pharma, music, banking, and government to pay the bills. I even went back to school to further my education. Simply put, being a single mother is hard, but I was determined to do anything to protect and care for my children. We single mothers encourage our children to dream big and never give up hope.

During a business trip to Suriname on March 1, 2021, at 5:00 AM I received the kind of call no parent ever wants to get. But let me tell you, the day before I somehow felt this call would come. There was an ominous presence I could not explain, and I felt ill all day. I saw a black butterfly in the window of my living room, and it all felt odd.

It was my son Brandon on the phone. At first, I could barely understand him. He was frantic and screaming.

"Mom! The police came to the door and said Gabriel died!"

"What? Gabriel? What do you mean? He has died? What happened?" I replied, breathless.

I was stunned, my heart dropped as if I had been punched in the chest, as if I breathed in but could not breathe out. I had a dream many years before that flashed suddenly through my mind. I had forgotten it until now. In this dream, Gabriel was five years old and just disappeared. I looked and looked for him but could not find him anywhere. I remember how sick I felt in the dream, and now that sick feeling returned with the call. I will never see him again. I was empty and full of horror. I realized why I wanted to keep him close all those years. I was numb, in disbelief that somehow my nightmare had come true.

Gabriel died in a tragic car accident that day and his life was lost at just twenty-three years of age. At his funeral we had over 400 guests—mothers, fathers, teachers, coaches, friends, and family. They all loved him so much. I was told how he saved lives and how he fed the poor. He was a walking angel. He left me with great memories. He used to call me his Superhero. He recorded music and left a catalogue of songs which I will release to the world one day. I wrote a letter to him that I would like to share with you:

Dear Son,

Thank you for 23 years.

I am writing this letter with tears running down my face but hope in my heart. All I can do is remember your voice and all the love you have shown me since birth. You would always run to my rescue when something was wrong. If I could turn back time, I would have taken more photos with you, traveled more with you, and hugged you more. You showed me a lot during your twenty-three years. You wanted me to be proud of you son, and I am.

You were always there for everyone, with so much kindness in your heart. On Thanksgiving you would bring meat for me to cook for your friends' mothers. You took a lot of risks driving hours from New York or Virginia just to be there for your friend's baby shower. You would say, "No mom, my presence is support and I need to be there." I would worry knowing

300

you are out there driving alone such long distances. No matter how old you are you are still my baby and it's the hardest thing not having you around.

There is a hole in my heart that will never be filled. Some days I go for walks alone and just cry. I still hear your voice, "You will succeed... you work hard... don't give up."

You were different, son. You are a mother's dream and a grandmother's too. Grandma always noticed your attentiveness ever since you were a toddler. You lived life as if you wanted to accomplish as much as you could.

I wish we could have done more things together, especially bring you to Jamaica and the Dominican Republic. Even though I cherish the memories we had in Europe, back then I felt like we had all the time in the world and many vacations ahead. I would give anything to bring you back to this earth to hug you, to see your smile, the glint in your eye when you joked and mispronounced my wine collection, it was hilarious.

Thank you for teaching your little sister Alexia wisdom as well as playing with her and making her feel loved; she cries for you often. It's been hard for everyone as you are an important part of this family.

I remember the time when I passed out and the ambulance came. You ran through the forest just to catch the ambulance before it left. When I had COVID you came and took care of me without a mask. Going to sleep and waking up has been hard without you around.

I can feel your presence at times. I see you in the wind and in the clouds. Thanks for showing your sister a sign when she asked. You had the computer playing the song you both made. I know when my ears ring and when I feel a chill beside me, you are there. It is becoming harder on your birthdays when you would have been older, as I can only imagine your maturity and growth at twenty-five. We should not question God or the universe as to why you left us so soon. Friends who are spiritual do say that when your mission is complete on earth, we leave. I know you want me to be a super mom, and I know you do not want me to break down and fall.

I was only with my father for twenty-three years, and now you passed away at twenty-three years as well. Driving in the car or walking on the street is a constant reminder of how you left us, and it is a constant sorrow. Sometimes I feel trapped in a box and cannot get out. A friend of mine recently lost his son too. Sometimes he calls me crying and I give him strength and peace.

I am sorry I was in South America when you had the accident, and I am sorry you were alone. I know you must have been scared. This hurts my heart. What gives me hope are the signs. I see them all around me.

I am proud and love you my beloved son, Gabriel. I will love you always and forever.

Love,

Mom

Japan

Chapter 44

Shonosuke Okura

Otsuzumi Player and Cultural Ambassador
of Japan Heritage

Shonosuke Okura was born as the oldest son of the late Chojuro
Okura and represents the sixteenth generation of his family. At
first, he learned to play Kotsuzumi, made his stage debut at the age
of nine, and switched to Otsuzumi at the age of seventeen. The
house of Shonosuke Okura is deeply embedded in the ancient roots
of Noh theater. The origin of Noh theater can be traced all the way
back to the sixth century and Hata no Kawakatsu, who created this
tradition upon request by Prince Shotoku. Hata no Kawakatsu was
the great ancestor of the Konparu and Okura families, who have
handed down Noh to the present day, including dance and Utai, as

well as the large and small hand drums and Kyogen, although the Konparu family ceased to exist during the Meiji era. The Okura school is said to be the originator of the Otsuzumi drum, and along with the kotsuzumi hand drum, the traditional Japanese instrument called the tsuzumi has been handed down to the present day.

While working in the world of traditional performing arts, Shonosuke collaborated with artists in various fields. In addition, he collaborated with an industrial designer to co-create a motorcycle in 2000 that was inspired by traditional themes and art. The drum solo style that became the basis of the design is a new production created by Shonosuke Okura based on traditional expressions. In December 2000, he was invited by the Vatican to hold an Otsuzumi ceremony at the Millennium Christmas Nazareth Concert. In 2001, he worked on the stage production of Nohgaku combined with projection mapping.

* * * * *

As an evangelist and ambassador of Japanese traditional culture and heritage it is my utmost goal to preserve the ancient values and culture of Japan. I believe a deeper understanding and more international exchange can be of great value for the sustainability of all cultures and I wish to create world peace through the power of our cultural heritage and traditions. I am the sixteenth generation of our family, which has preserved and cultivated the tradition of Nohgaku and Otsuzumi for more than 800 years. I feel a great responsibility for our old traditions and culture.

The essence of Nohgaku is an expression of a life in harmony with nature that Japan has inherited from generation to generation. This harmony is displayed on the Noh stage, the traditional clothing, and the different tools and instruments being utilized. The purpose of stage expression is to show gratitude to the source that created all living beings. Long before humans named the source power *god*, there had been a deeper understanding and deeper search for connecting with the true inner self. The Noh theater and Noh stage offers the viewer a revelation to find a connection to the deepest self. In Noh performances, wooden Noh stages are assembled in the precincts of shrines and temples and are dedicated to the gods and Buddha.

"Hono" (dedication) is the act of offering the best and finest items human beings create around their lives. Historically, in Noh the offerings made to the gods were

304

expressing gratitude towards nature and the creator, and these items were hand crafted and sourced locally in Japan. Nowadays, however, a lot of these are being imported and made from chemical ingredients.

The awareness of the performers is gradually shifting to the entertainment that is presented to the audience, and they are required to maintain their acting skills and form. Throughout the Edo period, the support system for the Noh world as samurai ceremonial music was protected across all the industries that supported it. During the Meiji era, the Zaibatsu corporate conglomerates provided partial support instead, but after the Second World War, the Zaibatsu were dismantled and the support was no longer received.

After that, there was only a small number of performers and supporters. In fact, artificial materials such as nylon and chemical dyes, which were cheap and easily available, came to be selected. The current situation is that the environment of Nohgaku, which is dedicated to the stage with the best authentic pieces, is collapsing. There are few skilled workers who have inherited them and there are few successors. This overlaps with the appearance of modern Japanese society.

When I was twenty years old, I lost my hope for the future and left my parents' house to live for one year with a farmer who applied traditional, natural farming practices. Based on that experience, I lived in a hut in the mountains near Izunokuni City and gradually made my return to the Noh stage while practicing natural farming methods for about three years. I was very shocked when I met the sons of skilled craftsmen such as carpenters, masons, and farmers. They all said in unison they wanted to quit the world of skilled craftsmen and become ordinary office workers.

I was devastated and thought it was a pity. It hurt my heart to see how these young men were ready to abandon the many skills they had learned at home and exchange it for life as a salaryman. Then it struck me that I was also one of them and realized this was not a problem for them alone, but a problem for the whole society.

Originally, Japan had largely established a sustainable, recycling-oriented living environment in the Edo period. A recycling system was built for all aspects of clothing, food, and housing, and the city had waterways and water for daily use, and manure was circulated as a growth accelerator for farms. Fertilizer expert Liebig, who read the Edo report written by Maron, a Swiss visitor during the Edo period, said, "The basis of Japanese agriculture is the complete circulation of all plant nutrients taken out of the soil as harvested products." Swiss consul Rudolf Lindau, looking at the townscape of Edo, said, "Many parks and gardens cover Edo, so when viewed from a distance, it gives the impression of an infinitely expansive park." Horticulturist Robert Fortune said, "The landscape is ever-changing and ever-beautiful. Hills and valleys, wide roads and shady paths, gardens and houses, inhabited by people who are industrious, toilsome, and apparently happy and content."

Observing the lives of these people, Alcock, the British Minister to Japan, said, "There is more freedom among the general public than we can imagine," and Austrian diplomat Huebner said, "Even in Europe, there is no example of a village organization with such freedom." It was Japan from the Edo period to the beginning of the Meiji era when the guests from overseas who saw the lives and scenery of the people had these kinds of impressions. It was described as a flourishing civilization. Exchanges with foreign countries have occurred, and the products of various civilizations have flowed in, so Japan has been gradually influenced by Western values.

When the country had been closed due to the national isolation policy during the Edo period, we encountered a variety of rare values and information, among which chemically synthesized alternatives that could be obtained without much effort. They were the envy of the people of the time. It has been revered as a special thing called imported goods. This is still inherited without change, and we obediently accept artificial chemicals surrounding various living environments.

This means that the value of traditional culture and traditional skills that have lasted for more than 2,000 years has been lost or almost lost over the past 150 years.

For example, we are involved in the production of costumes and tools (musical instruments) used in traditional Noh stages. Even if we take this one example, the production of madder, obaku, and indigo, which are the raw materials for dyes, will be delayed, and if chemical dyes are used instead, the process of making dyes that has been cultivated over many years will be omitted. Even the work has changed from before and has been simplified, and valuable traditions have been lost.

Even the lacquer applied to the drum is made through more than 100 steps of applying genuine lacquer, but now imported lacquer and synthetic lacquer are used, and the work has become simpler and cheaper, but the depth is the same as before. Some shades of lacquer are disappearing. As with lacquer, hemp cords are now nearly 90% imported, and since the hemp cords are soaked in bleach, the fibers are weak and cannot be expected to have the supple strength of the original hemp cords.

Those involved in traditional culture and performing arts do so within a framework of harmony, and we only use natural ingredients. This is because the traditional spirit of Japan is based on the foundation of Nohgaku expression, with the most important essence of being in harmony with the natural world. This spirit was established more than 1,400 years ago, during Prince Shotoku's Asuka period. As stated in Prince Shotoku's 17-Article Constitution, "Harmony is valued," it shows harmony between people and harmony with the natural world.

I believe now is the time to think carefully about whether it is a good idea to abolish various lifestyles and cultures based on ancient values that have continued for more than 1,000 years in the next 100 years. I am not the only one who is alarmed by the loss of these ancient principles and values.

As one way to deal with these problems, we launched the Otsuzumi Hono-no-kai. As I mentioned earlier, "Hono" (dedication) is the act of preparing the best and finest things for the Gods with gratitude for being alive by the great grace of nature and the Gods. Therefore, I am aiming to prepare the materials of the Otsuzumi, as dedication for the gods, as regenerated from the original ones, and the costumes are reproduced in the original manufacturing process, and the traditional tools are gradually arranged.

The basics of Otsuzumi performance consist of breathing, pausing, and striking, and if we do that in a larger group of people, we can all unite in the same rhythm and breath. Based on the ancient Japanese spirit of harmony that respects and cares for each other, we can create a stress-free and comfortable world for each other by uniting within each other's breathing and calling. Breathing is the basis of organic expression that transcends all races in the world. Based on that breathing, a pause is created, and a beat is born.

This is the oldest form of expression in human history, and through this performance, people will come face to face with the memories that lie deep within their bodies. It will restore the original form of human beings, and it will bring not only physical health but also mental rest.

It is my hope and goal that people of all races all over the world work together on this Otsuzumi drum, keeping their breaths in sync with each other and putting their hearts into it. It is my hope that Otsuzumi will be of great use as a tool for creating true world peace and unite humanity in harmony with sound and breathing. The sound of the Otsuzumi drum is called *Shirabe*, and it means that all harmony becomes sound. A variety of sounds are born due to changes in the environment such as the season, weather, and place, as well as differences in the temperament of each person.

My deepest hope, ambition, and purpose in life is to create a world in which people can live in harmony and peace by being an evangelist for our rich and deep Japanese cultural values.

Russia

Chapter 45

Masha Brodskaya
Musician and Nonprofit Organization

Masha Brodskaya is a Grammy-nominated multi-disciplinary multimedia artist, virtuoso violinist, singer, pianist, composer, and producer. She is a virtual reality and neuroscience music pioneer, ViolinBorg, innovator, educator, entrepreneur, and a winner of The Independent Music Awards. She has been featured by *Forbes* magazine, *The New York Times*, PBS NewsHour, CBS News, Fox News, and *Broadway World* magazine, to name a few. She has produced and taken part in shows featuring such artists as Pink Floyd, Gloria Estefan, Dionne Warwick, Public Enemy, B52, Al Di Meola, as well as at United Nations events. Masha has performed worldwide, from Independence Square (Maidan) in Kyiv and Freedom Square in

Kharkiv, Ukraine, to Carnegie Hall and Lincoln Center in the US, and across Europe and South America.

In her creative work, Masha bridges music with virtual reality, art, fashion, and neuroscience for artistic, educational, therapeutic, and cultural diplomacy purposes. As a frequent speaker on art and technology, she has shared the stage with Al Gore, Tim Berners-Lee, Vint Cerf, Edward Snowden, and many more. She is a Co-Founder and CEO of NEXVOX, a brain wave music therapy app and true peaceful creative collaboration between the human brain and artificial intelligence.

Masha is an activist, leader, and advocate for human rights and peace. She is the Founder and Director of GCI Planet, an interactive concert and smart education platform, a nonprofit organization utilizing music and arts as therapy and cultural diplomacy. GCI Planet is working with child prodigies from all around the globe and supporting children in hospitals, orphanages, and refugee camps worldwide. GCI is currently active in fifty-seven countries.

* * * * *

It dies last. It's hanging on a thin string. It gets lost and found. It gives life. It kills. It saves. It betrays. And sometimes it leaves without a letter.

Hope.

I hope my "hope" will stay long after I am gone.

The history of my family has been re-written, shot dead, burnt to ashes, kept in the Gulag, taken away with the names and lives—so it has also gone with hope. But it keeps on coming back stronger and louder, with a full realm of genetic memories, colors, and contrapuncti.

Before I continue, I want to say I don't mean to impose my opinion, but to simply share my own inner universe through this message of hope of mine. As a firm believer in fundamental oneness, I do believe we all are responsible for what is happening to us and around us. Also let me be clear, I do *not* believe in conventional *good* and *evil*. I believe in *nondualism*. Everything has its highest meaning and mission that, if it is to

310

rise above how much (or how little) we can see with human eyes from our dimension and density, comes back to *good* and *God*.

What we consider evil is the only security of the most precious gift we have: *free will*. And just that says it all. But also, *evolution*. There is no evolution and no growth without pain and struggle. That's where the work of evil becomes, if I may, even noble. And what about creativity and arts, after all? Hasn't it been historically true that the most powerful music and art are created out of big pain? As you see, everything, including the most horrible and terrifying, from the standpoint of a human life perspective, eventually leads to the better. Which means it gives and proves *hope* in everything and everywhere. No matter what. Always.

From the beginning of time, one of the main and most genius tools of so-called "evil" has been division. It creates separation, which leads to fear and hatred—division by culture, religion, race, politics, gender, and more. While we are busy inventing new ways of and reasons for killing each other, we become easily controlled and manipulated. I believe even "good" and "evil" are not opposites meant to fight, but are the two "sides" of singularity, to keep the universal balance, to intertwine in a passionate dance of love, giving birth to evolution, depth, and freedom.

I am grateful for being born as a hybrid of opposites, to experience a full range of beauty and challenges of being such. Born on the border of Russia and Ukraine, in a poor Jewish family of pre-and-post-Soviet intelligencia, growing up in Ukraine while speaking my native Russian language, I am culturally Ukrainian. Genetically I am half Ukrainian Jewish, half Russian North Asian. But it's not the only place where the opposites have found their unity in my veins. Half of my family comes from hard-core Communists and Red Army, and the other half is dvoryane (nobles) and White Army.

I know very little about the noble side, since the names and lives were taken, and archives were burnt, but the Communist part of my family I know well, even though the price was also paid in blood. And here I am talking about those Communists who are described in books as an example of humanity and selflessness. Extremely rare but existent, like my Jewish grandmother on my father's side, Babushka Maya, who raised me. A daughter of the "Enemy of the People" as her father, my great-grandfather, was pronounced by Stalin and shot dead in 1937. His wife, my great-grandmother spent seventeen years in the Gulag. Their four children, including my Babushka, were left on the street with no home, which was confiscated with everything in it by the state and picked through by different relatives, not one of whom wanted to deal with the kids of the "Enemy of the People." Antisemitism, harassment, poverty, World War

II—Babushka went from making bullets to saving wounded soldiers on the battlefield. What was her hope and her message to leave?

In the 1990s, in my hometown Belgorod where we lived, she created the Association of Victims of Illegal Repressions, and was fighting for the rights of those who, like her family, were repressed in 1937, imprisoned, and rubbed out by the State. She was fighting singlehandedly for every single person she could find, getting pensions and apartments for those old poor veterans, both men and women, many of whom lived in basements and balconies, barely having enough money for bread and milk (the USSR and Russia have been that generous to their own people).

One day the mayor of Belgorod invited her to his office. He put the keys of an apartment on the table in front of her and said, "Maya Moiseevna, you've been doing so much for people, and with no one's support, at the expense of your own small pension, getting apartments from the government for the victims of repressions, while sharing a room with your granddaughter in the apartment of your son and his wife."

My Babushka Maya replied, "I appreciate your generous offer, but I can't take it. I won't be able to look in the eyes of those who have it worse than I do." She left to go help more people.

Babushka Maya Brodskaya has been my inspiration behind GCI Planet, an interactive concert and smart education platform, a nonprofit organization I've created to help children and youth in need and isolation worldwide.

My mother's father, Dedushka Misha went to the front by lying about his age as he was too young. He was captured and imprisoned in a Nazi concentration camp. He escaped and came back to fight and went through the WWII from Moscow to Berlin as a sniper, receiving the highest medals and orders for courage, and was assigned the title of Hero of the War. And yet after the war, he was prosecuted for not dying in a Nazi concentration camp and was sent to Stalin's concentration camp in Siberia. From there he was sent to Yakutia in the far-eastern part of Russia, a place with an extreme climate, too harsh even by arctic standards. The seasonal temperature drop in Yakutia can reach 100 degrees Celsius. At the height of summer, it can get as hot as +40°C.

That's where my grandfather met my beautiful Asian grandmother Svetlana (Baboo), to whom I owe my blonde hair and hazel eyes, since it's the only Asian race on the planet with blue and green-eyed blondes. What was their message of hope? It was

312

enjoying small simple gifts of life, raising three children, and teaching music and dance to generations of kids.

As long as I can remember, in his safe my grandfather kept a little adorable boy-doll, only about six centimeters in length, that could close and open its eyes (to my admiration as a Soviet kid). It was given to him in 1945 in Berlin by a German woman as a talisman.

The heredity of the "Enemy of the People" in my family hasn't stopped there. My father, a virtuoso pianist and incredibly gifted composer, a man whose level of intelligence and talent was close to genius, was expelled from the conservatory in the late 1970s for writing "anti-Soviet" music. Well, also for being Jewish, of course. He lived in constant fear of being arrested. Alcohol had become his escape, and even though he had enough time to give life to two beautiful children, me and my beloved sister Ekaterina, and write two symphonies and many opuses for piano and voice, he died in his fifties from a heart attack, unable to overcome the strong addiction that consumed him and ruined his personal and professional life. What was his message of hope? I remember he told me once, "Mashkin, you must break this vicious circle. In your generation this must stop."

I grew up in a boarding school for musically gifted children in Kharkiv, Ukraine, living without parents since I was six. Besides being considered a child prodigy madly in love with music, it was also my mom's attempt to shield me from an unhealthy home environment caused by my father's addiction. While being very close with my father, and him being my first and most influential teacher, I had also been exposed to what a child, especially a daughter, shouldn't see or hear.

I was the youngest kid ever accepted to the school, majoring in violin, piano, and composition, with my first victory at international composers' competition when I was seven. Even though I was surrounded by other child-prodigies, kids are kids, with all their cruelty and jealousy. For being the youngest and so good at music, as well as poor and Jewish (even though I didn't look Jewish, but all my family did), I was bullied, bitten, and pretty much an outcast. Music was my escape and my salvation.

Things got better as I grew older. Girls still didn't want to be friends with me, but boys did (though I was sad they considered me their own pal, but I really appreciated it later). There was a turning point, though, with girls. One day when I was playing and singing my song "Prayer" (a pretty jazzy composition), one of the girls who was bullying me the most overheard it, walked into the room, and asked me to sing it again.

313

I did. It must have been some kind of magic, because after that she was my strongest admirer and protector. She even sang in a little vocal group I created, and which went on to perform in concerts and television programs.

Another story that has impacted my early understanding of the complexity of good and bad happened when I was going back to the dorms with another girl after our evening music practice. Just to remind you, I grew up in the 1990s, the times of banditry and armed street gangs, some of which included kids as young as 11–12 years old. My friend was ahead of me, and as I was catching up to her with my violin, I saw her surrounded by a circle of young men, the gang that was terrorizing the neighborhood. She was picked on and pushed around, and tears of fear were falling from her eyes. I am not sure what was in my head, but I walked slowly to the group and said something. They stopped being interested in my friend and switched their attention to me. She escaped, though I don't know why she didn't call for help.

I was standing there in the middle of the circle, lecturing the group of young criminals on morality and compassion. A boy half my height separated from the circle and walked straight up to me, looking up into my face. He was silent for a few seconds that felt unbelievably long, and then he said looking right into my eyes, "You have balls. I respect it." After that they were my friends and my "krisha" (roof), a slang word meaning protection from the mafia. They came to hang out with me after my evening practice, and that was where I learned for the first time that behind any troublemaker and so-called "evil" there is always a lack of love received from the family, or some other personal tragedy. It has formed my compassion for "evil" and understanding of a solution, which is love. And hope.

I finished my schooling early, graduated *cum laude*, and by age fourteen was already studying in Kharkiv conservatory. But my heart was calling for something more. So, I made up a story to get my documents, and secretly escaped to Moscow where I entered Gnesin's Russian Academy of Music as a singer and songwriter.

There I created my jazz band, started to write music for commercials, as well as doing surround sound for movies. In a quite short period of time, I managed to live a few totally different lives: I did some acting in movies and theater, a bit of modeling, and a couple of years of seriously doing poetry, getting published in five countries in four languages, and writing three books of poetry and prose. Meanwhile, I recorded three albums of my own original music. With those albums I went to many Russian producers and heard the same thing from all of them: "You are crazy. Your music doesn't have any Russian mentality," (whatever the heck that meant). That's when I decided, screw it, I am done here. I am going to America!

I left everything and came to New York City. It was the end of 2012. I had nothing—no friends, no place to live, no work, no money, barely any English. Alone and against the whole world again. But I did have one thing: Hope.

Little by little I started to perform and got into music production and teaching. Then virtual reality and neuroscience entered my creative universe, and then philanthropy. They have been overlapping and intertwining in my activities ever since. Even though I am still not checking any of the conventional boxes, I am working on developing my own.

Through all my family history and heredity, as well as my own experience as a misfit, I've learned a lot. It's made me who I am and has been reflected in all my creativity and artistry, feeling half of myself against the entire world, and the other half in league with that same world. That pain has found its embodiment in my debut album, *Enemy of the People*.

Then on February 24, 2022, my entire world changed, and the whole world itself has changed as well. For most of us, a war between Russia and Ukraine didn't seem possible, even in the most surreal of nightmares. I have family in both Russia and Ukraine, and my heart is bleeding on both sides, for Ukraine and for Russia, for all the lives lost, for all the families broken, for all the hatred spreading like the worst plague. It will take decades and generations to heal, if ever at all.

From the beginning of the war, I've been an active supporter of the people of Ukraine, with a focus on women and children. I have produced concerts and events, and have taken part and performed in many fundraisers, but always for civilians, not for the military. I wrote a piece for violin and orchestra and dedicated it to the people of Ukraine.

And now, my simple visit to Russia and my family may very well result in me being named a *foreign agent*, an "enemy of the people," and possibly twenty-five years of prison to go with it. Madness. Pain. But *not* without hope for peace, light, and healing Love. I do want and hope to sit down one day soon with Vladimir Putin, over a cup of tea, and have a human talk. I have no hate or fear towards him. I want to ask simple human questions. I want to discuss the possibility of cultural and spiritual diplomacy for peace and healing, because this is the one thing I believe in the most. It can go places where no military or politics can go. It can work miracles when everything else fails. This is my hope for my people of Ukraine, for my people of Russia, for my people of the world. But let me finalize it properly and without reference to specific nationalities or events.

I am sure all forms of life, both organic and inorganic, can peacefully co-exist together, including the relationship between humans and artificial intelligence, the antagonism of which is the next very real and biggest threat. And here again, creativity and cultural diplomacy are the *only hope* for humanity's survival and a peaceful future. I've had my very modest experiments with a peaceful, creative collaboration between the human brain and AI via NEXVOX. It's an AI-based software application developed by my creative partner Brian Forbes and me that translates human brainwaves into a musical score, and AI performs it in real time. And I can tell you, it works.

While writing my message of hope, I think I've just proved to myself what hope is for me. I am grateful for this opportunity. I wish you all love and hope. God Bless us all and let us always have our hope ever living within us!

China

Chapter 46

Peggy Liu

Environmentalist

Peggy Liu is Chairperson of JUCCCE, an NGO at the heart of the greening of China since 2007. Named the "Green Goddess of China" by the Chinese press and "Hero of the Environment" by *Time*, Peggy is one of the most impactful environmentalists on the planet today.

Her efforts have helped more than 1.5 billion people leap-frog towards personal and planetary health. For this, Peggy was awarded the Hillary Step prize, like a Nobel prize but for climate change solutions. *The Economist* called her "one of the most innova-tive thinkers in Asia."

Today, Peggy shares with communities, governments, and companies around the world the lessons she learnt in scaling societal movements by successfully tackling China's toughest environmental health challenges. Peggy's "Tornado Leadership" lessons empower visionaries to bring in a better future faster by accelerating the upward spiraling energy of a collective movement.

* * * * *

Something in me resisted writing this letter. Whereas words usually flow through me, this message of hope failed to be delivered swiftly.

The word "hope" is what had me stuck. It assumes a vast gap between a trauma of today and a glorious tomorrow. "Hope" itself is based in a fear we may not close the gap. This fear creates a downward spiral, drawing our attention to the worst apocalypse Chicken Little can imagine. But by focusing our energy on vividly painting that doom in a multitude of scenarios, we unintentionally give life to it. That isn't hope. That's drowning.

Let me not sugarcoat the suffering for humans and Mother Earth that is coming with man-accelerated climate change. Humans will have to adapt quickly to an increasingly inhospitable world or die. But I choose not to prioritize my attention on suffering. I choose to visualize humans thriving in balance with Nature, and I act in the knowledge that I have the power to bring that future about.

As an environmentalist, I do not carry hope. I carry a knowingness that humanity *will* get to this thriving future. Like a boulder on top of a mountain, that potential future already exists. It is waiting for us to give it a push to gather energy as it rolls down the hill. I create from this future that already exists, and reverse engineer shortcuts to it. Some may call me a pragmatic optimist. My friend Tbird Luv calls me an "evolutionary solutionary."

So, I don't want to give you hope. Hope is not helpful. I want to empower you and your communities to leap into a thriving future with secrets of how to nimbly ride the crests of these coming waves of inevitable environmental changes. They are secrets I picked up while catalyzing China's leaps into cleantech, smart grid, ecocities, efficient lighting, green bonds, sustainable diets, and a reimagining of prosperity. I visualize these movements as tornados that shifted a society of 1.4 billion people. They seemed destructive to a way of life at first but swept us into a much better life at warp speed.

318

These secrets have helped me open a series of portals to greater possibilities that were once unimaginable. As an example, one of the first China-wide impacts I catalyzed is a commitment of USD$7.2 billion from China's State Grid in 2009 to implement a new system of Smart Grid technologies across China's electrical grid. This is an enabler for the use of renewable energy and a dramatic reduction in energy loss. To start this movement, I had to first name the technology and envision how China would be reshaped for the better.

A fundamental rule of manifesting is "believe it to see it." This is the difference between an evolutionary solutionary and a skeptic. A skeptic must see and measure it to believe it. An evolutionary solutionary believes it is possible, makes it happen, then sees it. Think of Willy Wonka when he dreamt up and built his Wonka Chocolate Factory. Others may have called him crazy. But he already knew what the future looked like in glorious, delicious detail.

Detail is the key to making what you believe tangible so others can join you to build it. James Cameron spent ten years dreaming every detail of Avatar's Pandora world into being. What people dressed like, what they ate, how they lived in trees, how they commuted on flying beasts, how they went to war, and how they made love. The Pandora world was so richly painted that it was more real for the protagonist than his own life in a medical pod. Pandora could not be created by running away from "humanoid Earth" in fear. It was imagined out of love, by following James Cameron's sense of curiosity and wonder.

When we imagine the world we want, we need to be just as nuanced as James Cameron. We need a rainbow of colors in our palette. When our Creator painted rainbows, it didn't stop at seven colors. A rainbow contains an infinite number of nuanced colors. And on top of infinite colors, there is invisible ultraviolet and infrared light shimmering on either end. That's quite a palette to create with! The very existence of this variety is what makes life so wondrous and joyful. What would a jumbo box of crayons be without shades of orchid, alloy orange, three times red-violet, bittersweet shimmer, outrageous orange, and unmellow yellow?

Human emotions are our palette to shape the world in which we live. These tools are free and within every person's reach. Our reality is simply the emotional perception of our world. At every moment, we are unintentionally painting the world we live in with the emotions we feel. We are the canvas. Our curiosity is our paintbrush. Our wonder is our brushstroke. Our joy dries the paint. Do you want other people to trigger these emotions within you and shape your perception of the world, or do you want to choose how you react? We are not powerless. When we have control of our emotions, we can control our world.

Try it now. Focus on something that gives you wonder, joy, bliss, and ecstasy. Hold this emotion for a solid minute. Repeat this each hour. It's easy for someone to trigger you in a moment to fall into fear, fight, and flight. But it takes diligent practice to shape your emotions and shape your story of the world and of You.

In a world where AI is rapidly replacing humans in jobs, the ability to sense emotions remains an indispensable, marketable skill. Empathy allows us to sense nuance in relationships and be an effective cultural bridge. Empathy allows us to share love and compassion in healthcare and service jobs. Empathy allows us to sense the directional signals of a community so we can adapt agilely. Our current educational system churns out graduates who turn off their senses to be efficient cogs in a factory. To forward humanity, we need to transform educational systems to train visionary leaders who lead with their senses first and secondly execute with their brain.

Did you know a rainbow is completely unique to each and every person? Even if you are standing close to someone looking at the same rainbow, light will pierce droplets at different angles to create different prisms to create your own unique rainbow. Similarly, everyone views the world in their completely unique way through their emotions. There is no right or wrong way to perceive a rainbow. The polarization and friction we have today in geopolitics comes from not understanding how a rainbow is not black and white, and that it is okay for everyone to see the world differently.

In today's violent world, geopolitics is reduced to a black and white world of Batman versus Joker, good versus evil. It doesn't have to be this way. In a Monet pointillism painting, many colors come together in a masterpiece. In a symphony orchestra, many different instruments play together in harmony.

Because I founded an organization called Joint US-China Collaboration on Clean Energy out of the first public dialogues on clean energy between the two governments, I'm often asked to speak about China versus the US. In meteorology there is a phenomenon called a multi-vortex tornado. Many tornadoes all exist next to each other without dominating another. Each unique tornado spins around its own axis in a different way. But they all follow a central path forward. I see humanity as a collection of multi-vortex tornados. All equally valid in its existence. We don't need to conflict. We can all draft along with each other towards co-creating a better humanity.

320

Not only is each tornado valid in their differences, but the fundamental laws of Nature demand a balance of opposites. A tornado both destroys and creates a different world. If you run your finger through water, fluid dynamics will create equal and opposite vortices. Isaac Newton's third law of thermodynamics states "for every action there is an equal and opposite reaction." A pendulum, when pushed, will swing right back. Traditional Chinese Medicine restores health by restoring balance to organs. Buddhist monk Thích Nhất Hạnh taught there is no right without left, and no up without down, just interbeing. Daoism has both Yin and Yang. Our job in these chaotic times is to restore balance in ourselves and to society.

When I get a chance, I like to ask kids what they think of climate change and whether they are hopeful about the future. It saddens me to hear kids say, "It's happening and there is nothing I can do about it." This just gives away their power to others. They are but a puppet floating down a stream of life. Some kids say, "People will find a way, they always do." This makes them dependent on other people's strength as they shirk their personal responsibility to their community. Other youth express themselves with anger and protest. But if no better solutions are offered, they are inadvertently putting attention, and therefore life, into the world they are protesting against.

I share these secrets to empower our youth to build a new and better world; to paint a rainbow every day. These secrets are aspects of what I call *Tornado Leadership*—a method of leading societal movements. In a world that seems to be spiraling downwards, we need leaders who can create spirals of upward momentum. We need Tornado Leaders who can sense the direction of the wind and are brave enough to change with its unpredictability. We need Tornado Leaders who can align hearts around a central passionate vision of a better future. By drafting together like particles in a Tornado, we can more effortlessly and quickly leap through its vortex to a new world.

Rainbows and tornados bring in a better future faster. That is my emoji message of hope to you.

Acknowledgments

A huge thank you to everyone in "The Vine" community. Without you this book would not be possible, and without your giving nature all the global good this network has created would not exist. Thanks to my business partner Dave Conley for helping to bring my ideas around impact to life.

I would like to thank my mother (Cynthia) and stepfather (Bill) for teaching me to always keep hope in my heart and to stay the course.

To my loving fiancé, Paul Neumann, thank you for helping me through many tough times and medical issues I had during the making this book.

I would like to especially thank Brad Bandy for inspiring this book. Because of you, I know my life's purpose.

Finally, I would like to thank everyone who made selfless introductions to every writer in this book. You opened big doors to make it all possible and are why the wheel of giving keeps turning. The kind super-connectors for this book are listed below:

Laura Hearn
Mariam Azarm
Anuj Naheta
Miles Woodruff
James Guiang
Nandu Singh
Reem Khouri
Richard Le Poer
Karla Amtmann
Jose Baquerizo
Rash Huque

Charles Markeaton-Mundy
Yvonne Beri
Isaac Kattan
Henry Finnegan
Brian Menell
Danielle Mei-Lee Freer
Eric Omore
Gabriel Jimenez
Eduardo Burillo
Wendell Figueroa Ruiz
Scott Manthorne

Prince Palden Namgyal
Christian Schmitz
Evanthia Evangelou
Christopher Schroeder
Viviane Ventura
Nouriel Roubini
Tyler Wagner
Asher Jay
Religions for Peace

12625933R00186